American Culture in the 1960s

Twentieth-Century American Culture
Series editor: Martin Halliwell, University of Leicester

This series provides accessible but challenging studies of American culture in the twentieth century. Each title covers a specific decade and offers a clear overview of its dominant cultural forms and influential texts, discussing their historical impact and cultural legacy. Collectively the series reframes the notion of 'decade studies' through the prism of cultural production and rethinks the ways in which decades are usually periodised. Broad contextual approaches to the particular decade are combined with focused case studies, dealing with themes of modernity, commerce, freedom, power, resistance, community, race, class, gender, sexuality, internationalism, technology, war and popular culture.

American Culture in the 1910s
Mark Whalan

American Culture in the 1920s
Susan Currell

American Culture in the 1930s
David Eldridge

American Culture in the 1940s
Jacqueline Foertsch

American Culture in the 1950s
Martin Halliwell

American Culture in the 1960s
Sharon Monteith

American Culture in the 1970s
Will Kaufman

American Culture in the 1980s
Graham Thompson

American Culture in the 1990s
Colin Harrison

American Culture in the 1960s

Sharon Monteith

Edinburgh University Press

© Sharon Monteith, 2008

Reprinted 2009

Edinburgh University Press Ltd
22 George Square, Edinburgh

306.0973

Typeset in 11/13 pt Stempel Garamond by
Servis Filmsetting Ltd, Stockport, Cheshire, and
printed and bound in Great Britain by
CPI Antony Rowe, Chippenham, Wilts

A CIP record for this book is available from the British Library

ISBN 978 0 7486 1946 7 (hardback)
ISBN 978 0 7486 1947 4 (paperback)

The right of Sharon Monteith to be identified as author of this work has been asserted in
accordance with the Copyright, Designs and Patents Act 1988.

Published with the support of the Edinburgh University Scholarly Publishing Initiatives Fund.

Contents

Figures

Case Studies

Acknowledgements

This book is dedicated in memoriam to Dennis Brown (1940–2006) who lived through the sixties – in the UK, Nigeria and Canada, and who travelled to California for the 'Summer of Love' – and returned to the era in *The Poetry of Postmodernity* (1992) and in many of our conversations. Excelsior!

I would never have written this book if Martin Halliwell hadn't asked me to contribute to this series so thanks go to him and to Nicola Ramsey and Eddie Clark at Edinburgh University Press for their support. I would like to take the opportunity to acknowledge colleagues and friends in the School of American and Canadian Studies at the University of Nottingham, especially on this occasion those with whom I tend to talk about the 1960s – Tony Hutchison, Richard King, Peter Ling, Pete Messent, Dave Murray, Roberta Pearson and Graham Thompson – and those colleagues and friends who have travelled with me on research trips or supported me in other ways, including Tina Galloway, Allison Graham, Sharon Horne, Heidi Levitt, Alison Marsh, Judie Newman, Celeste-Marie Bernier, Ann McQueen, Helen Taylor, Jacqui Clay and Stuart Wright.

Some research that has found its way into this book was undertaken at the end of my period as a Rockefeller Humanities Fellow (Race and Gender in the Mississippi Delta) at the University of Memphis. I am also grateful for support at Nottingham, both in the School – and particularly from the Head of School Judie Newman – and from the Humanities Research Center which funded research trips to Birmingham, Alabama and to New York City.

Of the helpful staff in the libraries I visited during the course of this book's preparation, I would like to acknowledge Ed Frank and Chris Ratcliffe in the Special Collections in the McWherter Library at the University of Memphis and Wendy Murphy and Alison Stevens at the Hallward Library at the University of Nottingham, as well as staff at Memphis Public Library and the Museum of Radio and Television in New York.

Thanks go to Jim Burton (Salisbury University, Maryland), a friend as well as my former Ph.D. student, whose assistance over 2004–5 was invaluable. For library and computer assistance in Memphis, I acknowledge Jonathan Cullum and Manish Kubal. I thank Francisca Fuentes for allowing me to include a beautiful photograph taken at Arlington. I would also like to note my almost-student Daniel McKay and his father for copies of *Life* magazine so assiduously saved since the 1960s.

My love – and thanks for putting up with me across the different decades – goes to Nahem Yousaf.

Chronology of
1960s American Culture

Date	Events	Music	Performance	Literature
1960	President Eisenhower signs Civil Rights Act. John F. Kennedy defeats Richard Nixon in Presidential election by small margin. Kennedy emphasises a cultural 'New Frontier' on inauguration. Four black students from North Carolina A & T stage a sit-in at Woolworths segregated lunch counter, Greensboro, NC. The Student Non-violent Co-ordinating Committee (SNCC) founded, Raleigh, NC. Oral contraceptive approved for sale. Caryl Chessman's execution.	Stax Records founded in Memphis. John Hammond signs Dylan to Columbia. Alan and John Lomax, *Folk Songs of North America* Bob Thompson, *Gardens of Music*	Kennedy and Nixon participate in first televised debates between Presidential candidates Edward Albee, *The American Dream* *The Fastasticks,* Off-Broadway *Bye-Bye Birdie*, on Broadway	John Barth, *The Sot-weed factor* Richard Yates, *Revolutionary Road* John Updike, *Rabbit Run* Harper Lee, *To Kill A Mockingbird* Robert Lowell wins National Book Award for *Life Studies*
1961	Alan Shepard first American in space; Soviet astronaut Yuri Gagarin first person to orbit earth. President Kennedy establishes the Peace Corps. Kennedy requires federal contractors to take 'affirmative action' to ensure individuals treated without regard to race. CORE organises Freedom Rides. Birth-control pill comes into general use.	Ray Peterson, *Tell Laura I Love Her* Motown signs The Supremes Ben E. King, 'Stand By Me' 'I Fall To Pieces' by Patsy Cline is crossover hit	*Camelot* on Broadway Edward Albee, *Whose Afraid of Virginia Woolf?* Tennessee Williams, *Period of Adjustment* *How To Succeed in Business Without Really Trying*	Joseph Heller, *Catch-22* Henry Miller *Tropic of Cancer* unbanned and published in US Kurt Vonnegut, *Cat's Cradle* Walker Percy, *The Moviegoer*

Film	Television	Art	Criticism
Psycho *Primary* *The Apartment* *Sergeant Rutledge* *The Alamo*	*Andy Griffiths Show* *The Ed Sullivan Show* disallows Dylan from singing 'Talking John Birch Paranoid Blues' Hanna-Barbera's *The Flintstones* *Route 66* premieres on CBS	Museum of Modern Art, 'Art of Assemblage' Jasper Johns, *Painted Bronze* Robert Ryman, 'White Paintings' including *Untitled* Allan Kaprow, *Car Crash: Happening* Jim Dine, 'The Car Crash' Andy Warhol, *Dick Tracy*	John F. Kennedy, *Strategy of Peace* Paul Goodman, *Growing Up Absurd* Barry Goldwater, *The Conscience of a Conservative* Leslie Fiedler, *Love and Death in the American Novel* Daniel Bell, *The End of Ideology* Wallace Stegner, 'Wilderness Letter' C. Wright Mills, *Listen Yankee*
Shadows *Breakfast at Tiffany's* *A Raisin in the Sun* *The Misfits* *West Side Story*	Newton Minnow refers to television as a 'Vast Wasteland' President Kennedy holds first televised press conference *Mr Ed* debuts *Car 54 Where Are You?* on NBC	William Anders' photograph of earth from moon: *Earthrise* Martha Jackson gallery, 'Environments, Situations, Spaces' (including Allan Kaprow's *Yard*) Cy Twombly, *Bay of Naples* Dennis Hopper's photograph *Double Standard*	Marshall McLuhan, *The Gutenberg Galaxy* Clement Greenberg, *Art and Culture* Lewis Mumford, *The City in History* William F. Buckley, *Up From Liberalism* Wayne Booth, *The Rhetoric of Fiction*

Date	Events	Music	Performance	Literature
1962	The Soviet Missile Crisis. US intervention in Cuba known as the Bay of Pigs invasion fails. US explodes nuclear device near Christmas Island. Kennedy sends Special Forces troops to Vietnam to fight alongside ARVN troops. US Air Force first uses Agent Orange. SDS holds first national convention, Port Huron, Michigan. James Meredith desegregates University of Mississippi. Richard Nixon announces departure from politics.	Bob Dylan, *Bob Dylan* (debut album) Carla Thomas; 'Gee Whiz' Ray Charles, 'I Can't Stop Lovin' You' Booker T. and the MGs, 'Green Onions'	Edward Albee, *Who's Afraid of Virginia Woolf?* on Broadway *A Funny Thing Happened on the Way to the Forum* Cole Porter's 'Anything Goes' revived Off-Broadway	Philip Roth, *Letting Go* Edward Albee, *Who's Afraid of Virginia Woolf?* Ken Kesey, *One Flew Over the Cuckoo's Nest* Flannery O'Connor, *Wise Blood*

Film	Television	Art	Criticism
Advise and Consent	Launch of the satellite	*Artforum* inaugurated	Rachel Carson, *Silent*
Marilyn Monroe dies	Telstar	Castelli Gallery, 'Roy	*Spring*
To Kill A Mockingbird	Adam Clayton Powell,	Lichtenstein'	Michael Harrington,
The Manchurian	Sidney Poitier, Dick	Roy Lichtenstein,	*The Other America*
Candidate	Gregory and others	*Masterpiece*	The Port Huron
Promises! Promises!	testify to racial	'The New Realists'	Statement
That Touch of Mink	discrimination to	Andy Warhol, *Marilyn*	Dwight MacDonald,
Days of Wine and	House Committee on	*Gold* and *Marilyn*	*Against the American*
Roses	Labor and Education	*Diptych*	*Grain: Essays on the*
	The Tonight Show	Diane Arbus, *Child*	*Effects of Mass Culture*
	Starring Johnny	*With a Toy Hand*	James Baldwin, 'Letter
	Carson	*Grenade in Central*	From a Region of My
	The Beverly Hillbillies	*Park, New York City*	Mind', *New Yorker*
	premieres on CBS		Robert F. Williams,
	Hanna-Barbera's *The*		*Negroes With Guns*
	Jetsons		

Date	Events	Music	Performance	Literature
1963	Voter-registration drive begins in Mississippi. NAACP's Medgar Evers murdered in Mississippi by Byron de la Beckwith. March on Washington for Jobs and Freedom featuring King's 'I Have A Dream' speech. Nuclear test-ban treaty signed by US, UK and USSR. Bomb kills four black schoolgirls at church in Birmingham, AL. President Kennedy assassinated, Dallas, Texas. Jack Ruby murders Lee Harvey Oswald, jailed for Kennedy's murder. National Commission on the Causes and Prevention of Violence established. Buddhist monk self-immolates in Saigon to protest anti-Buddhist policies. University of Alabama desegregated while George Wallace 'stands in schoolhouse door'.	Dylan's first album, *The Freewheelin' Bob Dylan* Nina Simone, 'Mississippi Goddamn' James Brown, *Live at the Apollo* John Coltrane, *Live at Birdland*	Dylan duet of 'We Shall Overcome' with folk hero Pete Seeger at the Newport Folk Festival Dylan's 'Blowin' in the Wind' performed at March on Washington Cassius Clay, *The Greatest* *Oliver!* Broadway's most popular show	Sylvia Plath, *Ariel* Sylvia Plath, *The Bell Jar* Norman Mailer, *An American Dream* Sylvia Plath, 'America! America!' Howard Nemerov is poet laureate

Film	Television	Art	Criticism
Cleopatra *Hud* *Crisis: Behind a* *Presidential* *Commitment* *PT-109* *Shock Corridor* *The Thrill of It All*	President Kennedy's address to the nation on civil rights WLBT-TV in Jackson, Mississippi, brought before Federal Communications Commission Jack Ruby murder of Lee Harvey Oswald captured live on TV *Shindig!* premieres on ABC	The Foundation for Contemporary Arts established by Jasper Johns and John Cage Pasadena Museum, Marcel Duchamp retrospective Guggenheim Museum, 'Six Painters and the Object' (Jim Dine, Jasper Johns, Roy Lichtenstein, Robert Rauschenberg, James Rosenquist, Andy Warhol) Andy Warhol, 'Death' and 'Disaster' series Ed Ruscha's *26 Gasoline Stations*	Marshall McLuhan, *Understanding Media: The Extensions of Man* Betty Friedan, *The Feminine Mystique* James Baldwin, *The Fire Next Time* Martin Luther King Jr, 'Letter from Birmingham Jail' Martin Luther King Jr, *Why We Can't Wait: Chaos or Community? New York Review of Books* begins publication

Date	Events	Music	Performance	Literature
1964	Dr Martin Luther King Jr awarded Nobel Peace Prize. Lyndon Johnson defeats Barry Goldwater in Presidential election. Warren Commission report on President Kennedy's assassination finds Lee Harvey Oswald acted alone. President Johnson signs Civil Rights Act which outlaws all segregation practices. Freedom Summer voter-registration project. Civil rights workers James Chaney, Michael Schwerner and Andrew Goodman murdered during Freedom Summer. Free Speech Movement founded UCLA, Berkeley. The Wilderness Act passed. Equal Opportunity Comission established. Congress of Italian American Organizations (CIAO) formed. The ship USS Maddox is destroyed by the North Vietnamese. Congress resolution known as the Gulf of Tonkin Resolution allows Johnson to retaliate with force. President Johnson inaugurates 'Great Society' programmes and declares 'War on Poverty'	The Supremes' 'Where Did Our Love Go?' is their first Billboard no. 1 The Supremes, 'Baby Love' Dylan, 'The Times They Are A-Changin' *Meet the Beatles* (released in US)	The Beatles' first tour of the US Cassius Marcellus Clay defeats Sonny Liston for heavyweight boxing title and becomes Muhamad Ali Yoko Ono, *Cut Piece* premieres in Japan *Hello Dolly!* premieres on Broadway	Saul Bellow, *Herzog* Thomas Berger, *Little Big Man* Robert Lowell, *For the Union Dead* Amiri Baraka, *Dutchman* and *The Toilet* Shirley Ann Grau, *The Keepers of the House* James Baldwin, *Blues for Mister Charlie*

Film	Television	Art	Criticism
Mary Poppins	The Beatles debut on	Richard Avedon and	Susan Sontag, 'Notes
Dr Strangelove	*The Ed Sullivan Show*	James Baldwin,	on Camp', *Partisan*
Goldfinger	NBC's *I Dream of*	*Nothing Personal*	*Review*
My Fair Lady	*Jeannie* (1965–70)	Sidney Janis Gallery,	Leslie Fiedler, *Waiting*
Nothing But A Man	Soap opera *Days of*	'Four Environments	*for the End*
Cheyenne Autumn	*Our Lives* begins on	by Four New Realists'	Leo Marx, *The*
	NBC	Andy Warhol, *16*	*Machine in the*
	That Was The Week	*Jackies*	*Garden: Technology*
	That Was begins in US	Rauschenberg wins	*and the Pastoral Ideal*
		International Grand	*in America*
		Prize at Venice	Herbert Marcuse, *One*
		Biennale	*Dimensional Man*
		Robert Rauschenberg,	James W. Silver,
		Retroactive I and II	*Mississippi: A Closed*
		Edward Keinholz,	*Society*
		Back Seat Dodge-38	Howard Zinn, *The*
			Southern Mystique
			Ralph Ellison, *Shadow*
			and Act

Date	Events	Music	Performance	Literature
1965	Malcolm X assassinated at Audubon Ballroom, New York City. Democrat Party refuses to seat Mississippi Freedom Democratic Party delegation at the Convention, Atlantic City. 'Bloody Sunday' attacks in Selma, Alabama. Voting Rights Act signed into law. SDS protests Vietnam War in Washington DC. Racial disturbances in Watts, Los Angeles followed by protests in Cleveland, Chicago, Detroit and other cities. Operation Rolling Thunder authorised to allow aerial bombardment of North Vietnam. American ground troops sent to fight the North Vietnamese Protests against the draft begin. Federal law passed to make destroying draft card illegal. Federal Aid to the Arts Act institutes National Endowment for the Humanities (NEH) and for the Arts (NEA).	Dylan goes electric at Newport News folk festival in July Jimi Hendrix, 'Purple Haze' Tom Paxton, 'Lyndon Johnson Told the Nation' Phil Ochs, 'Draft Dodger Raag' Malvina Reynolds, 'Napalm' Rolling Stones, 'Satisfaction'	Ken Kesey and Pranksters hold first public 'Acid Test' Radio stations ban Rolling Stones' 'Satisfaction' as too suggestive	Ronald L. Fair, *Many Thousand Gone* William Denby, *The Catacombs* James Baldwin, 'Going to Meet the Man' Flannery O'Connor, *Everything That Rises Must Converge* (posthumous)

Film	Television	Art	Criticism
The Good, the Bad and the Ugly *The Greatest Story Ever Told* *The Sound of Music* wins Academy Award for Best Picture *The Cincinnati Kid*	*That Was the Week That Was* (NBC) NBC's *Get Smart* satirises spy genre *The Smothers Brothers Comedy Hour*	National Endowment of the Arts (NEA) founded Archives of American Art founded Susan Sontag, 'On Style' James Rosenquist, *F-111* Andy Warhol, *Four Campbell's Soup Cans* Warhol, *Electric Chair* Warhol, *Jackie* Sister Mary Corita (Frances Elizabeth Kent), *enriched bread* Wallace Berman, *You've Lost That Loving Feeling*	Mary McCarthy, *Vietnam* Truman Capote, *In Cold Blood* Malcolm X with Alex Haley, *The Autobiography of Malcolm X*

Date	Events	Film	Performance	Literature
1966	Warren Commission report on Kennedy assassination. James Meredith's 'March Against Fear'. National Organization of Women (NOW) founded, Washington DC. Human Be-In, San Francisco. Black Panther party founded, Oakland, California. 'Battle of Sunset Strip', LA. Medicare Act passed to support citizens over 65 with medical needs.	John Lennon states The Beatles are now more popular than Jesus Christ The Beatles farewell concert, San Francisco Police attempt to shut down James Brown concert because dancing is 'obscene'	Lenny Bruce dies of heroin overdose Dylan goes into seclusion for year and a half Warhol's film *Chelsea Girls* opens	Truman Capote, *In Cold Blood* Thomas Pynchon, *The Crying of Lot 49* Margaret Walker, *Jubilee*

Film	Television	Art	Criticism
Hollywood adopts age-based film ratings	*Star Trek* begins on NBC	The Artists' Tower of Protest, Los Angeles	Allan Kaprow, *Assemblage,*
Walt Disney dies	*Batman* (1966–8)	Noah Purifoy and	*Environments and*
The Chase	William F. Buckley	Judson Powell's *66*	*Happenings*
What Did You Do in the War, Daddy?	hosts *The Firing Line*	*Signs of Neon*	Susan Sontag, *Against Interpretation*
Khartoum		Robert Smithson, *Tar Pool and Gravel Pit*	Richard Dyer
Seconds		Larry Burrows'	McCann, *Hollywood*
		photograph 'Reaching	*in Transition*
		Out'	Charlotte Perkins,
		Robert Smithson,	*Women and Economics*
		'Entropy and the New	(1898) republished
		Monuments', *Artforum*	

Date	Events	Music	Performance	Literature
1967	Martin Luther King Jr's 'Riverside' speech in which he openly condemns war in Vietnam. The March on the Pentagon anti-war demonstrations. Astronauts Gus Grissom, Edward White and Roger Chafee killed during test launch, Cape Canaveral. The 'Summer of Love'. Inner-city riots Newark, NJ and Detroit. *Loving and Loving vs. State of Virginia.* Muhammad Ali refuses the draft. Senator Robert Kennedy calls for halt to bombing of Vietnam. Thurgood Marshall is first African American appointed Associate Justice of Supreme Court. George Lincoln Rockwell, founder of American Nazi Party, assassinated.	*Rolling Stone* magazine founded Monterey Pop Festival Beatles' *White Album* and *Sgt. Pepper's' Lonely Hearts Club Band The Monkees* wins Emmy	*Hair* premieres on Broadway Tom Lehrer's final concert Muhammad Ali stripped of heavyweight boxing title by World Boxing Association for having refused draft and boxing licence revoked. First Human Be-In staged in San Francisco.	William Styron, *The Confessions of Nat Turner* John A. Williams, *The Man Who Cried I Am* Richard Brautigan, *Trout Fishing in America* Wallace Stegner, *All the Little Live Things*

Film	Television	Art	Criticism
Bonnie and Clyde	Stones asked to change	Art in Public Places	Marshall McLuhan,
The Graduate	lyrics for *The Ed*	Program established by	*The Medium is the*
In The Heat of the	*Sullivan Show* to 'Let's	the NEA	*Message*
Night	spend some time	Los Angeles County	Roland Barthes' 'The
Medium Cool	together'	Museum, 'American	Death of the Author'
Planet of the Apes	Franceso Rosi's *The*	Sculpture of the Sixties'	published in the US
Don't Look Back	*Odyssey*	David Rockefeller	Maurice Tuchman,
Monterey Pop		funds Business	*American Sculpture of*
Cool Hand Luke		Committee on the Arts	*the Sixties*
The Dirty Dozen		Claes Oldenburg,	William F. Pepper's
		Placid Civic	'The Children of
		Monument	Vietnam'
		Chicago's 'Wall of	Susan Sontag, 'The
		Respect'	Aesthetics of Silence'
		Dennis Oppenheim,	John Galbraith, *How*
		Cut in Oakland	*To Get Out of Vietnam*
		Mountain	Arthur Schlesinger Jr,
		John McCracken, *Blue*	*The Bitter Heritage:*
		Column	*Vietnam and American*
		Michael Fried, 'Art and	*Democracy, 1941–1966*
		Objecthood', *Artforum*	
		Sol LeWitt,	
		'Paragraphs on	
		Conceptual Art',	
		Artforum	

Date	Events	Music	Performance	Literature
1968	Assassination of Martin Luther King Jr in Memphis. Assassination of Senator Robert Kennedy in Los Angeles. Democratic Convention, Chicago, Hubert Humphrey nominated, disturbances break out. Kerner Commision Report on Civil Disorders. Richard Nixon elected President. Poor People's March on Washington. Vietcong Tet Offensive. National Student Strike. Fair Housing Act passed. Shirley Chisolm first African American woman elected to Congress.	Otis Redding, 'Sitting on the Dock of the Bay' The Beatles, 'Hey Jude' James Brown, 'Say It Loud, I'm Black and I'm Proud' Alan and John Lomax, *Folk Song Style and Culture*	Tommie Smith and John Carlos' Olympic Protest *Hair* premieres on Broadway Neil Simon, *Plaza Suite* *The Boys in the Band,* Off-Broadway	Norman Mailer, *Armies of the Night* William Styron, *The Confessions of Nat Turner* John Updike, *Couples* Gwendolyn Brooks, *Come to Mecca* Tom Wolfe, *Electric Cool-Aid Acid Test*

Film	Television	Art	Criticism
The Green Berets	'Elvis' '68 Comeback	Musuem of Modern	Joan Didion, *Slouching*
2001: A Space Odyssey	Special' on NBC	Art, 'The Art of the	*Toward Bethlehem*
Finian's Rainbow	*Of Black America* on	Real 1948–1968'	Eldridge Cleaver, *Soul*
Night of the Living	CBS	Valerie Solanis shoots	*on Ice*
Dead	*Rowan and Martin's*	Andy Warhol	Walter Benjamin's 'Art
Wild in the Streets	*Laugh-In* begins	Dwan Gallery, New	in the Age of
Story of a Three-Day		York City,	Mechanical
Pass		'Earthworks'	Reproduction' (1936)
		(including Oppenheim,	translated and
		Oldenburg, Smithson,	published in the US
		De Maria, LeWitt)	Lucy Lippard and John
		Rauschenberg,	Chandler,
		Autobiography	'Dematerialization of
		Edward Kleinholz, *The*	Art', *Art International*
		Portable War	Guy Debord, *The*
		Memorial	*Society of the Spectacle*
			Eliot Porter, *In*
			Wildness is the
			Preservation of the
			World (Sierra Club)
			Stewart Brand, *Whole*
			Earth Catolog
			Ronald Berman,
			America in the Sixties
			John Barth,'The
			Literature of
			Exhaustion'

Date	Events	Music	Performance	Literature
1969	US astronauts land on moon; Neil Armstrong the first to walk on moon. Stonewall 'riots', Greenwich Village, New York City. Friends of the Earth founded. Massive anti-war demonstrations, Washington DC. The Manson 'family' murders actress Sharon Tate and friends, Los Angeles. My Lai massacre of March 1968 exposed in *New York Times* and *Life*. Nixon announces first withdrawal of troops.	Woodstock Festival Altamont Festival Diana Ross leaves The Supremes	Neil Simon, *The Last of the Red Hot Lovers* *Butterflies Are Free* on Broadway	Philip Roth, *Portnoy's Complaint* Symposium 'The Black Artist in America' N. Scott Momaday, *House Made of Dawn*

Film	Television	Art	Criticism
Easy Rider	*Sesame Street* on PBS	Leon Golub, studies	Theodore Roszak, *The*
Medium Cool	*ABC Movie of the*	*Napalm I*, *II* and *III*	*Making of a Counter*
Midnight Cowboy	*Week*	Metropolitan Museum,	*Culture*
Alice's Restaurant	*The Johnny Cash Show*	'Harlem on my Mind,	Vine Deloria, *Custer*
Butch Cassidy and the	*The Bill Cosby Show*	1900–68'	*Died for your Sins*
Sundance Kid		Formation of Art	Harold Cruse, *The*
The Wild Bunch		Workers Coalition	*Crisis of the Negro*
Marooned		(AWC)	*Intellectual*
		Formation of Women	Parker Tyler,
		Artists in Revolution	*Underground Film*
		(WAR)	
		Robert Smithson,	
		Asphalt Rundown,	
		Rome	
		Walter De Maria, *Las*	
		Vegas Piece, Tula Lake,	
		Nevada	

The Intellectual Context

C. Van Woodward described the 1960s as a 'twilight zone', caught between living memory and written history. This region of the mind and of record is the site where mythology is forged.[1] It is axiomatic to love or hate 'sixties' culture but it is much more of a problem to define a decade about which myths and images often masquerade as cultural history. Superlatives and provocative statements abound. The 1960s has been described as 'the most dynamic and icon-shattering decade of the twentieth century' when 'everything seemed possible for a brief shining moment' as well as the decade in which 'murder became an accepted form of political discourse'.[2] Music producer Jerry Wexler, the face of Atlantic Records since 1953 and its foremost promoter in the 1960s, dismisses the idea of the decade itself as a rhetorical impulse: 'We didn't know we were at some cosmic threshold . . . You never know that. I think that's all literary, all this business about decades. I think it's part of the bullshit rhetoric of rock . . . you know, the confluence of certain things, the myth period, the golden period . . . '[3] Looking back to the moment just before conglomerates controlled all mass cultural forms, Wexler reiterates 'the rhetoric of rock' even as he debunks it.[4] There is a significant difference between a rhetorical sixties and a historical 1960s but if it is difficult to escape re-accentuating those images legitimated by continual retelling in a set sequence of events, it is important to examine their persistence. The most important domestic crises – the fight for civil rights and the Vietnam War – and domestic policies such as the 'War on Poverty' and the 'space race' are examined here in some detail in the plethora of forms through which they found, and continue to find, representation.

This book also seeks to emphasise ways in which the local and the regional contribute to dominant images of the national. Rather than explore the 'global unbinding of energies' that Fredric Jameson summarised as the sensibility of the sixties, it looks to the South and also to the West in the making of the 1960s as myth and as history. It shows how often regions were the scourge of national faults. As the nation's mirror, its national conscience and the site of quintessentially 'American' dilemmas, the South was the primary testing ground for sixties ideology. The region would be demonised as America's 'counterpoint' with white southerners and African Americans – conceptualised as 'the South within the North' when residing outside the region – eluding assimilation into 'American' culture.[5] But it would also be mythologised as the hopeful site in which a national racial peace could be forged. Ellen Douglas' stories *Black Cloud, White Cloud* (1963) set in Mississippi were written, she says, against this background: 'corrosive hatreds, the crippled loves, the confusions, the flashes of nobility and heroism, the ways of making do, making room . . . '[6] In the South ordinary people were grassroots participants in what would become the most significant new social movement of the decade: the Civil Rights Movement. Other ordinary southerners formed the backbone of the conservative backlash that would help the Right of the Republican Party to successfully exploit what in 1968 Robert Sherill described as the 'gothic politics' of the Deep South, epitomised in the persons of southern Dixiecrats such as George Wallace, James Eastland and Strom Thurmond.

In Birmingham, Alabama – a city whose symbolism is explored in the Conclusion – white clergymen wrote an open letter entitled 'A Call For Unity' in an effort to resolve a racial stand-off at the *local* level when Martin Luther King Jr was arrested on 9 April 1963 but they found their words read and responded to as a *national* statement when King replied with his 'Letter from Birmingham Jail'. It was published in *The Christian Century* and in his book *Why We Can't Wait* (1963) as a measured defence of non-violent campaigning for black civil rights and has become one of the most famous documents of the new social movements, the cluster of mass protests that characterised the era's politics. Local events were never only that when Dr King was present. In 1967 when Chicago police confronted black children who had opened a water hydrant to refresh themselves on a hot day, the riots that ensued were linked to King having nailed his measures for improvement to the door of City Hall and cited as proof that non-violent principles could not be applied to the national (that is, northern) racial situation. The opening image in the photographic collection *The Movement* (1964) is indisputably southern: the road from Jackson to Yazoo City in Mississippi is the 'way in' to the Deep South, the heart of Movement territory. But organisers would also endeavour to break racial deadlock in northern cities, as the racialised battles in Chicago demonstrate so acutely. When Wendell Berry began writing poetry and fiction about environmental concerns in the late 1950s, his lens was intensely local, a smallholding in the border state of Kentucky, and his ideas were considered marginal. In a very few years with the publication of Rachel Carson's *Silent Spring* (1962) as a spur, the same ideas were news and Berry has repeatedly stated that the view from his window on the South encompassed not only the nation but also the world.

The possible meanings of the decade have been buffeted about on a sea of culture wars, in the media as well as in academe, and its legacy continues to be debated. This book is synedochic in its contribution in that it explores the ways in which selected events, texts and figures represent broader issues and trends. Sixties culture is explored through movies, fiction, photography, performances (musical, comedy, sporting, political), collective rituals and memorialisation. No case is made for a canon of representative texts or contexts. On the contrary, this book claims that what was often seen as marginal or socially peripheral can prove symbolically central to the cultural shifts of the 1960s. Although the aphoristic statement that 'history is made by the winners' might seem a safe guide to enumerating the major events of any decade, especially one already subject to a wealth of analysis, it does not adequately illuminate local flashpoints. Nor is it adequate to expect that biographical study of only those figures at the forefront of the decade's politics will stand in for a more nuanced cultural narrative. Presidents and government are often the least likely or reliable barometers of wider cultural concerns. To borrow Slavoj Žižek's phrase, the way to define 'the gist' of an epoch is not to pay attention only to the most explicit features that define 'its social and ideological edifices' but to investigate 'the disavowed ghosts that haunt it'.[7] Memory plays an important role in ghosting and mediating events that occurred half a century ago, in fiction, film and especially in memoirs where an individual's past is linked to the nation's history, because, as W. James Booth argues, 'memory time' can have a framework of seminal events and people but it is also 'an uneven topography of the past where "seminal" does not mean necessarily as a historian would rank them but rather ordered according to their felt importance in the ongoing life of the group'.[8] Paul Auster's memoir *The Invention of Solitude* (1982), for example, does not emphasise 1960 as the year of John F. Kennedy's election, but because Bill Mazeroski won the World

Series for the New York Yankees. A 'New York moment' supersedes any other decisive moment in (national) history.

The idea of a group or collective memory is itself subject to debate. For Joseph Roach, for example, culture exists in the 'social recesses of memory and forgetting' and as performed in vernacular forms.[9] The vernacular form and the social margin were spaces of choice and invention rather than only default positions in the 1960s. The significance of 'spectacular subcultures', as Dick Hebdige defined them, is their expression of socially forbidden content – 'consciousness of class, consciousness of difference' – in forbidden social forms – 'transgressions of sartorial and behavioural codes, law breaking' – and as seemingly 'profane articulations' when first raised as social critique.[10] Youth movements in particular showed that a culture can be most expressive at its boundaries. However, critique was not only initiated by the disenfranchised but also by established intellectuals such as economic sociologist John Kenneth Galbraith whose critique of consumerism, notably in *The Affluent Society* (1958), made him a member of the Kennedy White House. As Ambassador to India he was also voluble in his criticism of government policy, doubting Kennedy's course of action in Vietnam and the rightness of his advisors on defence and national security. By mid-decade, Galbraith was an anti-war activist. Dissent from 'within' as well as 'without' was a feature of 1960s intellectual life such as James W. Silver's *Mississippi: A Closed Society* (1964) in which the history professor exposed the persistence of white supremacist orthodoxy in a personal and social history. As Assistant Secretary of Labor under President Johnson, academic Daniel Patrick Moynihan's report 'The Negro Family: The Case for National Action' (1965) was a liberal's criticism of traditional welfare policy that would prove a rallying cry for a conservative counter-offensive. Moynihan left the White House in the same year and would become a senator in 1976 and remain a Democrat, but he continued to cross party lines, advising the Nixon White House and speaking out against Clinton's policies more than once in the 1990s.

While Moynihan was re-elected senator in the 1980s and 1990s, persons who failed in their bids for public office were sited more decidedly in the radical margins and their shot at the mainstream reveals much about the changing political landscape. When former student activist Tom Hayden ran for the California Senate in 1976 he failed. His slogan, 'The radicalism of the 1960s is becoming the common sense of the 1970s', for some connoted the bitter ends of an already long-lost ideal and, for others, the statement was synonymous with a false utopia. The 1960s would be re-made according to platform issues that both liberals and radicals advanced, but Hayden's mistake was to seem to believe that the 1970s was only 'a modish antique store of a decade that pilfered issues and styles from more vital times'.[11] Hayden would finally be elected to the California State Assembly in 1982, the decade in which conservative reaction to the 1960s took political hold with Ronald Reagan and in which the 'Woodstock Nation' was declared to have finally and quietly transformed middle America.[12] A glance at well-known figures who wanted to be President and failed, or who ran for Congress or Mayor in major cities, is to view the decade through the aspirations of not only George Wallace or Barry Goldwater, politicians who tried to advance from senator to President, but also figures who were *politicised* in the 1960s rather than politicians. Dr Benjamin Spock ran for President on a third-party ticket in 1972 and Ralph Nader, whose stand against corporate corruption and battles as a consumer watchdog led to the founding of an NGO called Public Citizen in 1971, ran for President three times in the 1990s and 2000s.

Controversial writers Gore Vidal and Norman Mailer each ran for office, Vidal for Congress in 1960 (and again in 1982 for the California Democrat nomination) and Mailer in 1969 as mayor of New York City on a Democratic platform to re-map the city as a series of 'villages' to create a deregulated, or indeed, from a different point of view, segregated, city. Mailer even suggested the city secede from the state, a libertarian position that also gained him support from the Right and indicates how closely he read US culture even as he railed against its 'soft' centre. His opposition to the state was, it could be argued, more conservative than William F. Buckley's platform in 1965 when he vowed to discharge a debt to black Americans and published his statement in his own *National Review*. Community activist and Yippie (Youth International Party) Jerry Rubin ran for mayor of Berkeley on an anti-war platform, espousing Black Power politics and promising to legalise marijuana, and 'gonzo' journalist Hunter S. Thompson ran for sheriff of Pitkin County, Colorado also promising the decriminalisation of drugs. While few celebrities had any chance of winning office, the media hook reinforced an image of a society in which dissent coincided with a certain braggadocio. Comedian and civil rights activist Dick Gregory began a campaign in 1968 to enter the 'Black House', a measure of the rhetorical as well as political leverage that a bid for President could engender. He was followed by a far more controversial Presidential candidate, former prisoner Eldridge Cleaver

whose *Soul on Ice* (1969) included the confession that he had used rape
as a weapon of racial hatred. Alongside Cleaver, fellow Black Panthers
Huey Newton and Bobby Seale ran for Congress as 'Peace and
Freedom' candidates. On the Far Right, George Lincoln Rockwell,
founder of the American Nazi Party and coiner of the slogan 'White
Power' as a counter to the Black Power movement, failed to attract
more than 200 members to his cause by his assassination in 1967 and
other reactionaries were equally unconvincing. General Curtis LeMay,
reputedly the inspiration for Dr Strangelove in the 1962 film, ran for
Vice-President to George Wallace but once he made it known he advocated using nuclear weapons in Vietnam their already doubtful double
act was doomed. It has become impossible to understand the 1960s
without examination of the groundswell that animated left-wing
dissent or the decade's conservative legacy which has influenced
culture wars debates ever since.

By the mid-twentieth century, with the wide acceptance of mass
cultural forms, 'culture' was designated 'ordinary', as in Raymond
Williams' 1958 celebration of lived experience over guardianship of
elite culture.[13] Examining the 'ordinary' exposes the ways in which
imaginative acts and representational objects define as well as interpret
the quotidian. Cultural anthropologist Clifford Geertz was progres-
sively aware through the 1960s that 'the line between mode of representation and substantive content is as undrawable in cultural analysis
as it is in painting' and that culture is the 'informal logic' of life.[14]
Williams' formulation of cultural practices as dominant, residual or
emergent succeeded in apprehending the alternative and oppositional.[15] 'Culture', always already as syncretic as it is declarative, began
to change as 'legitimate' arena – the theatre, the university, the art
gallery – transformed in relation to supposedly transgressive spaces
such as Off-Off Broadway, comedy clubs, or tenement walls such as
Chicago's 'Wall of Respect' (1967). Culture became a buzzword
largely because the rebarbative 'counterculture' forced a re-evaluation
and because the paperback revolution and the demise of the increasingly contentious Moving Picture Association seal of approval signalled that boundaries between 'high' and 'low' culture had indeed
crumbled. The 'counterculture' contained the tension between democratic ideals and undemocratic practices, a disillusion with a national
or 'official' culture as signified by government, the military and 'the
establishment' – in all its forms from stifling parents to party politics.
It also contained optimism about the idea of renewing that same
culture by reinvigorating as well as condemning the status quo.

The Turn of the Sixties

Exactly when the 1960s 'begin' and when the decade's salient preoc-
cupations 'end' continues to provoke debate. Should 'the long 1960s'
end around 1972-4, as Fredric Jameson argues in 'Periodizing the
Sixties', in order to allow for the withdrawal of US troops from
Vietnam in 1973? Should the end be tied to a key individual, such
Lyndon Johnson who died in January 1973 just as the last rounds of
America gunfire were fired in the war? Or do the 1960s run on until
the symbolic Saigon Airlift of 1975 – and indeed should the war in
Vietnam figure significantly as the 'end-stop' to an eventful decade?
The *Roe* vs *Wade* decision of 1973, legalising abortion as intrinsic to
the 'right to privacy' of any woman, was a result of women pushing
issues into the foreground in the 1960s. Yet pro-life vs pro-choice
antagonism has never ended; if one measures the decade according to
attempts by the disenfranchised to take possession of their histories, it
is not yet over. Or does the political and social impact end with
attempts to roll back gains when Affirmative Actions programmes
came under attack? There is no definitive answer to such questions;
much more important is the ways in which the 1960s remain high on
agendas where these issues feature.

Many important inroads into understanding tensions between
public and private in the 1960s were made in the 1950s. Galbraith
argued in *The Affluent Society* that the public sector was approaching
crisis because private consumer wealth dominated as the measure of
social success and hence public service funding was diminishing. Mike
Davis argues that the 1960s should be read as a 'fin-de-siècle' decade
because the postwar economic boom reached the height of its success
then prior to slumps in the mid-1970s.[16] C. Wright Mills posited in
The Power Elite (1956) that the nature of public life was decided by
the military machine and the corporate power base, as critics of the
war would reiterate, and that government could not be trusted to
resolve social inequities in the way of Roosevelt's New Deal. In his
chronicle of representatives of five million African Americans who
made the 'Great Black Migration' South to North, Nicholas Lemann
showed they were sustained by New Deal-initiated programmes that
Eisenhower or Truman put in place, their lives largely unchanged by
under-funded federal programmes such as the 'War on Poverty'.
Nevertheless, poverty underwent sustained review in the era.
Anthropologist Oscar Lewis coined 'the culture of poverty' in his
1959 study of Mexican families and reinforced his definition in the US

context in 1966.[17] Like Michael Harrington's *The Other America* (1962) in which he claimed complacency over technological progress was a contributory factor in the number of Americans living below the poverty line, Lewis emphasised chronic unemployment and the systemic low expectations of the underclass. The supremely controversial Moynihan report took its cue from both theses, as explored in Chapter 3.

While the 1950s is described as more conservative than the 1960s, quiescent, or even 'tranquillized' to borrow poet Robert Lowell's epithet, as Steve Whitfield, Pete Daniel, Brian Ward, Martin Halliwell and others have shown, that is far from the whole story. Leaning too heavily on the idea of the fifties as a conformist 'foil' for the effervescent sixties serves only to detach the era from all it built upon, as if Kennedy's inauguration initiated a new cultural frontier as surely as his rhetoric. It was, after all, Kennedy's advisor Arthur Schlesinger Jr who, following Lewis Mumford's depiction of suburbia in *The City in History* (1961), compared the Eisenhower era to a genuinely benevolent but bland company town. In contrast, it could be claimed that Allen Ginsberg's 'Howl' (1956) already connoted the radical cultural shifts popularly believed to characterise the 1960s. Or, as Morris Dickstein maintains, Dean Moriarty in Jack Kerouac's *On the Road* was the 'patron saint of the counterculture', an idea espoused by student activist Tom Hayden for whom Moriarty was the cowboy-explorer as rebel, breaking out of 'the new suburbia that now occupied the once-vast American frontier'.[18] Ginsberg's focus on dropping out, losing oneself in drugs, and chaining oneself to causes contains the seeds of despair and anomie that would tear apart the counterculture, even as he speaks of the generation that preceded it.

Similarly, in the 1950s parents and governments were caught up in a moral panic around juvenile delinquency, a fear that would be revisited throughout the 1960s. In 1957 *Cosmopolitan* launched a special issue asking 'Are Teenagers Taking Over?', describing them as 'blue-jeaned storm troopers, forcing us to do exactly as they dictate'.[19] Youth revolt was the subject of an intellectual *tour de force* which advocated breaking out of the 'mind-forg'd manacles' of the middle-class American family. Herbert Marcuse, Norman O. Brown and Paul Goodman, philosophers, a sociologist and neo-Freudians all, conflated a newly permissive erotic liberation with cultural and political radicalism as the fifties turned into the sixties writing, respectively, *Eros and Civilization* (1955, rev. 1962), *Life Against Death* (1959) and *Growing Up Absurd* (1960). Each emphasised youth forging beyond consensus by enacting what Marcuse called 'The Great Refusal', an act of revolutionary will explored in terms of movement culture in Chapter 5. The Civil Rights Movement had conservative roots in middle-class black respectability, as is made very clear by the Montgomery Bus Boycott of 1955 6 and the Southern Christian Leader Conference (SCLC) founded in 1957. The 1950s *was* a much quieter decade, in terms of civil rights successes. The Supreme Court decision to begin racial integration of schools in 1954 and the local decision to bring two of Emmett Till's killers swiftly to trial in Mississippi in 1955 were harbingers of cultural change that would gather force only in the 1960s.

Figure I.1 Dr Martin Luther King Jr acknowledges the crowd at the Lincoln Memorial for his 'I Have a Dream' speech during the March on Washington DC, 28 August 1963. Associated Press. Courtesy PA Photos.

Dr Martin Luther King Jr and the Turn of the Sixties

Dr King's political career was framed by social movement goals and local struggles, from the Montgomery Bus Boycott that brought him to national prominence to the sanitation workers' strike that brought him to Memphis in April 1968 where he was assassinated. Rev. Ralph Abernathy's eulogy at the funeral emphasised King's status as a signifier of hope denied, his death often seen as ushering in a period of declension: 'Let us slay the dreamer, and see what shall become of his dream'.

While 'I Have a Dream' is probably the best-known speech in or about the US, and its delivery was a bitter marking of the centenary of the Emancipation Proclamation, it is typically recalled as the hopeful high-ground from which the movement descended. Statements in *Why We Can't Wait* (1963) and *Where Do We Go From Here? Chaos or Community* (1967) are more illustrative of the complex 'American dilemma' that continues to inform US culture in which attention to race has been obsessive. King's essays like John F. Kennedy's speeches are renowned and revered. Down the decades they are a staple of school and college courses, 'The Letter from Birmingham Jail' (1963) often the text through which students are introduced to racial tensions in the 1950s and 1960s South. The open letter is a distinctive form of the radical essay and the short form was expedient for King who honed his rhetorical skills so that he might retain the oral and aural qualities of the sermon from the pulpit in the scribal form. When King writes, 'I am in Birmingham because injustice is here', as the reader pauses with him, it is possible to imagine an assenting 'Amen' rising against 'the dark dungeons of complacency' to light 'the bright hills of creative protest'.[20] King presented Birmingham as the nation's racial crucible and the larger significance of the city is explored in the Conclusion to this book. King's 'Letter', written during one of the twenty or so occasions he was imprisoned for non-violent agitation, was, he hoped, a 'creative psalm of brotherhood', but it was also a condemnation of the silence and/or gradualism of 'good people', in the persons of the churchmen to whom he directed his words. The white moderate was a primary recipient of King's disdain for the paternalism according to which 'he feels he can set the timetable for another man's freedom'.

Why We Can't Wait was published to coincide with the March on Washington and the paperback capitalised on Dr King winning the Nobel Peace Prize in 1964. It documents the hopes and ideals of the civil rights struggle as it warns of the rising anger that James Baldwin's *The Fire Next Time* (1963) also articulated. Polemical yet diagnostic, the publication of King's speeches in mass-market paperbacks ensured sales in the multi-millions and helped to secure his reputation as the greatest black leader the nation has produced. However, African Americans on the radical Left and the conservative Right could be critical of the strategies King had made his own in the 1950s. In 'Tear This Building Down', Julius Lester challenged King's espousal of agapic love in stark terms, declaring the March on Washington 'nothing but a giant therapy session', and asking, 'What is love supposed to do? Wrap the bullet in a warm embrace? Caress the cattle prod?'[21] Anne Moody working for voter-registration in Mississippi remembered that at the March on Washington, 'I sat there thinking that in Canton we never had time to sleep, much less to dream'.[22] Conservative George Schuyler was the most scathing in response to King becoming the youngest Nobel winner: 'Dr. King's principle contribution to world peace has been to roam the country like some sable Typhoid Mary, infecting the mentally disturbed with perversions of Christian doctrine and grabbing fat lecture fees from the shallow-pated'.[23]

In the three years before his death, King's philosophy of reform encompassed poverty at home and American foreign policy and international relations. His condemnation of the war in Vietnam maintained an emphasis on racial minorities barely considered citizens at home but deemed sufficiently American to die for their nation abroad. In the aftermath of the Watts disturbances when King began to urge Lyndon Johnson to withdraw from Vietnam, he made his most controversial speech, 'A Time to Break Silence' (1967) against 'the greatest purveyor of violence in the world today – my own government'.[24] King believed he was cowardly in having feared that speaking against the war would weaken his position as national spokesman on civil rights yet in *Why We Can't Wait* he was already asking, 'Why has our nation placed itself in the position of being God's military on earth, and intervened recklessly in Vietnam and the Dominican Republic?'[25] It was his avowed patriotism, 'to inject new meaning into the veins' of the nation, that first stirred King to ask the difficult questions that return in chilling echoes in the speech he delivered in Memphis the night before he died. It is infused with tragic prescience of his death that also recalls a statement when he first became a reluctant leader in 1955: 'Tell Montgomery they can keep on bombing and I'm going to stand up to them. If I had to die tomorrow morning, I would die happy because I've been to the Mountaintop and I've seen the Promised Land, and it's going to be here in Montgomery'.[26]

Dr King was the embodiment of moral integrity despite FBI attempts to discredit that image and in 1961 he was invited to be a star, playing a senator from Mississippi in Otto Preminger's *Advise and Consent* (1962) in which Charles Laughton played the senator from South Carolina based on Strom Thurmond. The Southern Christian Leadership Conference (SCLC) administrative committee voted unanimously that King should play the part and that the $5,000 offered should fund SCLC. King's image was the organisation's primary concern. King would fly to California for one day to film but a caveat was included: 'When the picture is finished, the producers have agreed to permit Dr. King and a Committee of three of his choosing to preview the picture and if it is thought to be too reactionary and damaging to Dr. King's image, then Dr. King will be eliminated from the picture'.[27] In the end, he never took an acting role but the attention paid to his image is indicative of how precious it was to the movement he spearheaded and how prized it still is. King has rarely been portrayed on screen as if to dramatise is to pastiche, rendering his messiah status less reverent. In 2001 the NAACP (National Association for the Advancement of Colored People) gave an Image Award to *Boycott!* In the film's coda Dr King (Jeffrey Wright) is resurrected; as Wright walks through the streets of Montgomery still dressed as King, the public does not commend the actor on his performance but experiences a shock of recognition: the implication is that 'King' could walk again down one of the 500 US streets named in his honour if only his moral suasion could be recovered in contemporary society. Dr King remains the yardstick against which other activists have been measured, despite Ella Baker's warning that 'The Movement made Martin' and repeated calls at the time for him to 'catch up' with the masses. King's career was also, as Peter Ling has argued in his biography, shaped by the counter-movement: not only the Dixiecrats who taxed him but also the liberals who thwarted or appeased him and the anti-war movement to which he finally added his not insubstantial voice.

The age and class of participants infused the Movement with the image of responsible integrity that followed those experienced in civic duties whose participation in the culture, were they granted full citizenship rights, could only benefit the nation. To begin with, black public figures who chose not to conform were replaced, as when the unorthodox Rev. Vernon Johns was superseded at Dexter Avenue Baptist Church by the more traditionally respectable Dr Martin Luther King Jr, and when King was elected leader of the Montgomery Improvement Association (MIA) instead of veteran activist E. D. Nixon. The rise of social movements after 1960, on the other hand, usually emphasised the youth and militancy of participants. The reification of youthful social protest risks denying a more complex picture, as argued in Chapter 5. In June 1963 when John Doar advised Vivien Malone, 'You should dress as if you were going to church, modestly and neatly', to integrate the University of Alabama, his words recalled the same index of black progress that underpinned the Montgomery movement in the 1950s.[28]

Vernon Johns died in 1965 but his talent for shocking congregants out of complacency would have served him well in movement culture in the 1960s. Speaking out is a key motif in this book. It is explored with regard to powerful phrasemakers as different as Norman Mailer, Susan Sontag, Leslie Fiedler, Pauline Kael, Rachel Carson, Wallace Stegner, Vine Deloria and Norman Podheretz. Novelists too acted as public speakers, so much so that John W. Aldridge would opine in 'Celebrity and Boredom' (1966), 'It sometimes seems that a "Kilroy was here" sign hangs over the literary life of our age'.[29] The expressive self was a cultural force in art, in position pieces such as Thomas Pynchon's 'A

Journey into the Mind of Watts' (1966), 'new journalism' and stand-up comedy. Comedians were particularly adept at catching the political Zeitgeist and hurling it back as acerbic satire, as explored in Chapter 1. The most controversial of cultural commentators worked hard to preserve a sense of speaking from the radical sidelines while situating themselves at the cultural centre; no one more than Norman Mailer.

Norman Mailer and Adversarial Cultural Critique

Mailer published *The Naked and the Dead* in 1948 when he was 25 but really set out his writerly stall in the 1950s as an adversarial commentator on contemporary culture. In *The Village Voice* (the paper he helped found), he defined what it was to be 'Hip', an ideology he argued could be traced back into 'all the undercurrents and underworlds of American life, back into the instinctive apprehension and appreciation of existence which one finds in the Negro and the soldier, in the criminal psychopath and the dope addict and jazz musician, in the prostitute, in the actor, in the – if one can visualize such a possibility – in the marriage of the call-girl and the psychoanalyst.'[30] In the 1960s he 'visualised' stories of these characters in his novels and promulgated these ideas in essays and journalism. Author of the audaciously entitled *Advertisements for Myself* (1959), he conjured the character 'Norman Mailer' in *The Armies of the Night* (1967) in a sleight of hand he attributed to reading *The Education of Henry Adams* (1918) as a high-school student.[31] Mailer exhibited a knack for ferreting out and commenting on the nation's psychoses. In *The Making of a Counter Culture* (1969) Theodore Roszak returns to Mailer's 'The White Negro' (1957) as 'still one of the best evaluations of youthful dissent' and Mailer's assertion that the use of chemical weapons in Vietnam 'might be the index of our collective instability' was a memorably provocative statement at the height of the war.[32] His instincts about readers were finely tuned so he inserted himself into each significant cultural event but projected a mock-modest impression of never having been at the centre: 'Mailer had an instinct for missing good speeches – at the Civil Rights March in Washington in 1963 he had gone for a stroll just a little while before Martin Luther King began "I have a dream" '.[33]

More than any other public intellectual, Mailer moved between factions whose social visions clashed. He portrayed himself as a political Everyman with his 'private mixture of Marxism, conservatism, nihilism, and large parts of existentialism', the kind of concatenation of affiliations that spans the political ages but privileges sixties ideology.[34] In Mailer's version of the anti-war March on the Pentagon in *Armies of the Night*, different shades of political opinion unite in common cause as citizens converge across generations, religions and classes.

Mailer was a publicity hound. *Time* condemned him as an 'anti-star' spewing obscenities as he performed the role of irascible know-it-all addressing demonstrators from the stage at Washington's Ambassador Theater.[35] The radical shift towards the use of 'bad language' and 'obscenities' epitomised by comedian Lenny Bruce found its way into the mainstream via his feisty commentary: 'Mailer never felt more like an American than when he was naturally obscene'.[36] Mailer followed Marcuse in yoking together sex and violence, 'the unspoken territories of sex', in novels such as *An American Dream* (1963). Having stabbed his wife some years earlier, Mailer shocked readers by making the apocalyptic orgasm the murder of a wife and rape of her maid, the protagonist a suicidal war hero friend of Kennedy, and the novel a dark disquisition on Kennedy's New Frontier. Topicality, the ruin of an otherwise good novel for many writers, was Mailer's primary tool and led to his appearances on TV shows such as 'Outrageous Opinions' hosted by Helen Gurley Brown. His opinion pieces were renowned, including 'An Evening with Jackie Kennedy' (*Esquire*, 1962), in which he described her hosting a television tour of the White House like 'a starlet who is totally without talent' in a 'phony' voice designed for 'selling gadgets to the grim'. Mailer was monitored by the FBI and CIA, receiving 364 pages of his FBI file in 1975.[37]

Re-reading *The Armies of the Night*, one is struck by the prescience of his commentary. Mailer's coruscating indictment of Lyndon Johnson's 'bad war' resonates with twenty-first-century criticisms of the war against Iraq. It is a reminder that George W. Bush was made in the crucible of the 1960s even as he modelled himself against presidential and almost-presidential figures Bill Clinton and John Kerry. Taking to the university lecture circuit in his eighties, Mailer's excoriation of Bush in *Why Are We at War?* (2003) derived much of its ideological shadowing from techniques he honed in the 1960s. Mailer once threw out the observation that 'Once History inhabits a crazy house, egotism may be the last tool left to History'[38] and while Kate Millett deemed him megalomaniacal and masculinist in *Sexual Politics* (1970), others celebrated his audacious intellectual presence. Diana Trilling compared him to the prophet Moses and Richard Poirier followed Mailer himself in arguing, 'men who become Presidents or champions of the world are . . . men very much like Mailer'.[39] His facility for catching the Zeitgeist and courting controversy made him a cultural phenomenon who is returned to in this book for the moments he intersects with the decade's key events.

The Myth of the 'New' Frontier

In 1960 President John F. Kennedy declared he would 'get America moving again' and his campaign and inauguration speeches forged the myth of an Arthurian Camelot, in which the youngest American president would serve in cold war-enforced peace and prosperity:

> And if a beachhead of cooperation may push back the jungle of suspicion, let both sides join in creating a new endeavor, not a new balance of

Figure I.2 Anti-war demonstrators run up against military police at the Pentagon in Washington DC on 21 October 1967, the events that Mailer describes in *Armies of the Night*. Courtesy PA Photos.

power, but a new world of law, where the strong are just and the weak secure and the peace preserved.

All this will not be finished in the first 100 days. Nor will it be finished in the first 1,000 days, nor in the life of this administration, nor even perhaps in our lifetime on this planet. But let us begin.[40]

By his death, having served the county for only 1,037 days, the Kennedy legend had taken shape. It was the image against which subsequent presidents would be measured and the Kennedy dynasty emerged as the nation's home-grown aristocracy.

The government's image of a 'New Frontier' emphasised personal and political courage with Kennedy the charismatic liberal figurehead. He was a magnetic media personality and in the 1960s the politician, like other celebrities, became an art form – as depicted by Andy Warhol and Robert Rauschenberg. Kennedy's star status was underlined by Arthur Schlesinger Jr and Theodore Sorenson in speeches they wrote for him and of direct popular influence was his own best-selling *Profiles in Courage*, awarded the Pulitzer Prize in 1957. Kennedy argued the challenges to political courage loomed large and celebrated US politicians he believed extraordinary in meeting them. The captain of a

PT-109, Kennedy had served with valour in Word War II and rescued marines, one of whom – Victor Krulak – he placed in charge of the special forces he called the Green Berets and sent to Vietnam in 1963. On 6 March 1960 Eisenhower announced the government planned to send 3,500 troops to Vietnam. Only a few months later, with Kennedy in power, the film *PT-109* (1963) dramatised his military courage and underscored in the run-up to war that what he might expect of others, he had been willing to undergo himself. The Peace Corps may seem the obverse of the secret troubleshooting Green Berets, but in their personification of Kennedy's rhetoric – 'Ask not what your country can do for you, ask what you can do for your country' – the young volunteers were equally the outward face of a cold war President around the world. Kennedy was most traditional, however, in his espousal of established liberal tenets. At the opening of the Robert Frost Library in 1963 Kennedy celebrated poets as disinterested observers, tellers of 'basic human truths' standing outside of ideology. The President's Romantic separation of culture from society, albeit couched in literary terms, would prove ironic in a decade when poets as different as Robert Lowell, Gwendolyn Brooks and Denise Levertov would engage specifically with contemporary issues, including the war precipitated during his Presidency, in avowedly political ways.

Different events have been proffered as *the* moment in which America lost its so-called innocence: the assassination of Kennedy or that of Dr King, the extinguishing of the last liberal hope with the death of Robert Kennedy, or the death of hope in a people's ability to change government policy and prevent the continual escalation of the Vietnam War. In Don DeLillo's novel *Libra* (1988), President Kennedy's murder is described as 'seven seconds that broke the back of the American century'.[41] On 22 November 1963 he was shot in Dallas and died within minutes. Lee Harvey Oswald, arrested the same day, was described by the press as a lone assassin despite conspiracies arguing the contrary and by 24 November he too was dead, shot by Jack Ruby, owner of a striptease club in Dallas and there was no doubt this time. Television cameras captured the crime and Ruby declared, 'I did it for Jackie Kennedy'. Kennedy's Camelot had spiralled into violence. His widow returned to the Broadway show *Camelot* again in the role of his Guinevere: 'At night, before we'd go to sleep, Jack liked to play some records; and the song he loved most came at the very end [of Lerner and Loewe's musical]. The lines he loved to hear were: *Don't let it be forgot, that once there was a spot, for one brief shining moment that was known as Camelot*'.[42]

Figure I.3 A boy reads Kennedy's inaugural speech at his grave site, Arlington Cemetery, Virginia. Courtesy Francisca Fuentes.

Lighting the 'eternal flame' to burn over his grave reinforced the image of the President as hero in power for only 1,000 days. In the weeks after his death, Jackie Kennedy declared: 'You must think of him as this little boy, sick so much of the time, reading in bed, reading history, reading the Knights of the Round Table, reading Marlborough. For Jack, history was full of heroes. And if it made him this way – if it made him see the heroes – maybe other little boys will see'.[43] One such boy would seize the folk dream she narrated; Bill Clinton used a clip of himself shaking hands with Kennedy and although he was not the first to align himself with the man and the posthumous myth, he would become the first Baby Boomer 'sixties' President, as explored in the Conclusion.

Others fell foul of comparison with Kennedy from Dan Quayle to George W. Bush but none more than President Johnson.[44] At his inauguration parade a young man could not unfix the image of Kennedy, dead or alive: 'a melancholy impulse had taken me back to the spot on Pennsylvania Avenue . . . where I had stood for the funeral procession the year before. When I try now to picture a triumphant LBJ going by, I see instead the riderless black horse. Same bands, different music'.[45] The inability to respond to Johnson in his own right is symptomatic of a wider cultural problem with which Johnson had to contend, suffering for his failure to *be* JFK and for his image as an elder*ly* statesman.[46] Youthfulness had been focal in defining the New Frontier and brother Robert took up the call, arguing, 'This world demands the qualities of youth; not a time of life but a state of mind, a temper of the will, a quality of the imagination, a predominance of courage over timidity, of the appetite for adventure over the life of ease in the world'.[47] He located President Kennedy squarely in the vanguard when he had actually been slow to act on civil rights, trying to contain unrest and maintain relations with the southern bloc of Democratic voters.

When Jackie Kennedy Onassis died in 1994 aged 64, her image remained, despite her second marriage, that of the First Lady gracefully carrying the nation's grief and upholding the Kennedy legend, not least via her silence on his romantic affairs. Even those who quickly became disaffected could identify with the utopian image embodied in the youngest President. Hunter S. Thompson argued, 'Student radicals may call Kennedy a phony liberal and a glamorous sellout, but only the very young will deny that it was Kennedy who got them excited enough to want to change the American reality, instead of just quitting it'.[48] Yippie activist Abbie Hoffman took up the same theme: 'Kennedy

often lied to our generation, but nevertheless he made us believe we
could change the course of history'.[49] Despite Kennedy sending some
15,000 military advisors to Vietnam, engaging with the internal politics of the Diem regime, and co-opting the nation into an unwinnable
war, cold warriors return to his Presidency as a moral highground.
Defense Secretary Robert McNamara resigned in 1966 but in the revisionist return to Vietnam that began with his 1991 memoir and continued in *The Fog of War* (2003), he looks back to the Kennedy
Administration as 'the best years of our life'. In 2007 McNamara
declared:

> 'I will tell you what leadership is . . . It's Jack Kennedy refusing to risk
> nuclear war when nearly everyone in the room is telling him to . . .
> Kennedy listened to the overwhelming advice of his so-called experts' –
> McNamara pauses, leaning back to add a touch of drama – 'and then he
> ordered the blockade instead'.[50]

In returning to the Cuban Missile Crisis, McNamara recalls the ubiquitous, if oxymoronic, Iron Curtain, the final frontier between life and
nuclear apocalypse. Kennedy's frontier metaphor was sufficiently
mobile to signify across real and imagined geographies; it could be
America saving South Vietnam from the horrors of Communism by
policing the 17th parallel, or even the terrain of North Vietnam which
Mary McCarthy described as 'still pioneer county'.[51] It could be the
gay liberation movement breaking the heterosexual frontier. It could
be rediscovered in the Native American past in N. Scott Momaday's
House Made of Dawn (1969) – or in outer space.

  The space race secured its dollars and democratic script from the
ideology of the New Frontier, as in Kennedy's 1961 speech to
Congress: 'I believe that this nation should commit itself to achieving
the goal, before the decade is out, of landing a man on the moon and
returning him safely to earth'.[52] Lynn Spigel has described the space
race as a way 'to transform the doldrums of national complacency and
sell the public on a sense of the future', as in the issue of *Look* entitled
'Soaring into the Sixties'.[53] For most of the decade space flights orbited
the moon and from the summer of 1969 to the end of 1972 lunar landings dominated the popular imagination. Astronauts featured in cultural productions as different as Hanna-Barbera's cartoon *The Jetsons*
(1962–88), Disney's *Moon Pilot* (1962), NBC's *I Dream of Jeannie*
(1965–70), *Planet of the Apes* (1968), *2001: A Space Odyssey* (1968) and
Star Trek, as discussed in Chapter 2.

Just as the space odyssey *Star Trek* returned to Shakespeare in its allusions to civilisation and culture, there was a return to Frederick Jackson Turner's frontier thesis of the 1890s in Kennedy's 'New Frontier', as there was in revisionist Western fiction and film. If Turner declared the Western frontier closed in 1893, Kennedy sought to re-open it by making a decade synonymous with a new cultural frontier. Turner's modern myth would be subject to new ideological scrutiny. In his 'Wilderness Letter' (1960), Wallace Stegner campaigned to ensure preservation of the California wilderness as the 'genetic reserve . . . against which our character as a people was formed'.[54] In *Little Big Man* (1964) Thomas Berger compared the attempted genocide of American Indians with US intervention in Vietnam. While the 1960s also saw the demythologising of the Western film in *Cheyenne Autumn* (1964), *Cat Ballou* (1965), *Paint Your Wagon* (1969) and *Little Big Man* (1970), Warren French argued that it continued to shape national mythology until *Easy Rider* (1969) ushered in the more problematic 'Southern'. It is an idea with which this study contends.[55]

Bonnie and Clyde (1967) is a central plank in any discussion of myth and revisionism, its *retro* style a component of its success, as made manifest when Theadora Van Runkle's versions of Faye Dunaway's costumes made their way into high-street stores. Like *Hud* (1963) and *Hombre* (1967), it rejected the image of an innocent America and the nostalgia (albeit self-consciously reiterated) that would texture films such as Sergio Leone's *Once Upon a Time in the West* (1968). Instead, petty and ruthless killers Clyde Barrow and Bonnie Parker, mock-heroic poor whites in the Depression Southwest, burn with a resentment that chimes closely with countercultural concerns. Comparing 1960s social unrest with Depression-era social upheavals, Arthur Penn could convey his fear that new social movements would fail to transform American life.

The myth of New World innocence was demolished in fiction too, including Richard Brautigan's *Trout Fishing in America* (1967) and Wallace Stegner's *All the Little Live Things* (1967), discussed in Chapter 5, which exposed the regenerative myth of the Western wilderness insofar as, like any other American place, it could be corrupted. *Easy Rider* (1969), a countercultural celluloid statement made on a shoestring budget of $375,000, grossed some $50 million worldwide on first release by tapping into the same archetypal 'American' dreams via the mythos of the frontier, with violence the consequence for any American who failed to conform to conservative mores on

Figure I.4 *Bonnie and Clyde* (1967). Courtesy Warner Bros./The Kobal Collection.

crossing the Mason-Dixon line. Instead of 'lighting out for the [western] territory', the protagonists travel from the West to the Deep South and their murder by southern 'rednecks' added the force and controversy that a tale of hippie bikers might not otherwise have had. The anarchic if laconic Captain America (Peter Fonda) and Billy the Kid (Dennis Hopper) are countercultural Adams. The film's legend, 'A man went looking for America and couldn't find it anywhere', is not only a eulogy for a paradise enlivened by drugs and lived out in rural places. The film's symbolic notion of 'freedom' also fails to imagine how black and white might live together even at the end of the decade. Sena Jeter Naslund's epic novel *Four Spirits* (2003) set in Birmingham in 1963 returns to the same impossible dreams when it opens with black children imagining that the gigantic cast-iron statue of Vulcan that presides over Birmingham might have a romance with the Statue of Liberty. As early as *Democracy in America* (1835–40), French commentator Alexis de Tocqueville had asserted that the danger of conflict between white and black would perpetually haunt the American imagination and the protracted struggle for racial harmony reached its apotheosis in the 1960s on the southern frontier. Historian Charles Payne even describes SNCC's (Student Nonviolent Coordinating Committee) entry into southern towns as 'reminiscent of the Old West, with one or two marshals coming to clean up Dodge City'.[56]

The South: The Eye of the Sixties Hurricane

An idea that was 'hot' in the 1960s was cultural mythopoesis, as posited by Richard Slotkin, which traces the ways in which stories, sometimes apocryphal, become accepted with repetition and solidify into myths and archetypes. President Kennedy, already mythologised in Mailer's *The Presidential Papers* (1963), fulfilled the tenets of Slotkin's myth-narrative: 'a protagonist hero with whom the audience is presumed to identify . . .; a universe in which the hero may act which is . . . a reflection of the audience's conception of the world . . .; and a narrative in which the interaction of hero and universe is described'.[57] Archetypes have helped to fix cultural ideas into decades. Myths were re-inscribed through structuring antinomies, to borrow Claude Levi-Strauss' terms, such as public vs private, individual vs community, Nature vs culture, garden vs wilderness – and the US vs Russia – as re-produced in political speeches and movies. New social movements would engage with such myths in their campaigns to change society; the frontier West and exceptionalist South would be especially tested and challenged.

The sixties was synonymous with the South, the region in which the Civil Rights Movement took its stand. As described by novelist Ellen Douglas: 'The separate black and white societies of the South and the country were grinding against each other with the agonized crunch of continental plates, preparing the earthquakes and volcanic eruptions of the sixties'.[58] Literary critic Fred Hobson remembers that as a southern student travelling West following a trail lit by *The Grapes of Wrath*, he was suddenly and ironically aware of going in the wrong direction. 'The nation's action and passion in 1964 . . . was to be found not in the West but in the South we were leaving behind'.[59] The eye of the Civil Rights hurricane was the South and as Freedom Summer played out in 1964 the nation would be confronted by evidence of massive resistance to racial integration in its most violent form. While African Americans were being killed for fighting for their rights, the murder of white northerners come south for the summer would create the media 'shock-stock' that had eluded black southerners, as explored in Chapter 5.

The national model of a north-south binary was particularly acute in the 1960s and has been described as both a second Civil War and a second Reconstruction. In *The Southern Mystique* (1964), Howard Zinn asserted the South represented the nation in its most concentrated form, functioning as 'a mirror in which the nation can see its blemishes magnified'.[60] Images of a 'savage' South ensured the region could be read as the nation's backward cousin with southern whites huddled together according to an enduring 'proto-Dorian bond', as W. J. Cash had described in *The Mind of the South* (1941). The 'South' was estranged from the nation, the image of the urban, liberal North dependent on a 'foreign' alien South. When Attorney General Robert Kennedy failed to find a discourse in which to convince George Wallace of the rightness of federal support of civil rights, he feared the South was 'like a foreign country'. Robert Drew's documentary film *Crisis* (1963) sets up a dichotomy between Robert Kennedy and Wallace, cutting from the Kennedy home where the children eat with their father and are persuaded by him to drink their breakfast milk to Governor Wallace's Alabama mansion where a black maid is left to care for his little daughter. Wallace's demagogic racism, descending from Herman Talmadge, Theodore Bilbo and James K. Vardaman, was a language that Drew presents Kennedy as unable to penetrate. The editors of *Time-Life* argued that 'The rest of the United States has been almost as ready to explain itself by contrast with Mississippi as by contrast with Russia' and African American comedian Dick Gregory remembers that when he worked for the Chicago postal service, he intentionally put mail to Mississippi in the foreign mail sack.[61] In 'Talking Birmingham Jam', folk singer Phil Ochs sang:

So I asked 'em how they spent their time
With segregation on their mind.
They said, 'If you don't like to live this way,
Get outa here. Go back to the USA . . .

And he lambasted 'The State of Mississippi': 'The calender is lyin'
when it reads the present time . . ./ Mississippi find yourself another
country to be part of!'

Turner's frontier thesis had argued the West was the nation's 'true
point of view' and supposedly regional points of view began to dominate in the 1960s as local grievances mapped on to national anxieties. In
the West grassroots organisations including the Industrial Workers of
the World united workers across racial and ethnic lines in the 1920s and
played a pivotal role in San Francisco's General Strike of 1934. The
West Coast was focal for the Beat Movement with landscapes such as
Big Sur and the Mohave Desert central to ideas of individual freedom,
as they were to the American Indian Movement. In 1960 California students led anti-HUAC (House Un-American Activities Committee)
demonstrations and UCLA Berkeley was the centre of the Free Speech
Movement (FSM), while in the Bay Area the National Farmworkers
Union, Black Panther Party and the hippie movement were all pio-
neered. The Watts rebellion of 1965 ensured that those who still deemed
American race relations a 'southern problem' were shocked into recognition that there were separate black and white cultures throughout the
US, strained and at odds. As Thomas Pynchon described, 'Watts is a
country which lies, psychologically, uncounted miles further than most
whites seem at present willing to travel'[62] and rebellions followed in
Newark and Detroit in 1967. This book pays special attention to the
West as well as the sea changes in American culture that began in
southern places.

When the Kerner Commission in 1968 reported 'our nation is
moving toward two societies, one black, one white – separate and
unequal'[63], a government-funded body finally announced the 'southern' problem was intrinsically national, as had been reiterated repeatedly across different cultural forms. *The Autobiography of Malcolm X*,
for instance, sees the 'southern' racial nightmare played out in rural
Oklahoma when Klan nightriders threaten Malcolm's father and burn
the family home to the ground. The movie *Love Field* (1992) critiques
Kennedy's America in terms of Kerner's separate black and white
worlds. A devotee of Jackie Kennedy (Michelle Pfeiffer) is confident
that all black people must be devastated by Kennedy's death. 'He did

so much for your people' she informs an African American mechanic at a gas station in rural Tennessee. His response is cutting: 'Take a look around, ma'am. Look like he done much here?' Watching Kennedy's funeral on the television, a well-meaning white southern woman is visibly affected. Her character fulfils Dr King's description of good people who remained silent on racist violence; she is shocked: 'I don't know when we started killing people to solve things'. The African American protagonist's rejoinder is as swift and sharp as the mechanic's: 'I didn't know we stopped'.

The 'savage' South acted as a synonym for larger social concerns, notably the nation's obsession with the fiction of racial purity. It is important to understand how the South was represented in order to apprehend the myriad ways in which it persists in sixties mythology.[64] In the rhetoric of the southern freedom struggle could be found the moral centre of the liberal nation, as in the freedom song 'We Shall Overcome'. Historian Sara Evans claims, 'The sit-in movement and the freedom rides had an electrifying impact on northern liberal culture'[65] and the influx of northern liberals into the 'conservative' South in 1964 was itself an indication that 'conservative' and 'liberal' are functional if nebulous terms. The assumption that citizenship was normatively white began to be dismantled in the South as African Americans represented themselves as 'the litmus test of the viability and reality of American democracy'.[66] Demands to tackle Jim Crow in the South and its residual forms in the North exposed a solipsistic racial blindness on the part of government and the extent to which Kennedy, Johnson or Nixon addressed race relations is one measure of their success in office. The dominant iconography was of good black folk versus evil white racists: rabid segregationist politicians, White Citizens Councils and Klansmen conspiring to ensure 'massive resistance' to gains made by blacks, inarticulate 'redneck' mobs stirred to violence, and corrupt tobacco-chewing sheriffs – an image explored in *In The Heat of the Night* (1967) and discussed in Chapter 2.

In order to understand an ideology one has to make it visible and mass demonstrations by black southerners showed in stark terms that protestors could not wait much longer for their civil rights to be enshrined in federal legislation. The role of newspaper journalists and television in reporting civil rights was essential. Until the mid-1950s events in the region had received sporadic coverage in the national press. The *New York Times* appointed Virginian John Popham southern correspondent in 1947, the first to fill that position for a national newspaper, but it was only in 1955 with the murder of Emmett Till that journalists such as William Bradford Huie ensured the South would receive national attention.[67] By 1961, it would be impossible for any paper to cover the nation's crises without a newsman on the southern 'beat' as the crisis in race relations came to represent 'America' for news agencies around the world.

Strong moral claims were made by the civil rights and anti-war protesters but the conservative backlash fomenting in the 1950s was heightened in the 1960s. While scholars following Lionel Trilling and Richard Hofstadter believed conservative thought had atrophied, the decline of liberalism was simultaneously the rise of the conservative right. The South and the West were significant both in the faltering of liberal ideals and the success of conservative opposition. Federal support of civil rights, slow in coming under Kennedy, was foregrounded by Johnson and the Democrats' loss of the 'solid' South was capitalised on by George Wallace whose courting of blue-collar middle America, in the North as well as the South, would help split the vote between Democrat Humphrey and Republican Nixon in 1968 and prefigure Nixon's 'Southern Strategy'. Therefore, it is all the more ironic that the Democrats' blocking of the Mississippi Freedom Democratic Party (MFDP) in 1964 first signalled the failure of the liberal democratic establishment. While the MFDP was loyal to Johnson, the all-white Mississippi delegates the Convention validated actually supported Goldwater. Mrs Hamer's famous statement that if the Democrats would not seat her Party, 'I question America', was the turn of the political tide.

Southern conservatives successfully blocked integration of schools and Gallop polls about the pace of change in southern civil rights swung decisively between 1964 and 1966 so that more than half the whites polled across the nation believed the Democrats were moving 'too fast' and too far. Also in 1966 SNNC's Julian Bond, elected to the Georgia House of Representatives in 1965, was subject to a 182–12 vote against seating him because SNCC had opposed US policy in Vietnam. It took the Supreme Court to ensure Bond's seat and right-winger Lester Maddox would be elected Senator the following year. The desire to voice opposition to Dixiecrats drew Bill Clinton into politics when in 1966 segregationist 'Justice' Jim Johnson campaigned for the governorship of Arkansas and Nixon's appeal to 'forgotten Americans' was a variation on George Wallace's populist electoral rhetoric. It would be reprised in 1980 when Ronald Reagan opened his election campaign in Mississippi associating the South with the place where 'Morning in America' would break were he elected to ensure 'special interest groups' would no longer be privileged and to restore states' rights. Brink Lindsey returns to the South as the distillation of the 'countermanding' of the counterculture when he demonstrates in *The Age of Abundance* (2007) that conservative Protestantism in the form of 'old time' Christian fundamentalism helped to forge audiences receptive to the proselytising that would underpin the New Right in subsequent decades. In the West, the John Birch Society amassed its strongest influence in Southern California. Only once Republicans had severed ties to such groups and shaken off the beleaguered, hostile and right-wing image they fostered would they capture lost ground – and the Grand Old Party.

In the 1990s George Lipsitz argued that California had become the 'new Mississippi'. Where white segregationists had failed to uphold racially exclusive politics in the 1960s, the presence of Mississippi's Trent Lott and of Haley Barbour at the head of the Republican Party in the 1990s was, he argued, the deferred triumph of their 'possessive investment in whiteness'. In the same period California successfully perpetuated the same racial exclusivity via Propositions 187 and 209.[68]

Media Culture

Television came of age during the 1960s, providing a cultural sound-track for Kennedy's New Frontier, replete with his family's dramatisation as early as 1962 in *The First Family* and the series based on his book *Profiles in Courage* that aired on NBC in 1964–5. Kennedy enjoyed a special relationship with the media, though one young man seeing his first transistor radio at Kennedy's inauguration remembers it as 'more of a marvel even than Kennedy's speech'.[69] When he lost the battle for the Democratic nomination for Vice-Presidential running mate on Adlai Stevenson's ticket in 1956, Kennedy was beaten by Senator Estes Kefauver who honed his presentation skills in the televised 'Kefauver hearings' tackling organised crime. Therefore, in the run-up to the 1960 elections, a photogenic Kennedy was very much aware of the importance of being seen regularly on television. Bright and cool, in contrast to Richard Nixon who sweated under the lights and whose complexion made him seem unshaven, in 1960 voters 'responded to Kennedy as they would to a famous athlete or popular movie star'.[70] This idea is underlined in Robert Drew's documentary film *Primary* and journalist James Conaway remembers that when Kennedy was inaugurated, 'He and the First Lady had about them a lightness associated with the new menthol cigarettes ads . . . caught up

in reports of Kennedy's youth and enthusiasm, I had dreamily imagined myself working in some way to help fulfill his dream without
knowing what that dream was or what Kennedy represented . . .'[71]
Nixon would only learn the media lesson later when in 1968 he remade
himself as the leader who could reunite the nation.

The 'instant book', or Extra, was a direct reponse to news. In
September 1964 Bantam and the *New York Times* published *The
Report of the Warren Commission on the Assassination of President
Kennedy* as an 800-page paperback within four days of the report's
release, even appending notes and an index, and *We Reach the Moon*
was on news stands almost immediately after Apollo 11 returned to
earth. The archiving of media images began as soon as television and
news reporting began shaping collective memories. The Nielsen
viewing ratings recorded that John Glenn's flight of 20 February 1962
was watched for more than five of its total ten-hour coverage by most
of America's television audience. There was four-day coverage of

Figure I.5 One of many demonstrations against segregated facilities, Memphis, September
1963. *Memphis Commercial Appeal*, photographer unspecified. Courtesy Mississippi Valley
Collection.

President Kennedy's funeral on all channels and the 1969 moon landings enjoyed wall-to-wall coverage around the world.[72] Packaging news as history is obvious in such cases but the representation of new social movements is revealing. Julian Bond, SNCC's communications director, has written repeatedly of the reciprocal impact of the Movement and the media. His task was to ensure that demonstrations against civil rights violations were reported, but under J. Edgar Hoover the FBI recruited around 300 agents to discredit the liberal press and to prejudice coverage of civil rights demonstrations.[73] While Movement drama harnessed the media despite Hoover, such media 'events' have also come to stand in for a more complex understanding of the extent to which grassroots organising made the Movement.

Life's 'America' in Transition

In 1964 *Life* was summarily dismissed by one critic as a 'supermarket' publication; 'everything glossily packaged and presented without emphasis and distinction'.[74] Throughout its history *Life* was more usually admired for its superb photo-journalism and its facility for reflecting middle American opinion. Pierre Bourdieu declared photography a middle-brow art that (re)affirms the continuity and integration of the domestic group, and *Life* can be seen as conforming to this model for much of its history. The white nuclear family was foregrounded as the dominant model of cold war consensus. Wendy Kozol, for example, examines the ways in which President Eisenhower was represented as husband, father and grandfather in photo-journalism underlining the connection between his political and domestic roles and Vice-President Richard Nixon was photographed by Hank Walker in 1958 playing with his daughters in the family garden.[75]

The emphasis on middle-class white families had to be adjusted when social schisms apparent in the 1960s became news. In 1955 *Life* had condemned the verdict that exonerated Emmett Till's killers for a racist hate crime but the photo-essay contained no images of the victim, his mother or his extended family, although it did include photographs of white defendants with their families: 'Apparently, *Life* found no way to represent the black family in the story of Emmett Till's murder trial that did not contradict its message of middle-class domestic life'.[76] *Life* was renowned for its roll-call of famous staff photographers from Margaret Bourke-White and Alfred Eisenstaedt to Lee Miller. When Gordon Parks started work at *Life* in 1948, the first African American to be employed by the company, he was expected to photograph the America that *Life* had failed to penetrate. Throughout his tenure in the 1960s he would do just that: his photo-essays of rebellion in Watts, Elijah Muhammad's Nation of Islam and Dr King's funeral were stark messages about a changing America, delivered in the images and the words of one of the polymaths of 1960s culture.

Photojournalism remained a dominant narrative of the era but its subjects would change along with photo-journalists' views. Freelance Jill Freed, for example, recalls that seeing photographs of Holocaust victims in *Life* made her a photojournalist; she would publish her first pictures not of foreign atrocities but of domestic victims of poverty in *Life* as 'Resurrection City', at the conclusion of King's Poor People's March.[77] In *Life* photographs remained the structuring principle that drove a phased feature article, whether on moral panics over teenagers, the warfare in Vietnam, or a Presidential day in the White House. However, the magazine saw significant ideological changes as in the case of Larry Burrows, whose photography of Vietnam is explored in Chapter 4, who moved from being a hawk in support of the war to an acerbic critic of it with each phase represented in *Life*.

Charles Moore's photograph 'Local Lawmen, Getting Ready to Block the Law', taken on the afternoon of 27 September 1962, is specific in context – James Meredith's attempt to integrate the University of Mississippi – but it is a documentary in miniature that also depicts the nation in transition. The white sheriff at the centre of the image smiles as he clenches a cigarette between his teeth and swings a baseball bat in menacing fashion while his associates encircle him. The picture is the subject of Paul Hendrickson's 400-page investigation *Sons of Mississippi* (2003) in which he traces these 'seven faces of Deep South apartheid' because the 'storytelling clarity' of Moore's image compelled his search.[78] Any understanding of a catastrophic history of the 1960s has its cultural roots in photo-journalism which was far more daring than *Life*'s history had promised or than its founder Henry Luce might have liked. *Life* featured profiles of Jimi Hendrix and it published a special edition on Woodstock. However, as John Gennari demonstrates, after achieving a $10 million profit in 1966, *Life* lost $40 million over the next four years as publication costs rose and subscriptions dropped.[79] *Life*'s position at the centre of photo-journalism lasted from 1936 to 1972 by which time it had lost ground to television. Due to slow production time, it could not cover breaking news in the way that television could nor compete with the immediacy of flagship documentary series such as *CBS Reports* and *NBC White Paper*. It was rededicated in 1972 as a semi-annual publication. While specialist publications could ride out the changes, the news reportage that TV stations provided was a more significant rival for *Life* although, as argued in Chapter 4, the still photograph would remain one of the most visceral records of the era.

National television was timorous in creating popular screen images of a changing nation, especially of racial integration outside of news coverage. When we remember that *Peyton Place* wasn't integrated until the 1968–9 season and the black Jeffersons didn't move into white Archie Bunker's neighbourhood until 1975, we gain a sense of how

mainstream television advanced cautiously. In 1963 ABC even refused
to screen the 1958 film *The Defiant Ones* in its film season. A close
examination reveals that programmes with plots incorporating civil
rights struggles began to find place in popular genres in what Richard
Schickel called 'the year of the problem', 1963 4. TV dramas including
CBS's *The Defenders* (1961–5) and NBC's *Mr Novak* (1963–5) began
to deal with race relations. *I Spy* (1965–8) was a breakthrough show for
openly dealing with civil rights themes and America's reputation
around the world. While it engaged with a cold war theme of espi-
onage, as did many other programmes from *Get Smart* to *Mission
Impossible*, its interracial heroes (Bill Cosby and Robert Culp) set it
apart from all other shows.

Musical and theatrical performances were often signature events in
their own right. Individual performances could be public statements
and news. Muhammad Ali's refusal of the draft, Lenny Bruce's arrest
for obscenity, the musical *Hair* and the music festival Woodstock were
all revealing of the 'adversary culture' of the 1960s, to borrow Lionel
Trilling's phrase, and each is explored in this book. Public spectacle
became an important, even expected or necessary, means of communi-
cating strong political feelings. Politicians, often promoting a rhetoric
of success and excess, expressed a politics of personalism on the Left
and the Right, from Kennedy's speeches to George Wallace's dema-
gogy, and Nixon's polarising rhetoric to 'Bring Us Together' by speaking for 'the Great Silent Majority'. The charismatic leader as visionary
was represented as spectacle, as when Dr King addressed the masses
from the steps of the Lincoln Memorial.

A politics of confrontation was interdependent on media performances of social crisis: Kennedy using national television to announce
the discovery of nuclear missiles in Cuba or Johnson's 1964 campaign
advertisement 'Daisy' or the 'Peace Girl', which implied opponent
Barry Goldwater might initiate a nuclear war endangering America's
children; and Nixon, of course, entitled an autobiography *Six Crises*
(1962). The image of the nation was the paramount consideration in a
politics of spectacle, explored in media forms from *Primary* (1960) to
Medium Cool (1968). By the end of the decade, however, a utopian
belief that acts of the political imagination could inspire social change
was dissolving into media frenzy. Even as early as 1960, New Orleans'
Mayor Delesseps S. Morrison proposed a three-day moratorium on
media coverage of school integration because he believed press reports
were exaggerated and he had witnessed cameramen setting up demonstrators to yell on cue.[80] The 'pseudo-event' was part of the cultural

'self-hypnosis' that Daniel Boorstin described in *The Image or What Happened to the American Dream* (1961) and the tendency to create pseudo-events only increased. During the 'Battle of Sunset Strip' in November 1967 when around a thousand people protested in orderly fashion against curfews – police action designed to prevent 'juveniles' from 'loitering' in downtown Los Angeles – TV crews were seen 'shouting to the youths to climb onto the buses and wave their placards so that they could be seen', and encouraging them to 'do something' for the cameras.[81] The desire to be famous would be characterised by Irving Howe as part of 'the psychology of unobstructed need' that he saw as irreverent and ironic but which by the end of the 1960s he feared had become socially corrosive.[82] Indian Rights activist and intellectual Vine Deloria called for an examination of movement tactics, arguing that 'the media's role in triggering and reporting events has been responsible for the rise in irrational fear experienced by our society'.[83] By the 1980s Michel de Certeau could write that society 'measures everything by its ability to show or be shown', an idea Don DeLillo explored in *Americana* (1971) in which culture has given way to images. The 'cancerous growth of vision' de Certeau identified was a long-term product of the 'symptoms' that Guy Debord explored in *The Society of the Spectacle* (1968) and that Christopher Lasch deemed 'fatal' in *The Culture of Narcissism* (1979).

Legacy: Heritage, Retro and Branding

In August 2003 when the hundredth birthday of the Harley Davidson motorcycle was celebrated, it was hippie Peter Fonda as Captain America in *Easy Rider* who marked the centenary. The bike was championed by Elvis Presley and Evel Knievel and on screen by Marlon Brando, James Dean and Steve McQueen, yet *Easy Rider* trumped all other iconic representations for its riders' 'American' dreams. The Stars and Stripes is clearly visible on the gas tank of Captain America's motorcycle and repeated in a striking motif on his jacket.

Capitalism and the counterculture were always interdependent; advertisers on Madison Avenue appropriated day-glo colours and psychedelic graphics and Stewart Brand's *The Whole Earth Catalogue* (1968) co-opted the space race as well as the counterculture as its launching pad. Branding sixties heritage began early. Freedomland opened in June 1960. This theme park in the Bronx incorporated a space-themed city in which visitors could take a simulated ride in a space rocket. By 1964, however, Freedomland had closed. In 1960s

Atlanta, Stephens Mitchell, brother of best-selling author of *Gone With the Wind* (1936), the late Margaret Mitchell, fended off real-estate developers who had bought the film set of the Tara plantation from Desilu Productions and a plot of land south of the city on Tara Road, named after the fiction. As the centenary of the end of Civil War neared, and segregationists cited the Lost Cause as a metaphor for massive resistance, developers hoped to recreate the fiction to attract tourists to visit 'Tara' for a $1.50 entrance fee. Despite Mitchell, in spring 1963 'Stone Mountain Plantation' opened and without any direct allusion to *Gone With the Wind* successfully harnessed its image, achieving its $1.50 entrance fee.[84] As early as April 1967, the Gray Line Bus Company began tours through San Francisco's Haight-Ashbury district so that even before the 'year of the hippie' was over, it was being commemorated. A heritage industry has grown up around the Civil Rights Movement that includes tours of places where racist atrocities were committed. Such tours promote history as peristaltic; events pulse through time as places are examined through a historical lens, whether romanticised, revered, reviled or researched.[85]

Figure I.6 *Easy Rider* (Columbia Pictures, 1969). Courtesy the Kobal Collection.

As time passes, the era is both more commodified and more highly prized, as John F. Kennedy's golf clubs sell for $772,000 at auction, far more than Sotheby's estimate, and Norman Mailer's literary archive is bought by the Harry Ransom Humanities Research Center for $2.5 million. However, the branding of the era was not only recognised but also critiqued by contemporary cultural critics. In 1959 poet Randall Jarrell described celebrities as a disposable consumerist phenomenon, 'not kings . . . but Representatives' with 'only the qualities that we delegated to them'. In the cold war context he argued celebrities were 'bought' as any other commodity to make Americans feel better:

> One imagines as a characteristic dialogue of our time, an interview in which someone is asking of a vague gracious figure, a kind of Mrs. America: 'But while you waited for the Intercontinental Ballistic Missiles what did you *do*?' She answers: 'I bought things.'[86]

If the threat of nuclear war influenced consumerism, in the early 1970s *US News and World* declared that Americans, 'increasingly disturbed by the frenzy of the space age', were 'looking back at the nation's past with fascination and longing'.[87] Don McLean's song 'American Pie' (1971), which begins with the death of fifties icon Buddy Holly in 1959, traces popular music through a representative of the generation 'lost in space' when 'in the streets/ the children screamed/ The lovers cried, and the poets dreamed'. A retro style was created almost immediately. In the movie *American Graffiti* (1973), over a single night in the summer of 1962 California teenagers say farewell to childhood to a soundtrack of fifties rock and roll. Bob Dylan quickly became 'the voice of a generation', and Ray Charles and James Brown competed for the title of 'The High Priest of Soul'. The musical revolution was managed by record executives as part of what would be a billion-dollar industry by 1968 but, nevertheless, conservatives worried that music could be harnessed to 'ridicule religion, morality, patriotism, and productivity – while glorifying drugs, destruction, revolution, and sexual promiscuity' largely because advertising images were so successful in selling the idea of a counterculture.[88] Now, *Revolution 9* by the Beatles is a Nike advertisement and as one character moans in Christopher Buckley's novel *Boomsday* (2007), 'The anthems of my revolution are now background music in TV commercials for cholesterol pills, onboard navigation systems for gas-guzzling SUVs, and hedge funds. Everyone sells out. Boomers just figured out how to make it an industry'.[89]

In 2005 the widow of Black Panther Party founder Huey Newton was accused of exploiting the Panthers' legacy by producing Burn Baby Burn Revolutionary Hot Sauce, 'a taste of the 60s', under the aegis of the Black Panther Foundation, the 'guardian of the true history of the Black Panther Party'. The phrase 'Burn Baby, Burn' recalled the Watts rebellion of 1965 which left thirty-four people dead and although the Foundation protested that the sauce was a fundraiser for community drives, former Panthers and Los Angeles residents lodged complaints. Contestation over ownership and curatorship of images can be bitter when the sixties remains an experiential channel that can be mined, revised or looted. Malcolm X, for example, is commodified as a bristling separatist militant when in the final year of his life his adherence to a racially inclusive Islam rather than to ideologue Elijah Mohammad is overlooked. Computer game 'Battlefield Vietnam' (2004) has so far received criticism from Vietnamese veterans in Birmingham in the UK and from journalists in the US but is a hit with game players who want a 'first-person shootout'.[90] The game provokes ironic contemplation, especially when representing the Vietnam War can be a psychic morass patrolled by historian 'cops'.

In the 1990s, for example, film critic Michael Medved became exercised over the ways in which the era was represented, believing left-wing crusaders 'bashing America' were taking the place of John Wayne-styled heroes in the 'flag-waving' films of his childhood.[91] Conservative cultural forces such as Walt Disney and Wayne influenced young people who had grown up with *The Wonderful World of Walt Disney* providing a moral centre and Wayne's films evoking patriotic zeal for fighting 'good' wars. Medved's criticism recalls the Department of Defense press release of 1966 ordering that movies and television productions should be made in 'the national interest', following the Department's directive on two counts: (1) Authenticity of the portrayal of military operations, or historical incidents, persons or places depicting a true interpretation of military life; and (2) Compliance with accepted standards of dignity and propriety in the industry.[92] Wayne's *The Green Berets* (1968), discussed in Chapter 2, followed such a script. He wrote to President Johnson for endorsement in December 1965, just seven months after troops began fighting, stating that the film would 'help our cause throughout the world' and would 'inspire a patriotic attitude on the part of fellow Americans'.[93] Medved's concerns are illustrative of a wider backlash that distinguished the culture wars of the late 1980s and the 1990s. Oliver Stone was criticised, for instance, for depicting a student anti-war demonstration at Syracuse that did not happen in *Born on the Fourth of July* when 200 other campus revolts around the country provide dramatic licence.

The influence of the 'Baby Boomers' born between 1945 and 1964 and especially those who 'came of age' during the 1960s – and in Vietnam as Stone did – is unprecedented in its cultural impact on how the decade is represented and remembered. The intellectuals who have drawn and policed cultural boundaries and the media practitioners who have worked across culture industries to render the decade in autobiographical detail are usually Boomers. Todd Gitlin asserted that the 1950s 'expired' in 1960 between the sit-ins in February in Greensboro, North Carolina and the anti-HUAC demonstrations in San Francisco in May.[94] In other words, he privileges the chain of events in which direct action taken by young people like him established the era as a culture of dissent. The mix of autobiography and history privileges where Boomer authors stand not only politically but also personally – a central trope of the decade in which the personal supposedly *became* political – as indicated in the very titles of books such as Mary King's *Freedom Song: A Personal Story of the 1960s Civil Rights Movement* (1984) and James Farmer's *Lay Bare the Heart: An Autobiography of the Civil Rights Movement* (1985). The feeling of emotional continuity with the decade's concerns is continually emphasised, as when Andrew Young describes watching footage of the march in Chicago's Gage Park, when bottles and bricks were hurled at Dr King, himself and others, thirty years later and still feeling frightened.[95]

A desire to 'know' more about it compels us to revisit the decade through each available cultural and political lens and to assess its legacies. This book's title *American Culture in the 1960s* holds parenthetically within its spurious clarity a multiplicity of cultural forms that locate the decade within a network of discourses that are continually evolving new emphases. Wallace Stevens once observed that the end of an era is a peculiarity of the imagination and Frank Kermode declared the sense of an ending a recurring cultural myth. 1960s American culture was not decided in the era but continues to ignite debate; with each revision the era becomes more compelling.

Chapter 1

Music and Performance

This chapter considers the cultural significance of music, comedy and other types of performance – including theatrical and sporting. It explores the idea that a culture can be defined according to those performers and performances that initially seem to violate its norms. The formative phase of celebrity culture developed out of the emergence of mass culture, as the silent-movie star Rudolph Valentino made clear. Women fainted in the aisles during movies in which he appeared and thousands attended his funeral in New York in 1926. In the 1960s celebrity culture was celebrated and, as this chapter will explore, celebrity status could have serious political consequences. The cultural emphasis on fame can be seen in Andy Warhol's commercial realism whereby he reproduced celebrities as artifacts and both memorialised and commodified them as the wallpaper against which future images of fame would be measured. From Elvis Presley to Marilyn Monroe and Jackie Kennedy, Warhol made celebrities into myths, replicating their image as he did mass-market products such as cans of Campbell's soup. Shortly after Monroe's death in 1962, his *Marilyn Gold* and *Marilyn Diptych* ensured her image would be idolised and consumed just as the actress had been in life.

Situating himself between images of Marilyn Monroe, as in Figure 1.1, Warhol became as iconic as the icons he assembled; a Svengali-like creator in the way that Hollywood had perfected star-making in the 1920s.[1] With The Factory in New York City his artistic headquarters, his 'discoveries' were showcased in 'musical reviews' called 'Up-Tight' and 'Exploding Plastic Inevitable', art installations that combined dance and film with light shows. They included Nico and The Velvet Underground and their orchestration by Warhol was what endowed them with celebrity status – at least for a while – while his own fame escalated, with Susan Sontag defining taste in ways that personified

Figure 1.1 America's pop-art painter and filmmaker, Andy Warhol with his 1962 double portrait of Marilyn Monroe, The Tate Gallery, London, 15 February 1971. AP Photo. Courtesy PA Photos.

Warhol's style in 'Notes on Camp' (1964) and a single screen print of Marilyn Monroe selling for $17 million in 1998.

In 1968 Warhol famously declared, 'In the future everyone will be famous for 15 minutes', a prescient comment that looked forward to the disposable media-made celebrities of late twentieth- and early twenty-first-century popular culture. However, established icons could also remake themselves quickly and effectively using media such as television. Neither adversarial nor countercultural, in the 1950s Elvis Presley was a musical style-setter but had neglected R&B to become one of the most highly paid actors in Hollywood in the 1960s. He remade himself on the NBC ''68 Comeback Special'. The live television audience is young and 'cool' and when he snarls, 'If you're lookin' for trouble/ You've come to the right place', their reaction helped to transform 1956's biggest-selling single 'Heartbreak Hotel' for a new generation. Elvis's fashion sense had been forged early in his career during trips to Memphis's Lansky Brothers on Beale Street which marketed what kids wanted to wear but on the 1968 show a figure-hugging black leather suit marked a turn in fashion as the way to brand a new sound. This statement echoed another departure in musical style when Bob Dylan dressed in leather motorcycle gear to signal his independence from the folk scene at the Newport News folk festival of 25 July 1965.

Celebrity status would become an important focus of new social movements striving for media platforms, as when folk-singer and Yippie activist Phil Ochs famously quipped that 'If there's any hope of a revolution in America, it lies with getting Elvis Presley to become Che Guevara'. Such quips were trumped by John Lennon's famous comment that the Beatles were 'more famous than Jesus' which incensed middle America as well as the Christian right but which may be acknowledged now as social commentary on the excesses of populism that the music scene fuelled in the 1960s, so that Lennon could state later 'I don't believe in the Beatles' in an attempt to extend the metaphor. By the 1990s, philosopher Richard Rorty would have thoroughly intellectualised Lennon's comment about the Beatles, whose members had originally come together at a church fête in Liverpool. When Rorty argued that 'the novel, the movie, and the TV program have, gradually but steadily, replaced the sermon and the treatise as the principle vehicles of moral change and progress', he might have more accurately included the importance of popular song and its performers, or sport and its heroes.[2] For example, the political impact of singer Aretha Franklin and a song such as 'R.E.S.P.E.C.T' is neatly summarised by comedian Dick Gregory, 'You heard her three or four times an hour. You heard Reverend King only on the news'.[3]

While the emphasis on self-expression was a cornerstone of new social movements, this chapter also focuses on figures whose performances blazed a trail, and whose meaning derives from the era's key 'sounds'. The decade was a musical rollercoaster in which different sounds came to prominence as others receded. Folk and blues traditions are paramount in understanding where sixties music began and the excesses of psychedelic rock help us to understand where the decade's music ended up. At the beginning of the decade, music integrated audiences before desegregation laws made that possible in the South, as Attorney General Robert Kennedy quickly realised, gathering performers including Harry Belafonte and Lena Horne at his New York apartment to discuss how he might best address southern segregation. In 1961 to 1964 as she toured the South, Joan Baez refused to sing to segregated audiences and when she performed at the traditionally all-black Tougaloo College in Mississippi to an integrated audience, she was investigated by the Mississippi Sovereignty Commission.[4] However, in his history of the relationship between music and civil rights struggles, Brian Ward emphasises the variety and impact of the many musical crossovers that combined in 'a new inter-racialism of the airwaves' in the early 1960s and that would infiltrate other media as when Sam Cooke sang Dylan's 'Blowin' in the Wind' on *Shindig*'s inaugural programme in 1964 and black Memphians went wild for Elvis Presley when he played a 9,000-strong audience along-side BB King and Ray Charles.[5] Andreas Huyssen has argued that postmodernism 'began' in the 1960s, energised by countercultural trends such as musical crossovers and by the reclamation and celebra-tion of folk culture and rock and roll.[6]

While the machinery of Motown successfully engendered musical stars as well as hit records, Curtis Mayfield in albums such as *There's No Place Like America Today* and hits such as 'Grow Closer Together', 'People Get Ready', 'Move on Up' and 'Keep on Pushing', emphasised the decade's race relations and prophesied their further deterioration. Eddie Thomas, a member of the Impressions, recalls that Mayfield was 'like a factory all by himself' and Mayfield explained that 'it was impor-tant for me to own as much of myself as I could'. He therefore registered each song he wrote with the Library of Congress and founded publish-ing companies to earn him royalties.[7] The 1960s saw a shift in emphasis from artists recording songs written by others to the singer-songwriting craft epitomised by Bob Dylan and Lennon and McCartney. The 'cult' and unorthodox Randy Newman is a further example of an under-explored performer who when he calls himself the 'dean of satire' is self-deprecating as well as ironic. His simple songs first heard in the 1960s chronicle complex issues, as in the 'concept album' *Good Old Boys* (1974) which combines irony and the sentimental in a journey through the South. Iconic figures such as Bob Dylan and musical phenomena such as Motown reveal much about a changing climate but so do the countless others who contributed performances in an unpredictable decade.

Like a Rolling Stone: Musical Heritage and the Folk Movement

The 1960s saw musical returns as well as innovation. Even its most innovative performers were dependent on the revival of traditional musical influences, as underpinned by musicologists such as Harry Smith whose *Anthology of American Folk Music* released in 1952 so influenced Bob Dylan. The Basement Tapes he recorded with the Band in 1967 may be understood as Dylan finding his foothold in a contin-uum of traditional music traced from the early nineteenth century. In ballads and broadsides, Dylan found an 'American idiom'. Alan and

John Lomax famously reclaimed an American folk heritage and
embodied it in African American bluesman Leadbelly, contextualising
that heritage in cultural histories such as *Folk Songs of North America*
(1960) and *Folk Song Style and Culture* (1968), groundbreaking extensions of the classic *Folk Song USA* (1947) which Alan Lomax had
introduced with a rhetorical flourish: 'A people made a three-thousand
mile march between the eastern and western oceans . . . Songs traveled
with them . . . Every hamlet produced its crop of ballads of murders,
disasters, and scandals . . . Every fiddler put his own twists on the tunes
he learned from his pappy'.[8] The vernacular tradition was reinforced
by the Greenwich Village folk boom epitomised by the coffee house
and folk club performances of Karen Dalton, Joan Baez and the young
Bob Dylan. The image of an 'authentically' American music of the
people was criticised early by Toni Cade Bambara in her short story
'Mississippi Ham Rider' (1960), in which an elderly bluesman based on
Mississippi John Hurt is persuaded to cut records for New York
backers who hope 'folkway-starred sophisticates' will 'absorb' the
native music of 'Mr. Ethnic-Authentic'.[9]

Similarly, the image of the troubadour, whose ballads and broadsides exemplify the romance of being 'on the road' was successfully
harnessed by Dylan who began as an acolyte of Woody Guthrie and
who created a story he later described as 'hokum' of being kicked out
of home and riding freight trains to New York City.[10] It took
Newsweek until 1963 to 'out' Dylan as Robert Zimmerman, a middle-
class Jewish boy from Hibbing, Minnesota and it would take much
longer before performers would be as self-conscious as Bambara about
the musical minstrelsy Dylan addresses in his 2001 album *Love and
Theft*. Folk performers were often 'urban kids trying to sound like hill-
billies and sharecroppers' because, as Louis Menand has described,
'artifice was the price of authenticity'.[11]

Columbia Records surpassed RCA Victor by 1960 as the most successful record company, and veteran producer and impresario John
Hammond who had discovered Billie Holiday, Count Basie and other
musical greats, has described scouting for talent that year and signing
up the old (Pete Seeger) and the new (Aretha Franklin). More bizarre
was Hammond's visit to hear Texan folk singer Carolyn Hester with
then husband/agent writer Richard Fariña – and discovering Bob
Dylan playing harmonica in the background. 'I watched him for a
while and found him fascinating', remembered Hammond in 1977,
'although he was not particularly good on either guitar or harmonica'.
Hammond had hoped to sign the 'Queen of Folk Music' Joan Baez,

Figure1.2 Bob Dylan in 1967 with Allen Ginsberg in the background. Leacock
Pennebaker/The Kobal Collection.

but thought Dylan's 'Talking New York' showed sufficient promise
to sign him to Columbia.[12] Dylan's duet with folk hero Pete Seeger at
the Newport Folk Festival in 1963 would bring two eras into convergence: what had become the Civil Rights Movement's foremost
musical expression of hope recalled the Popular Front from which
Seeger had emerged in the 1930s. Dylan revered the American music
of the old heartland as performed by Seeger and Guthrie, and the
nineteenth-century songs of Stephen Foster, 'handed down songs' or
'rebel songs', as Dylan calls them in his memoir.[13] During Woody
Guthrie's protracted death in 1967, Dylan and Seeger would visit and
play his songs. It is a sad scene of commemoration made iconic in the
movie *Alice's Restaurant* (1969) in which son Arlo is protagonist, combining a desire to carry on his father's music with his own youthful
quest for meaning.

Across different musical forms, new artists declared allegiance to
musical 'ancestors'. Wilson Pickett referred back to the Soul Stirrers, a
gospel group that began in the 1930s and included Sam Cooke until he
went solo. In turn, Aretha Franklin made clear how Cooke had influenced her; Johnny Cash admired the Carter Family even before he met

Bob Dylan

Dylan's first song was 'Song to Woody' written for Guthrie whose music was an epiphany 'It was like the land parted', so much so that Dylan came out of 18 months of seclusion to perform at Guthrie's memorial concert in January 1968, leading Pete Seeger to say, 'Woody wants you to take this music to the world, because if you do, maybe we won't have any more fascists'.[14] Dylan was expected to carry the burden of representation – not only as folk successor and troubadour, but as bard of a generation. To begin with, his songs combined the qualities he admired in Guthrie – poetic tough balladry – with those he discovered in Robert Johnson's delta blues but his musical legacy runs to some 500 songs that stretch from folk to blues to rock, and back to folk. Influenced by Poe and Rimbaud and celebrated himself by poets such as Archibald MacLeish, Dylan has been studied by music historians, cultural commentators and literary critics, from Griel Marcus and Peter Guralnick to Mike Marqusee and Christopher Ricks. His revisionist memoirs, the first volume published as *Chronicles* in 2004, prompted the first interview in two decades and his reputation as a post-sixties recluse has had to contend with his incessant touring over recent years. Dylan is a complex constellation of contradictions.

It is ironic that he should be so keenly associated with the politics of the 1960s when he has spent so much time repudiating any equation between his songs and political events.[15] Songs such as 'Oxford Town' about James Meredith's attempt to integrate the University of Mississippi, or 'Only a Pawn in Their Game', an elegy for Medgar Evers, and the bardic 'Chimes of Freedom' which celebrates the SNCC (Student Non-violent Co-ordinating Committee) activists he spent time with in Mississippi, are not among the songs that have endured as *the* classics but other songs were sixties political events in their own right. 'Blowin' in the Wind' was performed at the 1963 March on Washington and Dylan received the 1963 Tom Paine award for his contribution to the Civil Rights Movement but, even as he released them, Dylan bridled at the idea that 'A Hard Rain's Gonna Fall', a response to the Cuban Missile Crisis, and albums such as *The Times They Are A-Changin'*, with the title song's plea that senators and congressmen 'heed the call', should be construed as protest. Dylan bristled at being tied to his times, an idea which recalls his interest in the 1850s and 1860s honed in New York Public Library because – he says – the songs he wrote 'wouldn't conform to modern ideas' and an earlier century became 'the all-encompassing template behind everything that I would write'.[16] Typically, what drew Dylan to that period, however, was the idea of a nation creaking and cracking as the Civil War began and it is more than coincidental that similar schisms characterised the 1960s. Dylan continues to return to issue-based politics in the spirit of protest, and the film he scripted, ironically entitled *Masked and Anonymous* (2002), may be read as evidence that he has not escaped the 1960s.[17]

As a global phenomenon, Dylan was made in Britain. Even at the height of Beatlemania, he was mobbed after a London gig, 'already regarded as a pop star, a sex symbol, a sybaritic prophet – all rolled into one'.[18] Hits such as 'It Ain't Me Babe' and 'Mr. Tambourine Man' were first performed in the UK and in 1965 Dylan's international star status was secured just as the Beatles were securing theirs in the US. 'Subterranean Homesick Blues' was a Top Ten hit and *Bringing It All Back Home* was number 1 in UK album charts in May 1965 whereas Dylan didn't achieve the same market recognition in the US until later.[19] *Don't Look Back*, D. A. Pennebaker's film of Dylan's UK tour, tracked his success including the pseudo-religious frenzy that fans exhibited. Despite the consensus view that Dylan was criticised throughout the period in which he introduced electric and amplified sets – negative reception at concerts described as a year of booing that began at Newport in 1965 and continued to Manchester Free Trade Hall in 1966 – it is invidious to fantasise Dylan's career as such cleanly sliced segments in which he was alternately fêted for folk 'purity' or slated for 'folk rock'. His is a career that rides the punches ('I'm a trapeze artist') even it he did not always roll with them. The cliché that he is 'the voice of a generation' has been purposely worn down by Dylan rather than seen as something to live up to.[20] More revealing is the heightened emotion his music provokes: to Gary Allen in a tirade against 'That Music' he was a communist 'crimson troll'; for Griel Marcus, he is a dreamer whose 'Like a Rolling Stone' can be compared to the Declaration of Independence.[21] Marcus argues in typically suggestive rhetoric that by 1967 the nation was 'a faith and a riddle . . . a threat and a plea, a church and scaffold'[22] and Dylan's lyrics have been read as the riddles of a prophet though which national metaphors might be best apprehended.

The cult of personality that underlined 1960s performance politics can be effectively explored through Dylan, Muhammad Ali and others such as Jimi Hendrix and Abbie Hoffman. If disaggregating the man from the times would seem an exercise in futility, the attendant risk is that they become ciphers if attention is not paid to the contradictions they lived out in a turbulent decade. Dylan seems to be addressing that worry: he has returned to his musical roots and the first years of his success as folk guru and protest singer in *Chronicles*. And he is talking. Martin Scorsese who made a movie about The Band, *The Last Waltz* (1977), was granted Dylan's time for interviews underpinning the biopic *No Direction Home* (2005) which returns to his early career. Todd Haynes' postmodern 'biography' *I'm Not There* (2007) is a choral film in which six different actors, women and men, interpret different stages of his life and career. The many faces of Dylan and the many directions in which he has travelled musically have influenced performers as different as the Beatles, Jimi Hendrix, Marvin Gaye, Bruce Springsteen and James Blount. As Luc Sante has succinctly summarised, 'even when he has been at pains to make himself transparent', Dylan 'has given grist to the interpretation mills, which have rarely been idle in forty years'.[23]

and married June. In 1972 Diana Ross played Billie Holiday in *Lady Sings the Blues,* locating her own star image with that of the 'authentic' jazz and blues diva. Sixties musicians demonstrated a facility for mining the seams of literary and cultural history as well as past musical forms. Columbia records, in the person of Chris Albertson and with the support of John Hammond and others, re-recorded for a new generation the 78rpm records Bessie Smith recorded in the 1930s. Songs passed across generations as parables, sometimes in coded language in which class or racial protest was implied. The boundary between musical culture and politics was porous. Metaphors of struggle occurred in Appalachian mountain ballads, African American spirituals, free jazz such as Max Roach's *Freedom Now* suite and Yiddish folk songs. The 'shouting poem' that began with Ginsberg's 'Howl' was taken up by performance poets Nikki Giovanni and Sonia Sanchez who were joined by bluesmen poets such as Leroi Jones (Amiri Baraka) in singing out loudly and proudly an emancipatory critique, not least of the war in Vietnam. Giovanni's hard-hitting poem 'Nigger Can You Kill?', for instance, is influenced by music such as John Lee Hooker's 'I Don't Want To Go To Vietnam'; Giovanni is resolute that domestic issues such as racism and poverty needed to be resolved before focusing on war. Similarly, Nina Simone's vehement 'Mississippi Goddamn' (1963), the first protest song this Juilliard-trained classical pianist wrote, was triggered by the 1963 racist bombing in Birmingham of a black church in which four little girls died. It includes the desperate, angry, vengeful lines: 'Oh, but this country is full of lies/ You're all gonna die and die like flies/ I don't trust you any more/ You keep on saying "Go slow!"'.

Protest and Politics as Melodrama and as Theatre

From the March on Washington to the March on the Pentagon, political demonstrations harnessed media interest. The masses gathered in one place would itself form a spectacle memorialised in photograph and documentary footage. The 1968 Democratic Convention hosted in Chicago was a spectacle containing all the ingredients of a melodrama. US party conventions have traditionally been colourful and even violent. Historically, the major responsibility at the Party convention was choosing nominees to go forward on the Republican or Democrat 'ticket' but by the 1960s candidates were expected to battle each other for nomination in Presidential primaries. In advance of the 1968 Convention, however, Vice-President Hubert Humphrey manouevred himself into the position of Presidential nominee and delegates discovered it had already been decided that he would be put forward. This twist galvanised what was already a volatile situation. Abbie Hoffman, Jerry Rubin, Dick Gregory and others combined New Left and hippie philosophies. Their public theatre had helped put the Youth International Party (Yippies) on the media map. Fifty thousand people gathered in October 1967 to dramatise Hoffman's dream to levitate the Pentagon through the power of communal meditation in order to exorcise its power and precipitate the ending of the war. So excessive a performance that it sounds apocryphal, it was 'theatre of everyday life' as Erving Goffman has described: it was not that the bizarre idea could succeed but that a phenomenal demonstration would send a message of dissent. The 1960s saw a number of overblown gestures or 'pseudo-events', manufactured as photo opportunities even if they retained more meaning than this would imply for participants. At the 1968 Chicago Convention, Yippies produced a pig declaring it should be President, its platform garbage. While the satirical humour was effective there were warning undertones: an earlier 'Yip-in' celebration at Grand Central Station in New York City had turned violent and the Convention would dissolve into the similarly overblown 'Battle of Chicago' with some 660 arrested, 1,000 injured and American Indian Dean Johnson killed.

The cultural leverage that comes with celebrity status can be seen in a very different and international context during the 1968 Olympics when African American sprinters Tommie Smith and John Carlos won gold and bronze medals in the 200 metres. In and of itself, Smith's world-record-breaking performance brought African Americans to centre stage. When the two athletes mounted the podium to receive their medals, what followed is generally reported for its function as a Black Power salute and for the furore it caused. However, what also made Smith and Carlos's protest memorable was its synchronicity as performance art, a symbolic image of black nationalism as Smith has described:

> I wore the black right-hand glove and Carlos wore the left-hand glove of the same pair. My raised hand stood for the power in black America. Carlos's raised left hand stood for the unity of black America. Together they formed an arch of unity and power. The black scarf around my neck stood for black pride. The black socks with no shoes stood for black poverty in racist America. The totality of our effort was the regaining of black dignity.[24]

Banned from the Olympic Village and suspended from the national team, the immediate judgment on Smith and Carlos was that protesting domestic politics was anathema at an international sporting event. Only with hindsight, as when Smith was celebrated as the 'Sportsman of the Millennium' in 1995 and San José State University erected a statue of its famous alumni in 2005, would the politics of their performance be fully acknowledged. The Olympic Project for Human Rights (OPHR) influenced by sociologist Harold Edwards at San José State is usually cited as the sole inspiration for Smith and Carlos's protest. Australian Peter Norman, who stood with Smith and Carlos on the podium, wore an OPHR badge next to his silver medal to indicate his support of their protest. However, the cultural context in which the performance should be understood was much wider than reference to OPHR alone suggests. The form the protest took was not new: before he became a comedian Dick Gregory had used the same salute at Olympic try-outs in St Louis.[25] More significantly, when Carlos and Smith decided on their demonstration of Black Power politics, the most vocal of African American sporting heroes was banned from performing. Recalling the Olympic Protest in the 1990s, Arthur Ashe was convinced that Muhammad Ali was Smith and Carlos's inspiration: 'Ali had to be on their minds. He was largely responsible for it becoming an expected part of a black athlete's responsibility to get involved. He had more at stake than any of us'.[26] Winner of fifty-one tennis titles, including the US Open in the year of the Olympic protest, Ashe too staked a claim for the underprivileged throughout his career and the addition of Richmond-born Ashe's statue in 1996 to those commemorating the Southern Confederacy lining Monument Avenue was an ironic post-Civil Rights addendum.

Initially Muhammad Ali professed himself to be apolitical, boasting that he had never fought for integration and vowing that he would never protest a cause. But he would become a signifier of protest and courage for having refused to fight in Vietnam. His trajectory through the decade is epic and controversial: he grew up in Kentucky and won an Olympic Gold in Rome; when he was stripped of his boxing title, he won it back; he would be world heavyweight champion three times. Vilified in the 1960s for his religion and politics, he has since been mythologised as a peace emissary, negotiating the release of US hostages in Iraq, and commodified as a brand: he has been used to advertise Coca-Cola and Adidas.

Muhammad Ali

The cultural impact of Cassius Marcellus Clay (1942–64) and Muhammad Ali (1964–) reflects the divisions of the 1960s and unlike most sporting figures he has been the charismatic subject of writers who have little to do with sport: Alex Haley, Joyce Carol Oates, Gary Wills and Ishmael Reed. When he fought Joe Frazier in what was heralded 'the fight of the century' he was so iconic that Frank Sinatra took photographs for *Life*. In April 1960 he was registered for the military draft. Two years later he was called but when he failed the aptitude test, he was reclassified ineligible ('I was the greatest, not the smartest'[27]). That decision was challenged in 1966 by which time he was world heavyweight champion (from February 1964 when he defeated Sonny Liston). When the aptitude requirement was lowered as President Johnson's government increased the volume of young men called, Ali refused to go, stating unequivocally that 'I ain't got no quarrel with those Vietcong'. In more measured tones he explained at the hearing at which he failed to gain exemption as a conscientious objector: 'It would be no trouble for me to go into the Armed Forces, boxing exhibitions in Vietnam or traveling the country at the expense of the government . . . not having to get out in the mud and fight and shoot. If it wasn't against my conscience to do it . . . if I weren't sincere'.[28] Ali was sincere in his belief that to fight a 'Christian' war as a 'Muslim' who had not been attacked by the Vietnamese was to deny all that he had learned from the Nation of Islam; after the Hon. Elijah Muhammad had been denounced and died, Ali remains true to his beliefs.

Norman Mailer's profile of Ali which appeared in *Life* in 1971 was entitled 'Ego' and Ali's self-fashioning as the conscience of young America was as, if not more, important than his boxing prowess. He was mythologised as a boxer by Mailer: 'What separates the noble ego of the prizefighters from the lesser ego of authors is that the fighter goes through experiences in the ring which are occasionally immense, incommunicable except to fighters who have been as good'.[29] But he was a sign of the times rather than solely a sporting hero. The famous statement 'I don't have to be what you want me to be. I'm free to be me' is indicative of the choices he made that led to the ban on practising his sport. Ali was prohibited from boxing from 1967 to 1971, some forty-two months during which he sharpened his political performance speaking on college campuses around the country. When he returned to prizefighting, Mailer could claim Ali as the most prominent American after the President, 'the prince of mass man and the media' and 'the first psychologist of the body'.[30] The psychology of the body was a neologism coined to describe how Ali would 'psyche out' opponents. This was one facet of Ali's theatricality and had been part of his persona from the beginning.

Ali was a showman, his own promoter as 'The Greatest' through a variety of media, including his 1963 album of pugilistic poetry, talk show appearances and photo opportunities. His famous monologues drew on movies, music and comic books for popular cultural resonance and the public performances in which he insulted and antagonised opponents drew on African American oral traditions of 'playing the dozens'. Ali successfully harnessed facets of black performance history. He was a media star throughout the decade but his star status changed when he converted to become a Black Muslim. Repudiating his 'slave name' of Clay, Ali was demonised by the press just as the 1959 television documentary *The Hate That Hate Produced* had demonised the Muslims. Gordon Parks remembers driving along with Ali in Miami in 1966 when he was training for his upcoming fight with Henry Cooper in London and hearing a radio announcer report his return to training. Ali's reaction was: 'Cassius Clay! I'm on everybody's lips. But still they won't call me by my right name'.[31] The *New York Times* and other publications refused to recognise his change of name throughout the 1960s and journalist Robert Lypsyte has described submitting features on Ali only to discover an editor had changed every reference back to Clay prior to publication.[32] By 1966 Floyd Patterson could publicise that in beating Ali he would bring the heavyweight title 'back to America', as if by becoming a member of the Nation of Islam, Ali had also become a foreigner. Historically, the black sportsman had been caught between two racially polarised audiences, as indicated by the success of black prizefighter Jack Johnson and the vaunted need to find the next 'Great White Hope' to beat him. The black boxer was often reductively envisaged as a dupe of white-owned sports and entertainment industries. Ali's self-fashioning as a celebrity and a political spokesman set him outside of such stereotypes.

Ali even became an actor. In 1979 he played Gideon Jackson, a former slave who becomes a South Carolina senator, in the film based on Howard Fast's Reconstruction-set novel *Freedom Road* (1944). Publicity emphasised 'the power of a dream and the triumph of the human spirit' and the scene in which Jackson speaks up at the State Convention to rewrite the constitution is typical of the quietly measured tones beneath which Ali subsumed his familiar bluster. The moral leader of former slaves and poor white sharecroppers, his character is killed by Klan, the violent arm of landowners who renounce the claims of freed men. Gideon is waving a white flag of submission in a final attempt to protect his people when he is shot dead. The camera pans around the slain until the final image is of Gideon's grandson staring into the camera with a look of bitter accusation. Ali's presence ensured that while the film dramatised the struggle of the Black Convention in Charleston South Carolina in 1865, it would simultaneously recall the black freedom struggles of the 1960s. Dick Gregory has called Ali 'a monument of a human being' and explained: 'There were a lot of us against the war . . . but nobody heard us because we didn't command the worldwide attention that Ali engaged'.[33] Ali would help any event resonate of the 1960s as powerfully as the present, as evidenced in his lighting the torch at the 1996 Olympics in Atlanta, a tower of strength despite Parkinson's disease.

Figure 1.3 Pugnacious cultural critic Norman Mailer arm-wrestling with heavyweight champion Muhammad Ali on the terrace of their San Juan hotel, 1 August 1965. Mailer came to watch José Torres, world light heavyweight champion, fight Tom McNeeley. Ali boxed four exhibition rounds after the Torres fight. AP Photo. Courtesy PA Photos.

Ali's star status underpinned *Freedom Road*. The movie as 'event' depends on the convergence of different factors and the synergy between different culture industries in the 1960s in which performances of all kinds are relevant. For example, the success of *The Graduate* in 1967 was based not only on Dustin Hoffman's performance but underlined by its soundtrack. It was the first film to include songs that had previously been released, notably 'The Sound of Silence' by Simon and Garfunkel. Arthur Penn in deciding on the soundtrack for *Little Big Man* wanted his story of discrimination to have the *sound* of discrimination. The achievement of that sound is a typically sixties cultural crossover. Penn felt that even for a film about American Indians, the dominant 'sound' of discrimination in the 1960s was African American. A white musician John Hammond, son of the record producer, whose musical career began as an interpreter of Robert Johnson and classic and forgotten blues songs, created an original score.[34] He cleverly preserved and interpreted the sound and of an earlier era in a movie that would also equate the ideology of the massacred Cheyenne with the utopian counterculture of the 1960s. By the 1970s, the movie soundtrack would be a staple and a promotional must-have for the successful marketing of many films.

Examining the cultural character of the era through attention to performance style is revealing on all levels. Fashions in clothing are expressive of changing youth values and the significance of youth as a target demographic. In any public performance dress was key, as in Elvis's 'comeback'. Dashiki wearing poets performed black cultural nationalism and the sombre respectability of the Nation of Islam under the leadership of Elijah Muhammad is recorded in monochrome photographs of a phalanx of black men in crisp white shirts and sharp black suits. In the South SNCC volunteers dressed down in denim coveralls while attempting to register poor black people to vote. They chose not to present themselves as formal or officious to blend in, rather than be easily marked by the police or the Klan. Nevertheless, the black members of SNCC were romanticised by Norman Mailer as having a reckless style and élan. In his view, their courage on voter registration drives was reinforced by a 'tasty choice in what they wore, a long thin feather in the hat . . . or an old pair of boots' with turned-up toes. They had flair'.[35] The civil rights worker as black cavalier is an image that exudes the kind of 'cool' that Mailer championed in his writings about the hipster.

Cultural productions in which youth culture was prominent provoked media coverage of generational and other tensions. The musical *Hair* was an entertainment event that challenged and changed censorship laws in the theatre. It premiered Off-Broadway on 29 October 1967 but by April 1968 it was Broadway's biggest hit, racking up 1,873 performances at the Biltmore Theater. Its distinctive location in New York City would be emphasised in the 1979 film of the stage musical by scenes in Central Park. However, the stage play was a huge success on Sunset Boulevard, Los Angeles and would be easily adapted to different American cities where youth rebellion and resistance to the draft challenged the status quo. On the one hand, the musical entered the mainstream: the Broadway cast's album stayed in the Top Ten of the Billboard charts for 150 weeks. On the other hand, *Hair* was subject to censorship in the South and sometimes only staged after legal appeals against its banning. In Chattanooga in 1972, the directors of the Tivoli theatre refused to allow the show to be performed and a civil ordinance prevented its staging. The appeal for the right of free speech went all the way to the Supreme Court and was not resolved until 1975. At the heart of the clash was a definition of the role of community theatre. The Supreme Court ruling records that of those who initially opposed *Hair* as an offence to decency, 'None of them had seen the play or read the script, but they understood from outside reports that the musical, as produced elsewhere, involved nudity and obscenity on

Figure 1.4 The Memphis State University production of *Hair*, 1970, directed by Keith Kennedy. Courtesy the Mississippi Valley Collection.

stage. Although no conflicting engagement was scheduled for the Tivoli, respondents determined that the production would not be "in the best interest of the community" '.[36]

When Memphis State University produced the musical in February 1970, it caused a furore, even though it did not include scenes of nudity. Protests that followed were largely made on religious grounds and the banners, though easily mocked as absurd – 'God Hates Hair' and 'God Made Clothes' – are a vivid reflection of an older generation's fear of youthful excess. A 'free' lifestyle challenged rigid definitions of Christian morality and the racial conformity on which southern culture rested so precariously was defied by scenes of race-mixing. The same issues that divided citizens in other cities were brought into sharp relief by baffled, placard-carrying young conservatives outraged by their long-haired peers. The scenes of protest in Memphis were an indication of the strength of feeling that this musical about draft-dodging hippies could provoke. The controversy was so spectacular that Craig Leake, Memphis State graduate of film production in 1969, returned home to make an NBC documentary called *When Hair Came to Memphis*.

Figure 1.5 Protests against the staging of *Hair* in Memphis. Dave Darnell, staff photographer for the *Memphis Commercial Appeal*, 22 February 1970. Courtesy the Mississippi Valley Collection.

Hair epitomised 'The Age of Aquarius' which – except in circum-
stances like those above – travelled very successfully under the aegis of
the theatrical spectacle, as evidenced in London's Shaftsbury Avenue
production which opened in 1968 and almost made 2,000 performances, closing in 1973 only because renovation of the theatre building forced its run to end. London's Gate Theatre updated the musical
to place the War in Iraq at the centre of its satire and again the musical
ran successfully from 2003 to 2005.

In the 1960s, demonstrations, live art, street and 'guerilla' theatre
and political spectacles were legion. Alan Kaprow is the academic and
artist usually credited with coining the term 'Happenings' to describe
the revolutionary and participatory process that was a desire to impro-
vise around ideas and events, 'to paste-up action, to make collages of
people and things in motion'.[37] Susan Sontag defined a 'Happening' in
terms of what it was *not*, to reflect the impossibility of agreement over
conventions, aside from the modernist mantra 'Make It New' according to which a Happening takes place in a continuous present.[38]
However, the concept was not new. In its original conception in the
early twentieth century, the 'happening' was designed to shock, antag-
onise or revolutionise, as in the re-enactment of the storming of the
Winter Palace on the third anniversary of the event in 1920 when it is
estimated that around 11,000 Soviet people took part in the performance. American examples include the music and dance of John Cage
and Merce Cunningham and Cage's conducting of a mimed and silent
interpretation of his music in the 1950s.

Living theatre, poetry readings and other kinds of 'happening' really
took off in the 1960s and the 'theatre' of war was one of the determin-
ing factors in public demonstrations, the anti-war movement being particularly adept at dramatising currents of dissent. The spectacle depends
on a collective hermeneutical understanding of the event even when
unpredictability may be its central feature, as in 'The Battle of Chicago',
or in Living Theater created in cultural opposition to the play culture
of Broadway. Playwright Neil Simon's success across the decade may
be usefully read as a control in an otherwise unpredictable experiment.
Ruby Cohn may seem to give Simon short shrift when she alleges, 'His
plays ignore not only wars but also racial violence, drug abuse, energy
depletion'.[39] However, her assessment points up the tendency to
measure theatre of the 1960s according to the issues it espoused in
openly politicised ways. Theatre seemed to be sliced into seemingly
separate cultural segments. Only streets away in New York City, a burgeoning radical theatre could be discovered Off-Off-Broadway. It has

been represented as if it 'just happened' with no manifesto except a desire to represent what 'living in the now' felt like, with no charge to audiences except what they chose to contribute when a hat went round. The best-known theatre group, Living Theater, did outline the key tenets of an Off Off Broadway performance so that even the most fluid performance theatre began to operate within generic expectations: 'No curtain/ Performers circulate among audience/ Everyday clothes/ Performers circulate among audience/ Everyday clothes/ Performers become part of the audience/ Contacts'.[40] However, as Stephen J. Bottoms demonstrates, if live theatre was conceptualised as studiously amateur, it soon began to creatively intervene and self-consciously critique countercultural idealism, as in *The Hawk* (1967) at Theater Genesis, an improvised play in which a drug dealer murders his clients.

While New York would remain the symbolic centre of American theatre, no matter how radical its precepts, on the countercultural West Coast, the Diggers were founded by a group of displaced New Yorkers, their theatrical enterprise evolving out of the San Francisco Mime Troupe which in the late 1950s sought to use guerilla theatre to undermine capitalism and shake the status quo. Emmett Grogan, Peter Berg and Peter Cohon (actor Peter Coyote) were central figures and their theatre movement dramatised what a 'free' life might involve, not just via ticketless theatres but 'free stores' and free food for the poor, disdaining what they saw as cynical or delusional 'countercultural' hype as much as asphyxiating bureaucracy. Individual writers and performers were also noteworthy for their inventiveness. Amiri Baraka combined theatre as provocative, issue-based agit-prop and a keen sense of the Black Aesthetic in ways designed to make cultural waves. Kimberly Benston has asserted that 'Baraka entered the American consciousness not merely as a writer but as an event'.[41] Early plays such as *The Toilet* (1964) and *The Baptism* (1966) set out to shock, the former set in a high school's public toilet reeking of excrement, in which a fight breaks out between a black boy and a white, and the latter yoking together religion and homosexuality. While in the 1950s conservative critics such as Anatole Broyard had disdained the idea of a 'Negro theatre' as encouraging belief in the difference of blacks from whites, Baraka's plays were firmly situated within black cultural agendas.[42] *Dutchman* (1964) is the story of a white woman (Lulu) and the black man (Clay) she stabs to death on the New York subway in the middle of the day with no consequences. It is one of the most disturbing parables, presenting 1960s race relations as an inferno; once dead, the rest of the subway car's passengers dispose of Clay's body by dragging it out of the car.

Figure 1.6 Citizens Against Busing, Barney Sellers, staff photographer for the Commercial Appeal, 22 March 1972. Courtesy the Mississippi Valley Collection.

Often in the 1960s the politics of performance was carnivalesque or media-hyped, publicised as 'the rhetoric of re-enactment' that Paul Connerton has described as one of the ways in which individuals present themselves as a collective.[43] While the anarchic left was renowned for eccentric performances galvanising countercultural youth, the conservative right could sometimes be equally creative in dissent. In Memphis, for example, a publicity stunt saw segregationists burying an old school bus to protest the busing of white children across town to ensure the integration of city schools. In Figure 1.6, children pose and a man dances on the bus roof as protestors smile and laugh. Susan Sontag described 'Happenings' as surrealist with surrealism being 'the farthest extension of the idea of comedy, running the full range from wit to terror'.[44]

Standing Up, Speaking Out and Singing Loud: From Gestalt to Geeky

Smiling and laughing about civil rights issues is rarely associated with massive resistance to desegregation. Laughing at segregationist ire was traditionally the province of stand-up comedians whose politically

inspired performances combined commentary on the news (Mort Sahl
has appeared with a rolled-up newspaper in his hand since 1953) with
a bitter, contorted idealism (Sahl also wrote speeches for Kennedy
before idealism turned to criticism). The importance of stand-up
comedy in the 1960s cannot be overestimated. It featured across the
culture industry. Frank Gorshin and Rich Little typically performed
on television, Gorshin playing The Riddler in TV's *Batman*, and both
demonstrated the art of impressionism. Little's seemingly plastic face
would be contorted into an uncanny impersonation of Richard Nixon
throughout the 1970s. As an outlet for populist and radical sentiments
over the issues that beset the country, however, clubs and small theatres were more significant than television in first bringing fame and
notoriety to comedy performers. The boom in satire was the 'one-man
show' typified by Lenny Bruce's comic monologues, as in one that
forms a blistering critique performed in the character of an American
Indian complaining, 'Oh Christ! The white people are moving in! You
let one white family in and the whole neighbourhood will be white!'
Bruce pushed comedy performance to extremes never before experienced in American culture with routines such as 'Who Killed Christ?'
and 'Are There Any Niggers Here?' flaying anti-Semitism and racism
to the bone.

The legal trials that Bruce underwent divested comedy of the social
safety nets that had seemed to tacitly allow the comedian free speech,
and were followed by his death in 1966. The aura of Bruce's celebrity
was partly the result of the dead comedian as fetish. A nation's stories
invest in death and, as Michael Taussig claims, the most controversial
artists succeed in bringing 'the fetish character of the modern state into
a clear and sensual focus'.[45] Lenny Bruce in life and legacy existed at
the nexus of postwar America's 'revolutions'. The theatrical trailer for
the 1979 film *Lenny* for which Dustin Hoffman was Oscar-nominated
marketed its subject as the 'conscience of America', stating, 'It is ironic
that he was prosecuted for acts that have become a part of today's life',
largely the idea of humour as social indictment. This reverses one facet
of Bruce's reception in the 1960s, as when *Time* magazine famously
declared him 'the sickest of them all'. However, Bruce's appeal was
much more complicated: the *New York Post* eulogised him as 'a kind
of prophet' and TV stalwart Ed Sullivan called him 'dynamic and original'.[46] Britain's Jonathan Miller and American critic Lionel Trilling
took on the debate in the *New York Review of Books* in 1968 and the
meaning of free speech and sexual freedom continues to rage around
Bruce's 'martyrdom'.[47] When Bruce was first arrested for obscenity,

Judge Axelrod was ready to find him guilty right away and Bruce pleaded with the US judiciary not to 'take away my words'. Bruce's career was the most controversial case of free speech in the 1960s. Fetishised as a 1950s jazz- and Beats-inspired hipster who intersected with the counterculture – as in 1966 when he performed with Frank Zappa and the Mothers of Invention – his death from a drug over-dose on a bathroom floor, like his performances, proved a big photo-opportunity that has been compared to the way photographers fed on gangster John Dillinger's death.[48]

Comedians who opened themselves to public approbation or dis-approval demonstrated an almost preternatural talent for distilling the cultural moment. One of the most unusual was a university professor: mathematician Tom Lehrer. His satirical musical repartee began in the 1940s when he wrote songs while still a student at Harvard. In the 1950s he recorded studio and live albums and toured the US, Britain, Australia and New Zealand. By the beginning of the 1960s, as Lehrer entered his thirties, he was a huge hit both sides of the Atlantic and spent the decade supposedly saying farewell to his fans. He chose Glasgow as the venue for his first 'final' concert performance in 1960 and Copenhagen as the site of his final farewell in 1967. Lehrer had decided that, 'I never had the temperament of a performer . . . I do not require anonymous affection, such as that manifested by the applause of large groups of strangers. I wanted the audience to leave thinking *Weren't those songs funny?*, whereas most, if not all comedians want them to leave thinking *Wasn't he (or she) funny?*'[49] This distinction between writer and performer sets Lehrer apart from Bruce and self-publicists such as Mailer and provides a way into understanding why such idiosyncratically reserved figures as Lehrer – and Randy Newman, whose career took off the moment Lehrer's ended – should attain cult status. That Lehrer tried and failed to say farewell to his audiences more than once is reflective of the times: there was always one more event or issue he could not allow to pass without excoriat-ing satire.

In many ways, Lehrer combined the music hall of earlier decades with the explosive satire of the cold war – or what he called the *derrière-garde* of American popular music. Although he only recorded around fifty songs, stating that his standards were so high that rela-tively few were 'keepers', it would be difficult to conceive of 'alterna-tive comedy' without Lehrer. He was at the heart of one of US television's most popular cult shows *That Was The Week That Was* – even though he never appeared on screen. *That Was The Week That*

Was was inaugurated in Britain under the aegis of broadcaster David Frost, and when exported to air on NBC in 1965, the American version stormed the Nielsen ratings chart. Lehrer wrote the songs for the show but they were sung by the show's team of presenters. Lehrer's best known song, 'National Brotherhood Week', had its first outing on the show and encapsulates the sharpest of his sharp satire.[50] Racism, religious intolerance and hypocrisy are targets, including a poke at his own Jewish heritage: 'Oh the Protestants hate the Catholics/ And the Catholics hate the Protestants/ And the Hindus hate the Muslims/ And ev'rybody hates the Jews'. In mock democratic harmony, he imagines African American entertainer Lena Horne and segregationist southern sheriff Jim Clark dancing cheek to cheek. The more ludicrous Lehrer becomes, the more barbed his critique. 'We Will All Go Together When We Go' was a cold war anthem, a satire on the 'grand incineration':

> We will all fry together when we fry.
> We'll be French fried potatoes by and by.
> There will be no more misery
> When the world is our rotisserie,
> Yes, we all will fry together when we fry.

Despite what happened to Bruce, comedians continued to be among the most outspoken critics of American culture on everything from race relations and the war in Vietnam to local issues. Dick Gregory is a case in point. Lehrer remembers that when looking for an 'in' at a San Francisco nightclub to test some new 'sixties' material, he got one because Gregory, the club's regular booking, was out 'picketing somewhere'.[51] Gregory's career began in 1961 working small clubs until his first real gig at Hugh Hefner's Playboy Club in Chicago. He was swiftly lauded for biting political satire and straight-talking about racism. Although Hefner had booked Gregory as a temporary replacement for a white comedian, he signed him for a three-year stint. Gregory described himself as bilingual in English and Profanity, in similar fashion to Lenny Bruce. However, he adapted his act and was a significant television presence in the decade in which civil rights initiatives coincided with the medium's focus on news. In 1962 with African American congressman Adam Clayton Powell presiding over a hearing on employment practices in television and news media, Gregory testified to discrimination against minorities before the House Committee on Labor and Education alongside Sidney Poitier and Sammy Davis Jr. At a 1963 charity auction in which a stellar cast raised money from a TV audience, Gregory was pointed: 'A hundred years ago, I would have been for sale'. Television provided one of Gregory's iconoclastic moments when he demanded to sit down with host Jack Paar on the *Tonight Show*. Having noted that black artists performed and left the stage without joining Paar, Gregory determined to break the intractable code of *de facto* segregation before a huge TV audience.

If Gregory enjoys an iconic status it is because he is famous for having been present at each key event, such as the March on Washington of 1963 and the 1965 disturbances in Watts, Los Angeles when he took a bullet in the leg trying to calm the crowds. He made explosive comedy of civil rights while proving himself a dedicated foot soldier because he believed that even the most bigoted individuals were ripe for conversion. He told a roomful of white southern men at the Playboy Club, 'Last time I was down South, I walked into this restaurant and a white waitress came up to me and said, "We don't serve colored people here." I said, "That's all right, I don't eat colored people. Bring me a whole fried chicken!" ' Three white men approach his table to tell him, 'Boy, we're givin' you fair warnin'. Anything you do to that chicken, we're gonna do to you.' And Gregory comes in for the kill: 'So I put down my knife and fork, I picked up that chicken and I kissed it. Then I said, "Line up boys!" '[52] The shift Gregory made from performing in nightclubs to lecturing on university campuses emphasises his chosen role as a peripatetic teller of truths; 'don't pass your poor white brother by' he has advised black members of his audiences. In Memphis in 2001, he returned to some of the same stories. One of the most famous occurred in Jackson Mississippi in 1962 when an elderly black man had just been released from jail for protesting his right to vote; while imprisoned his wife had died, on only the second night they spent apart. Gregory has declared that the courage and dedication of the old man changed his life. Gregory was a comic innovator whose stand-up routines about the hard facts about black life in America in the 1960s opened the doors for those who followed such as Richard Pryor and Bill Cosby.

African Americans were still denied the title, when Leslie Fiedler referred to The Beatles as 'imaginary Americans' and in this seemingly throwaway remark captured something of the group's fascination with American popular culture as it invaded their British sensibilities.[53] The transatlantic trajectory of the Beatles is a key motif of the global phenomenon that was pop music in the 1960s. In Thomas Pynchon's gloriously satirical *The Crying of Lot 49*, the pop group The Paranoids is instructed to cultivate English accents and to watch British TV in an effort to ensure that they become mimics. Studies of the group always emphasise their function as myth and history.[54] In his memoir *Dixie Lullaby* (2006), Mark Kemp remembers that as an eleven year old southern boy he had only understood rock and roll as 'the stuff of modern British mythology . . . Mama had told me that Elvis Presley was somehow connected to the birth of rock & roll, but in 1971, I couldn't see it'.[55] Kemp knows the Beatles are the apex of a mythical rock and roll even though he is too young to experience the excitement that their appearance on *The Ed Sullivan Show* evoked on 9 February 1964. Sullivan was the most powerful doyen of music television. His Sunday evening show was live while most music programmes were taped and he invested the British pop 'invasion' with media credibility, as did Bill Eppridge's photographs of the group in *Life* and journalist Larry Kane's interviews with the band during their US tours of 1964 and 1965.[56]

To assume a nativist strain to the biggest record sales of the decade would be to ignore the Beatles' *White Album* released at the end of 1968 which beat the top sellers of all the preceding years. It has been argued that the tensions between the 'Fab Four' that are commonly supposed to be revealed in the album's structure and that would see them head in different directions also reflect some of the strains apparent in the fraying years of the 1960s. It is certainly possible to graft the Beatles on to each cataclysmic event – as it is Dylan – as if the highs and lows of the group track the decade, but it is at least as revealing to look behind them to the media-made Monkees who had a different introduction to their US fan base also through television. This group was conceived as the first 'boy band' when producers Bob Rafelson and Bert Schneider (before successful careers in movies) lined up Peter Tork, Davey Jones, Mike Nesmith and Mickey Dolenz after successful auditions for an NBC TV series, conceived as a small-screen version of Beatles films *A Hard Day's Night* (1964) and *Help!* (1965). It was axiomatic to assume that the Monkees, who only became a 'real' group following TV success, had no real talent, especially when their music was originally played by session singers and they were marketed for children both sides of the Atlantic. Yet the series won an Emmy and in 1967 the boys even outsold the Beatles. Mike Nesmith was significant in pushing his own compositions into the mix and when they succeeded in wresting some creative control from music manager Don Kirschner (of Brill fame) they both toured and recorded their own

Figure 1.7 The Monkees pose with their Emmy award at the 19th Annual Primetime Emmy Awards in California on 4 June 1967. They won for best comedy series and best comedy direction for *The Monkees*. The group members are, from left to right, Mike Nesmith, Davy Jones, Peter Tork and Micky Dolenz. Courtesy PA Photos.

songs. This shift is epitomised by a single song, 'Sugar Sugar', the song the Archies released under Kirschner's direction that became a cult hit for the cartoon group made up of session singers. The Monkees had disdained to record the song and the Archies who existed for fans only in animated form were unable to follow the Monkees' example of musical rebellion.

The Sounds of the Sixties

It would be a mistake to assume that Dylan, Motown, the Beatles or the Woodstock generation were always the dominant sounds when the best-selling artists were often those who maintained established musical traditions into the 1960s or whose talent lay in producing 'Easy Listening' such as Andy Williams, or who were country stars, such as Glenn Campbell. Best-sellers included Herb Alpert and the Tijuana Brass and The Fifth Dimension whose 'Up Up and Away in My Beautiful Balloon' has become the height of 'muzak', and the 'golden oldie' was introduced in the 1960s. The 'Singing Nun', aka Sister Luc-Gabrielle, spent ten weeks at number 1 in 1963 and in 1969 the Carpenters' ballad version of the Beatles' 'Ticket to Ride' was hugely popular and at the 1971 Grammy Awards, following hits such as 'Close To You' and 'We've Only Just Begun', they beat Simon and Garfunkel. In the album charts, *Hair* did amazingly well but so did Barry Sadler's album *Ballads of the Green Berets*, which stayed at number 1 for five weeks in 1966. The pop boom of the 1960s endured not only because the music reminds so-called Baby Boomers of their youth but also because of the professionalisation of the industry in the decade. Entrepreneurs found a niche in the music business as producers and talent scouts so that the term 'music industry' began to be applied and John Hammond, Jerry Wexler, and Berry Gordy, Herb Alpert and Phil Spector began to corral music into different 'sounds' for different record labels. Phil Spector's 'Wall of Sound' had begun topping the US charts in 1958, his debut single as producer 'To Know Him is to Love Him' selling a cool million for the Teddy Bears, but from 1960 Spector's distinctive sound also served to define the girl group. Teenage girls came together as the Crystals, the Shirelles, the Ronettes and the Shangri-Las and were phenomenally successful, their harmonies recalling groups such as the Andrews Sisters who would so successfully blend harmonies with the Supremes on Sammy Davis Jr's TV show. The girl group was one of the most enduring musical sounds of the 1960s and, as academic studies of musical trends have argued, also a non-threatening means of securing crossover success. Many girl groups found a home in Motown, such as the Vandellas, the Marvellettes and, most successful of all, the Supremes.

The charts were the industry's measure of best-selling products or brands and a general, if flawed, reflection of changing musical tastes that cultural historians may follow. Billboard began ranking the industry's most popular albums and by 1958 had become the industry standard for singles too, though there were scandals over 'payola' or 'pay for play', denoting the financial inducements record companies could use to persuade radio stations and television programmers to promote their records. Both celebrity disc jockey Alan Freed and tastemaker

Dick Clark fell foul of 'payola' scandals in 1960 and 1962. Promoters such as Sam Phillips of Sun Records in Memphis had already established connections between particular cities and particular musical sounds and Stax Records was founded in Memphis in 1960 as 'Soulsville USA'. Based in a former movie theatre at 926 East McLemore, it became the home of southern soul, between 1962 and 1967, its record sales increasing by 500 per cent in what would later be celebrated as 'the soul decade'. Claims for the significance of soul are legion. Aficionado Gerri Hirshey summarises its force: 'Soul blew a huge hole in *Leave It To Beaver*-land . . . soul played black activist centers, and white fraternity bacchanals; soul cassettes went to Saigon in rucksacks . . .'[57] Carla Thomas' self-penned 'Gee Whiz', a Top Ten hit in 1961, inaugurated the Stax sound in Memphis just when Detroit became Motown's 'motor city'. Chicago, traditionally associated with the blues, was rivalled by Los Angeles, the city which produced 99 per cent of the blues by the end of the decade.[58] While the sounds of Chicago and LA were eclectic, the most memorable harnessed a 'house' sound via a house band. The Funk Brothers of Motown are discussed below and at Stax, Booker T. and the MGs were known as the groove engine on tracks by Otis Redding, Wilson Pickett and many more, as well as hitting the charts with their own 'Green Onions' in 1962.

A 'hit factory' neglected until recent studies revived interest was the one publisher Don Kirschner founded when he saw a niche in the music market that could be filled in New York's Brill Building, which he leased to songwriters. It was the working home of a gallery of hit-makers from Burt Bacharach and Hal David to Carole King and Neil Sedaka. Music critics have recently begun to recover the Brill song-writing teams' significance in professionalising hit-making – or, more negatively, as producing similar sounds in an assembly-line music factory. Some have seen the Brill sound as purposely taming the raw rock and roll of the 1950s. Influences included not only R&B but also doo-wop, Gershwin and Irving Berlin, and it has been posited that the Brill sound 'feminised' the love song. The presence of Carole King and Cynthia Weil is simplistically cited as evidence of this when in fact King's partner and husband Gerry Goffin was the lyricist on many of their hits. In the context of New York's Brill teams, Ken Emerson's thesis is the most culturally suggestive when he posits that success lay in the songwriters' ability 'to assimilate and project rock & roll into the mainstream of American popular music, thereby extending and expanding both'.[59] The Brill Building was home of the 'Great

American Songbook' of the 1960s but while the term might seem to restrict the songs to a seamless continuity, the effect was a promiscuous mix of styles, producing hits for the Drifters, the Righteous Brothers, Dionne Warwick, the Animals and Herman's Hermits, what Emerson summarises as a 'smorgasbord of African American, Afro Cuban and European flavorings'.[60]

The best-known hit factory, however, was further north, in Detroit. The music that began there travelled around the world and provided one of the most distinctive and enduring sounds of the decade, a phenomenally successful racial crossover that combined soul and R&B with pop.

The Motown Sound

What was formerly known as 'race music' enjoyed a phenomenally successful crossover over in the music of the Temptations and the Supremes, the Four Tops, Marvin Gaye and Smokey Robinson. In Europe where Motown artists were fêted, theirs was American music, but in the US music could appear as segregated as any southern city in the early 1960s. A putative difference was distinguished further by two types of music charts, the R&B chart differentiating most 'black' music from 'white' Billboard charts. The success of African American performers, however, would be a global phenomenon. Motown even battled the 'British invasion' with some success in the UK. Thanks to a number of factors, including Dusty Springfield, the British blues and pop singer who publicised Motown acts so assiduously to the UK media, the Supremes' 'Baby Love' was the sole American hit of 1964.

The legend of Motown is that black kids from the Detroit projects were spotted, groomed and manufactured as stars at 'Hitsville USA' and while this simplifies a complex organisation, the 'Sound of Young America' was produced under the orchestration of one man. Detroit is the 'Motor City' and the motor of the Motown machine was Berry Gordy. He began as a songwriter but as a musical entrepreneur he was an icon of African American capitalist success. His artists, usually from the working classes, represented that success in obvious ways. The Supremes, who were brought up in Detroit's Brewster housing projects, were draped in furs and evening gowns. One critic called them 'artificial' in their 'sequin-spangled angst'[61] but for Gordy the fashions were expressive of conspicuous black consumption and the cultural power that Motown could wield. He auditioned hopefuls such as the Supremes (called the Primettes when first trying their luck at Motown) and 'discovered' most of the musical entourage including Stevie Wonder, who was only nine when he joined the 'family'. Mary Wilson of the Supremes addressed the central trope of the Motown family in her memoir *Dream Girl* (1986), its close community as well as the potential for unproductive tensions: 'we really believed we were one big family. But success separated us from the other artists, and the industry started calling all the shots'.[62] Gordy saw the Supremes as 'the vehicle to lead Motown into a whole new world of music' that included the Las Vegas lounge circuit; after fearing 'our music' wouldn't be seen as 'good enough for places like that', he made sure the Supremes were a storming success at the Copa and that other of his acts would follow.[63] The Supremes were the height of mainstream success, even appearing as nuns in an episode of TV's *Tarzan*.

Motown had its first Top Ten hit in 1960 and Brian Ward counts up some 174 Top Ten hits during the decade[64] with the Supremes from 1962 to 1970 celebrating 12 number 1s from some 30 singles and 25 albums. The factory comprised of two distinct labels – Tamla and Motown – and subsidiaries such as Miracle Records. It brought together a host of songwriters, producers and arrangers as well as singers and musicians but it was the writing and producing team of Brian and Eddie Holland and Lamont Dozier (HDH) whose talents first secured the hits that would help build the sound. Motown produced dance music with memorable, if repetitive, lyrics. The singers gained most publicity but it was the definitive sound that set them apart. The rhythm section with bass guitar, tambourine and snare drum so effectively characterised a Motown track that within one or two beats it was instantly recognisable. The snare drum came in on every down beat and the drum and guitar were back beats, with percussionist Jack Ashford playing some 12 instruments. Potential competitors for hits are most revealing in that more than anyone else they needed to understand the Motown sound. Carl Davis, producer of Chicago soul including Curtis Mayfield and the Impressions, believed the Motown sound was built from the bottom up, the singers the icing on a very rich cake. The metaphor he chooses, though, is painterly: 'Motown used to put a picture frame together, paint in all the background, and then they would take the artist and put him in the picture. They would make a complete record, record it in a certain key that they thought would fit the song. Then the singer had to come in and sing the song'.[65]

The documentary film *Standing in the Shadows of Motown* (2002) tells the story of the musicians jamming in the basement in Studio A. Allan Slutsky, who undertook a fifteen-year project to get it funded, called them 'the last great music story of that era'. Representing the Funk Brothers as 'the soul behind the sound' reawakened interest in Motown's history, especially that of neglected heroes: one Funk Brother, Joe Hunter, describes with emotion 'the pleasure of being discovered after fifty years as a working musician'.

In 1968–9 the Motown 'family' fell out when the Holland brothers and Dozier were refused more money or control by Gordy and left Motown, suing and being counter-sued until an out-of-court settlement was reached. The songwriters continued working in various guises (including the labels Invictus and Hot Wax) but the classic Motown era was all but over. When Motown moved its business premises from Detroit to Los

Angeles many key contributors from the early years were left behind. Martha Reeves, who had been with Motown from 1958 when she began work as a secretary before fronting the Vandellas, remembers that there was 'no warning, no announcement, and no way of preparing for it'. In *Standing in the Shadows*, bassist James Jamerson is portrayed as the tragic symbol of the end of a musical era – having followed Motown to LA, he dies poor and unrecognised by Motown fans.

Many tragedies ensued after the Detroit era ended, as in the murder of Marvin Gaye, but at the height of success Tammi Terrell collapsed on stage while singing a duet with Marvin Gaye in 1967 and died in 1970 of a brain tumour, and Gaye stopped touring for three years. The Temptations' Paul Williams shot himself in 1973 and, most famously, Florence Ballard, mainstay of the Supremes until 1967 when she was dismissed by Berry Gordy, died in poverty. Diana Ross's relationship with the Supremes has always been controversial and her 1969 'farewell performance' which launched her solo career was managed spectacularly as a Motown extravaganza with its own hit single, 'Someday, We'll be Together', masking tensions within the Supremes that would be dramatised in the 1981 Broadway musical *Dream Girls* and again when the show was adapted into a movie in 2006.

Figure 1.8 The Supremes during at a reception at EMI House, London, 1969. (left to right) Cindy Birdsong, Mary Wilson and Diana Ross. Courtesy PA Photos.

From the Human Be-In to Helter Skelter

Griel Marcus, who began as reviews editor with *Rolling Stone* in 1967, is one of the most inventive of cultural critics. By yoking together what appear to be dissimilar elements of the 1960s music scene, he conveys the shift from an ideal of participatory democracy to the dangerous solipsism that was a distinct cultural current at the end of the decade: 'Finally the Beach Boys held hands with Charles Manson as the sixties ended freedom from tradition, the freedom to invent cuts deeply and all across the board. There's no way to separate the Beach Boys' smiling freedom from Manson's knife'.[66] A seemingly shocking statement is illustrative of the importance of southern California in understanding the cults and clashes that broke the counterculture and the anomie that a cultural project of individual emancipation would inevitably involve. Brian Wilson described meeting Charles Manson as a 'horrific footnote in the career of this band' and it is possible to trace connections between the pop group Charles Manson and the Family and the Byrds, Led Zeppelin, the Stones and the Beatles, all of whom met the right-wing psychopath at gigs or through members of the Family or the group's producer.[67] When Manson and followers murdered actress Sharon Tate and friends in Los Angeles on 9 August 1969, words from The Beatles' song 'Helter Skelter' were scrawled in blood on the walls of the house on Cielo Drive. The conflation of the 'revolution of the head' (to borrow the title of Ian MacDonald's study of the Beatles) and drug-fuelled paranoia and anger helped paralyse the utopian hopes of the counterculture. Apocalyptic themes became evident in psychedelic and acid rock that focused on alienation and excess. Mike Marqusee argues, 'Hendrix took Dylan's rock 'n' blues poetry to orgiastic heights'[68] and that Jean Luc-Godard's *One Plus One* (1968) with the Rolling Stones as its subjects made culture synonymous with war; as Godard filmed the development of the song 'Sympathy for the Devil', he changed the lyrics to incorporate the assassination of Robert Kennedy, 'Who killed the Kennedys? After all, it was you and me'. An escalating sense of hopelessness and madness was dramatised in Martin Gaye's 'What's Going On?', the Temptations' 'Ball of Confusion', Edwin Starr's 'War!' and the Living Theater's picture of a cruel and barbarous culture in *Paradise Now* – and not least in the form of the music festival.

The 1960s pop festival has become synonymous with Woodstock. That the festival did not take place there but some 50 miles away is an indication of the mystique of the name: 'Woodstock' is a cultural signi-

Figure 1.9 Woodstock, a still from the 1970 Academy Award-winning documentary directed by Michael Wadleigh and edited by Martin Scorsese and Thelma Schoonmaker. Warner Bros./ The Kobal Collection.

fier, idealised and memorialised for the mass appeal 'three days of peace and music' in upstate New York held for some 400,000 'flower children'. Captured in 120 miles of film shot by some 16 cameras, Michael Wadleigh's film was deemed a 'culturally significant' document by the Library of Congress in 1996. In November 2007 a spat between Democrat and Republican hopefuls for the 2008 Presidential election Hillary Clinton and John McCain brought Woodstock's cultural meaning back into the news. They clashed over Clinton's idea to dedicate a $1 million federal grant to the Woodstock Museum, the Bethel Woods Center for the Arts, with McCain retorting that since he was a prisoner of war in Vietnam he was 'tied up' at the time. The images he used in his campaign to become Republican nominee, editing together a picture of himself in a Vietcong prison with images of hippies cavorting at Woodstock, dramatised a continuing cultural divide over the memory and meanings of the sixties. The legend for Wadleigh's movie, 'No-one who was there will ever be the same', was made to resonate with the bitter memory of one who was not.

Despite Woodstock's claim on popular memory, the festival 'movement' began and ended in California. In June 1967 the first mass countercultural musical performance was the 'Human Be-In', staged in San
Francisco in Golden Gate Park at the height of the so-called 'Summer
of Love'. The event was designed to be a peaceful psychedelic pop sen-
sation to 'shower the country with waves of ecstasy and purification'
via its three key tropes: Music, Love and Flowers. The seeds of destruction were already present. It was followed by Monterey at which
the song 'San Francisco (Be Sure to Wear Flowers in Your Hair)'
became a signifier of the hippie movement discussed in Chapter 5. It
has been described as the 'first great congress of youth'[69] and may be
seen as the birth of the revolutionary musical 'Happening' in the specific form of a festival of music. The pop festival quickly became a
media event as signalled by D. A. Pennebaker's fly-on-the-wall film
Monterey Pop for the ABC network which showcased the Grateful
Dead, The Byrds, The Who, Ravi Shankar, the Jimi Hendrix
Experience – and Otis Redding who famously converted an audience
of white rock fans to his stomping soul and blues just prior to his death
in December of 1967. Redding's performance was one of the last
musical crossovers that would reflect the integrationist principles of
the declining Civil Rights Movement.

California's Altamont festival, with the Rolling Stones topping the
bill, was made notorious for the murder that took place just a few feet
from the stage when Hell's Angels were accused of killing a young
African American audience member. Like the Manson murders it epitomised a music scene spiralling out of control. Taking place on
6 December 1969, it is also a conveniently symbolic 'end' to a decade
in which the 'sense of an ending' is a recurring cultural myth, an idea
to which this book will return. A more meditative sense of the lost
hope of a countercultural frontier is epitomised in Joni Mitchell's
paean to 'California' in which the protagonist 'too cold and settled in
Paris, France' knows that California will 'take me as I am' while at the
same time: 'They won't give peace a chance/ That was just a dream
some of us had'. The proximity of dream to nightmare captured here
and in personal essays such as Joan Didion's *The White Album* (1971)
is not only a continuing theme but has also burgeoned into an
American genre.

Rock and pop casualties of the 1960s are renowned, infamous for
their starburst deaths (Jimi Hendrix and Janis Joplin in 1970, Jim
Morrison in 1971), their burnouts, such as Mama Cass Elliott's sad
demise in 1974 , as well as for quietly disappearing from view, such as

heroin-addicted Karen Dalton who died in 1993. Those who survived sixties excesses have often suffered, like the Beach Boys' Brian Wilson emerging from the best part of two decades of depression to carry the 'Sixties Sound' to new fans in a new millennium. Sixties performers enjoy continuing resonance in new contents and with new audiences. The myth of Motown is reinvigorated in Irish writer Roddy Doyle's *The Commitments* (1987), for example, where young working-class Dubliners co-opt the Motown sound to create their own 'Dublin soul': 'If "soul" is about escapism and revolution (as one character says), then music must be the politics of the people – the plebian voice raised in protest'.[70] Protest songs that came out of the 1960s were revived when Carole King provided the soundtrack for John Kerry's presidential campaign in 2004 and Bruce Springsteen recorded an album of Pete Seeger's songs in 2005. Gospel singer Mavis Staples revisited and updated the freedom song soundtrack of the Civil Rights Movement fifty years later in *We'll Never Turn Back* (2007), aligning sixties musical protest with the government's failure to respond to the devastation that was Hurricane Katrina.

Chapter 2

Film and Television

An examination of the cinema reveals a changing film industry at the end of the 1950s as cinema's role as provider of classic family entertainment was lost to television in what Samuel Goldwyn called the 'third era' of cinema history.[1] As Marshall McLuhan made clear in his studies of the new 'cool medium', the regular trip to the movies was replaced by selective and more infrequent movie-going to enjoy big-budget spectacles in the 1950s – and this too would decline in the 1960s. It became important to target audiences for each new film and to make that film an 'event', rather than to assume the public would turn out to see a film programme at a local cinema whatever its components. Filmmakers also had to begin to think beyond the box office as the measure of film industry success. Hollywood opened its doors to television as early as 1955 when each week a segment of *Warner Bros. Presents* entitled 'Behind the Cameras at Warner Bros.' gave viewers a glimpse of the studio in action. The Hollywood 'Walk of Fame' was created in 1958 and although the Boulevard district wouldn't be listed as a historic site until the 1980s, it was in the 1960s that Hollywood staked its claim on tourism. Hollywood studios opened to tour parties and British film critic Charles Higham, visiting in 1965, discovered:

> At Universal, candy-striped trams slide along the streets resembling Paris, London or Rome, or take a minor detour to the sinister little hill where stands the *Psycho* motel. At Warners, the crowds cluster in a giant marquee where vintage cars and uncomfortable-looking waxwork drivers advertise *The Great Race*. At Universal, Frankenstein's monster may, if you are in luck, actually pick up and kiss your child.[2]

As corporate conglomerates replaced the studio system, the industry invested in its star system to maintain the Hollywood mystique, but the role and definition of the 'star' would change too as notions of celebrity developed, as outlined in Chapter 1. The TV chat show host became a celebrity – Jack Paar, Ed Sullivan and Johnny Carson – and presenters and news anchors Chet Huntley, David Brinkley and Walter Cronkite were household names, and in the case of Cronkite 'the most trusted man in America'. If the twentieth century was 'the century of the common man' as Vice-President Henry A. Wallace had predicted in 1942, he was celebrated on prime-time television in the 1960s. Hugh Downs, Paar's foil on the *Tonight* show, was fronting NBC's *Today* and *Concentration* for more than 12 hours a week by 1963. Interviewed in *Look*, he asserted, 'Our heroes today come out of the common ranks. . . I am paid more for acclaim than for merit. I am not in the least haunted by conscience or impelled to give the money back. This is the age of the lionization of the common man'.[3] The star of motion pictures was only one in a new constellation of new media personalities.

Film and television were bound tightly together in a network of businesses and markets that drove production. By the end of the decade 90 per cent of Americans had access to television sets and Hollywood would be a 'clearing house' as well as a 'dream factory'. A film's copyright was the intellectual property studios controlled and distributed to television and in the 1950s licensing a studio's film library was judged the most profitable way to ensure cinema would be embedded in television programming. *Warner Bros. Presents* on ABC remade films such as *Casablanca* as television series and advertised Warner's cinema releases to television audiences. Walt Disney agreed to host a weekly television programme on ABC that helped finance the Disneyland theme park in Anaheim and ensured Disney Productions would be advertised on television. Even Alfred Hitchcock, renowned for his condescension about the small screen, was persuaded to star in a hit series for CBS: *Alfred Hitchcock Presents* (1955–62). In 1965 US television converted to colour and the film industry magazine *Variety* began to review small-screen successes. Film re-runs were no longer in the purview of distributors and exhibitors; television hosted re-runs of films and the situation would not be challenged until the video revolution of the 1980s when home entertainment was changed by the VCR and home-video rental business.

In the 1960s, Desilu and MGM became the bright stars of film and TV mergers, especially in terms of filmed television programming with Desilu making hit series *Star Trek* (1966–9). Programming wouldn't really make the shift from (white) family entertainment such as *Leave*

It To Beaver and *Father Knows Best* until well into the 1960s but the key demographic was changing. Children raised on *The Wonderful World of Walt Disney*, *The Mickey Mouse Club* and Dick Clark's *American Bandstand* had been schooled in democratic social values, an idea represented in the movie *Hairspray* (1988), in which a white teenager in Baltimore in 1962 uses her new-found fame as a dancer to racially integrate a TV show. When the children of the 1950s became the voters and consumers of the 1960s – and draftees to America's war in Vietnam – they rebelled. Social outlaws Robin Hood or Rob Roy were hardly negative characters in Disney films and the 'television generation' had learned much about tensions between the generations from cartoons and live-action features in which adults were ambivalent at best, and evil at worst, absent parents or too preoccupied to notice their children's needs (*Alice in Wonderland*, *Pollyanna*, *Mary Poppins*). When adults were represented positively, as in *The Absent-Minded Professor* or *A Tiger Walks*, they took a stand against a conformist or cruel community.[4] Disney died in 1966 but the industry he represented remained controversial throughout the decade,[5] not least in 1969 when Richard Schickel's *The Disney Version* conceptualised his media empire as backward-looking, sexist and colonialist. Endorsed by Pauline Kael as 'the story of how Disney built an empire on corrupt popular culture', Schickel's carefully argued study may be read as a countercultural attack on an American institution. Disney's contribution to cultural history was savaged again when Ariel Dorfman and Armand Mattelart's Marxist critique asserted that the fantasies Disney manufactured were reactionary, bourgeois at best. Despite academic condemnation at the time, with hindsight, it is possible to recoup the unquestioningly conservative Walt Disney, as a Capra-like grandfatherly influence on the ideology of the counterculture as Douglas Brode shows in *From Walt to Woodstock* (2003).

Larger social forces are reflected in the growth of media. Despite global media, and the Supreme Court's sympathetic response to challenges against censorship, cold war apprehension drew the nation back from internationally collaborative possibilities promised after the launch of the satellite Telstar in 1962. The cultural forces that dominated were domestic. In the days following President Kennedy's assassination, the National Commission on the Causes and Prevention of Violence was established according to Executive Order Number 11412. It would influence the way in which violent movies were deemed to impact on America's cultural life. Later, in the wake of *Bonnie and Clyde* (1967), Jack Valenti, President of the Motion Picture

Association of America (MPAA) had a meeting with producers, writers and studio heads. The meeting took place after the assassination of Senator Robert Kennedy in 1968 and he urged upon all present an 'increased restraint and heightened responsibility in portraying violence'.[6] To begin with television looked to the movies as a guide but quickly found its feet and forged new genres that fitted the medium and played to those participatory qualities that Marshall McLuhan valued, such as the talk show. Hollywood began hiring directors who had cut their teeth in television as a way to bridge the gap between the media industries and, it was hoped, draw TV audiences back to the cinema. And while film critic Pauline Kael was scathing about those who began film careers making TV commercials, her pithy observation that the visuals of the typical commercial were 'almost a one-sentence résumé of the future of American motion pictures' looked forward to the crisp visuals typical of 'high concept' movies that began to be associated with New Hollywood by the late 1970s.[7]

At the end of the 1960s, the first academic programmes in film studies were instituted. Film aesthetics as explored in cultural commentary and industry magazines supported discussion of a film's formal qualities and style, especially as elucidated through *les politiques des auteurs* and ideas of canonicity, and in parallel, there was developing interest in the sociology of film, its cultures and ideology. Dwight MacDonald in *Esquire*, Manny Farber writing for *Artforum* in the1960s, Stanley Kauffman in the *New Republic*, Bosley Crowther in the *New York Times* and Andrew Sarris of *The Village Voice* wrestled over what film theory and criticism should entail. Pauline Kael disagreed with all of them most of the time.

Pauline Kael and Film Culture

Kael was an iconoclastic cultural commentator and the least esoteric of her peers. Movies were her barometer of social change and public taste but, mostly, she wrote what she liked, her passions and prejudices couched in a vernacular produced in resistance to whichever film theory was gaining credence in critical circles. Kael baited as well as rated films with a talent for aphorism and for invective. Her review of *Joanna* (1968) demonstrates the latter: '[W]e are getting the howling banalities of the past brought back in creamy Panavision and fruity DeLuxe color and enough Mod clothes to choke a clotheshorse, and they're brought back not with irony but with moronic solemnity. There's a less publicized side of the generation gap: we remember this stuff from the last time around . . . A movie like *Joanna* makes one want to throw up . . .'[8] As Renata Adler's devastating attack on her in 'The Perils of Pauline' (1981) showed, Kael was a celebrity courting controversy in a decade that courted celebrities and she could infuriate cinéphiles with her opinions almost as often as she entertained.

Kael started in public radio in Berkeley, California and wrote notes for film programmes. She contributed to *City Lights*, *Kulchur*, *McCall's*, and British journal *Sight and Sound* until she was given a weekly column in *The New Yorker* in 1967 and stayed there until she became ill and retired in 1991. She influenced younger critics, such as Roger Ebert and Manohla Dargis, largely because of her smart and smarting criticism but also because she more than any of her contemporaries personalised the role of the film critic. She was combative, celebrating movies that other reviewers disparaged and that her *New Yorker* readers might even disdain to view, and savaging those others admired. In this way her criticism is also resonant of the ideological yardsticks against which films of the 1960s were measured. Kael was scathing about the reductionism of *The Green Berets* (1968) and the vigilante clean-up movie *Dirty Harry* (1971) and although she described the conventions of 'bad student films' as 'random footage, shaky zoom shots, the inevitable girl with a bubble-gum bubble, and people eating flowers and cutting up for the camera',[9] she was never as cutting about the pretensions of New American Cinema as she was about blatant propaganda. She celebrated films that criticised American culture from the inside, such as Martin Ritt's *Hud* (1963) which she described as located 'deep in the divided heart of Hollywood'.[10]

Kael's anti-theoretical stance is epitomised in her review of Siegfried Kracauer's *Nature of Film: The Redemption of Physical Reality*, translated into English in 1961. Its title 'Is there a cure for film criticism?' typifies the 'disease' she believed was caused by the imposition of film theory that she feared was overwhelming appreciation of cinema.[11] Kracauer was one of many targets. One of Kael's *bêtes noire* was a tendency to idolise classic films as sacred cows, as she lamented in an essay on *Citizen Kane*, and she took Andrew Sarris to task for taking his lead from *Cahiers du Cinéma*. While Manny Farber had championed underrated directors and producers since the 1940s following the *Cahiers* critics in France, the development of auteurism had entered American film culture largely through Sarris, in essays that began a critical feud between him and Kael. In 'Circles and Squares' (1963) in *Film Quarterly*, she was adamant that reworking auteur theory in the American grain was a mistake. It may seem ironic that in a film culture in which elevating the role of the director as auteur also emphasised the role of critic as aesthetic judge, Kael should bristle. However, auteurism is a conservative and somewhat romantic approach to cinema and Kael was prescient in signalling that filmmaking is a collaborative and industrial process. As Howard Hampton summarised in Kael's obituary in 2001, she 'cut through the tendrils of cant and bullshit that engulfed film criticism in posturing pseudo-intellectualism and auteurist hero-worship'.[12]

The closest Kael came to advancing a theory of film criticism was in 'Trash, Art and the Movies' (1969) which celebrates the vitality of mass culture and the importance of plotting change in movie habits and tastes – especially her own. She saw the state-of-the-nation reflected in cinema, and was an advocate of breaking down divisions between 'high' and 'popular' that taxed other visual media. Kael's *Deeper into Movies* (1973) won a National Book Award and the battles of film reviewers, especially those in which Kael was involved, could be loud and influential enough to unnerve filmmakers and magazine editors, as when Kael was fired from *McCall's* for referring to *The Sound of Music* as 'The Sound of Money'. A review could make or break a movie. *Bonnie and Clyde* was condemned by Bosley Crowther for violence in one of his last reviews before retirement in 1968, an indication perhaps that as films changed in the 1960s, film criticism did not always keep pace. However, it was lauded by Kael whose 9,000-word essay sealed director Arthur Penn's importance. It is ironic, therefore, that Penn should criticise Kael for not recognising him as the sole creative force on the movie because of her disdain for auteur theory.[13]

Kael remains controversial because of her excess: she would enthuse or excoriate but she hardly ever wrote a balanced review. While she felt the need to champion the 'trashy' or kitsch, as film director Paul Schrader observed on her death: 'The pop films Kael most loved, such as *Hud*, if made today, would be considered art-house fare. Who would have thought the Establishment would crumble so easily? That, forty years after Kael began writing, Harold Bloom would be standing outside the multiplex like a lonely Jeremiah? It was fun watching the applecart being upset, but now where do we go for apples?'[14]

Changing Places

It has been argued that the 1963 $40-million epic *Cleopatra* was the last classical Hollywood film. Certainly with Elizabeth Taylor, a studio-manufactured star, in the leading role and Joseph L. Mankiewicz as director, it seemed set for success because of its pedigree as well as the 'scenes of unparalleled spectacle' Mankiewicz described for *Life* prior to the film's release.[15] As Cleopatra enters Rome, for example, she wears $6,500 worth of gold dress and some 6,000 extras including snake handlers and belly dancers cavort in her presence. When she closes her eyes thick with black eyeliner as she winks at Marc Anthony (Richard Burton), it is clear that the most powerful woman in the ancient Roman Empire is being represented for her times. Neither Theda Bara in the 1917 version nor Claudette Colbert in 1934, who smoulder just as sexily, would have been directed to wink so audaciously.

However, the epic spectacle that rejuvenated the box office in the 1950s was to prove a more ambiguous cinema product in the 1960s.

Figure 2.1 *Cleopatra* (1963). Courtesy the Kobal Collection.

Charlton Heston managed to rescue *The Greatest Story Ever Told* (1965) and *Khartoum* (1966) yet they did not enjoy the box office success of *El Cid* (1960). Despite its tagline 'The motion picture the world has been waiting for!' *Cleopatra* almost bankrupted Twentieth Century-Fox. It was then sliced opened and gutted, and all its problems laid bare, in Nick Cominos' short film *Première* that dissected its Hollywood opening, and in producer Walter Wanger's book *My Life With Cleopatra* (1962) in which he charged that he had been sidelined.

If *Cleopatra* signalled the end of the historical epic, it also signified a loss of continuity with the studio system of classical Hollywood. In fact, the television mini-series was on hand as a new form through which ancient history could be reproduced as entertainment with Franceso Rosi's *The Odyssey* successfully exported from Italy in 1968.

Some contemporary critics put a positive spin on seismic changes in the movie industry, as in Richard Dyer McCann's *Hollywood in Transition* (1966), but despite Twentieth Century-Fox leasing Cleopatra to ABC for $5 million, the box office failed to mop up production costs. As they rose and studios threw in their lot with the new medium, they made fewer films in a diminishing market, placing their hopes in a more broadly defined blockbuster that might arise in any genre, whether *Goldfinger* (1964) or *Mary Poppins* (1964), and prove to be the spectacular family fare that might lift the industry. By mid-decade the blockbuster was an established product via a consistent volley of commercial hits: *My Fair Lady* (1964), *Doctor Zhivago* (1965), and *Thunderball* (1965), conservative narratives in a decade in which conservative vs radical definitions of culture vs counterculture would often determine a film's success or failure

Despite changes in the media industries in a transitional decade, the film industry survived. As the decade opened, fifties themes were legion with Doris Day at the height of success in frothy romantic comedies in which she tussled with Rock Hudson or James Garner and *The Apartment* (1960), an acerbic comedy about the 'organisation man' of the 1950s carrying the day at the Oscars. Day and Hudson in their Technicolor brilliance did not seem far removed from John F. and Jackie Kennedy; the fashions Day shows off to best effect in *Pillow Talk* (1959) – figure-hugging suits and pillbox hats – were Jackie Kennedy's trademark and Hudson's playboy antics now seem prescient of the glamour (and the scandal) that the President and his First Lady would represent. Day remained a star throughout the decade and in 1967 turned down the opportunity to play Mrs Robinson in *The Graduate*, a role that would have sealed her significance as a sixties icon, while Hudson played a middle-aged man who is surgically changed to begin life anew in *Seconds* (1966). John Frankenheimer's monochrome nightmare may be read as a critique of Hollywood studios trying to change themselves to reflect a new, youthful image.

One of the reasons television was so successful was that news-conscious TV networks *defined* national issues as well as reporting them. Television's facility for non-stop coverage as events unfolded changed the nature of reporting as well as entertaining. Perhaps the most important cultural change was the facility of television news to transform events and people into 'history' in the moment of their media coverage. Obvious examples include the televised shooting by Jack Ruby of Lee Harvey Oswald. Re-enactments of the event have helped the public to feel part of a national culture. In *The Chase* (1966), the shooting of Bubber (Robert Redford) in front of an amassing crowd recalls the shooting of Oswald and when Oliver Stone's film *JFK* (1991) and Jonathan Demme's *Love Field* (1994) re-enact the emblematic moment of Kennedy's assassination, they deploy TV footage, including a choked Walter Cronkite announcing Kennedy's assassination, to signal the moment's impact on the nation's idea of itself. Serious journalists and commentators felt their professional position under threat from the medium's focus on entertainment. Extrapolating from his own experience of *The Morning Show* which he presented on CBS, even Walter Cronkite has said that he visualised the television industry as 'a huge building dedicated to the business of entertainment' with journalism in 'an attached annex next door. In that door between them is a huge vacuum that runs twenty-four hours a day threatening to suck into the larger building anyone who comes too close'.[16]

In local television, the so-called 'pastel programming' that set family shows against news and current affairs could be especially powerful. For example, African American television audiences in the South noticed how frequently there were 'racial blackouts' in the 1960s. Steven D. Classen demonstrates the extent of these in his case study of WLBT-TV in Jackson, Mississippi, the most infamous of examples. The interviews he conducted reveal that southern consumers suffered the strategic omission of black faces from their screens. *The Nat King Cole Show*, for example, was banned by WLBT and other Southern stations. However, much more insidious tactics were also used. Viewers remember the station would announce 'technical difficulties' each time black people featured on NBC- or CBS-franchised programmes and would switch to locally agreed programming. The WBLT case was brought before the Federal Communications Commission which prosecuted the station for manipulation of consumer access to programming and disallowed it from renewing its licence to broadcast in 1969. The Tougaloo students' committee which brought the case, and the Jackson Movement which supported it in 1963–4, also ensured that the cast of top-rated TV show *Bonanza* was sufficiently aware of the TV station's 'policy' as to rescind its agreement to visit the state once made aware that fans would be segregated.[17] Much more seriously, Medgar Evers, a civil rights activist and the head of the NAACP in Jackson, was assassinated the day after he appeared on WLBT. In an interview condemning racial segregation, he reached more people in a few minutes than he could have done through other means. However, the TV also made him recognisable to his murderer, as discussed in Chapter 3. Evers mobilised the power of television but his killer did also, spurred by the uncustomary sight of an articulate black man on local news to end Evers' life.

One particular way in which racial tensions affected local film programming was in decisions southern censors made and the ways in which race relations in the South affected self-censorship on the part of filmmakers. For example, *And God Created Woman* was banned from exhibition in black movie theatres because Brigitte Bardot was deemed 'too exciting for colored folk'.[18] Similarly, when scriptwriters Irving Ravetch and Harriet Frank adapted Larry McMurtry's novel *Horseman Pass By* into *Hud*, they altered the black cook with whom Hud (Paul Newman) has a sexual relationship so the part was played by white actress Patricia Neal. In 1963 the US was not considered ready to watch the affair McMurtry had imagined. At the stage of exhibition, local censors could be all-powerful. In Memphis, for example, city censor Lloyd T. Binford was renowned for his outrage at any and all representations of sexual desire and kept a tight grip on censoring even the most anodyne of images of race relations. Having been re-elected twenty-eight times as censor, he retired in the late 1950s fearing that the demise of the Production Code had opened up a Pandora's box of unspeakable images.

Screening the Space Race

Two of the most powerful visual images of the 1960s were filmed by amateurs. The first was bystander Abraham Zapruder whose seven-second home movie documentary of President Kennedy's assassination included the moment bullets entered his head. The footage was initially deemed too shocking to be broadcast on television and instead *Life* magazine successfully negotiated for rights, as discussed in Chapter 4. The second 'home movie' was film of the 1969 moon landings. To begin with there had been controversy over televisual representation of man orbiting the moon. NASA had allowed TV stations to film a simulated flight during rehearsals but on the day slated for the attempt, the orbit was scrapped due to poor weather. As TV news networks covered this, they also used clips from the rehearsal, stating that they were an 'exact simulation', but they found themselves subject to typically cold war suspicion. When the orbit did take place, pre-recorded footage was used again. After the fakery associated with television quiz shows in the 1950s, audiences were sceptical and TV stations in search of powerful images to boost their bulletins were contrite.[19]

Even in the 1960s, conspiracy theorists were quick to charge that the moon landings never took place and a favourite thesis argued that they were a cinematic hoax. It was argued that images showed no evidence of a blast crater on the moon and that when we watched astronauts taking off from the moon there was no exhaust plume. Accusations were based on the inconsistency of precisely those visual images that have marked out the symbolic territory of the moon landings as recorded on film. Conspiracy theorists used their knowledge of films and filming to challenge the veracity of documentary footage, arguing, for example, that the astronauts' moon walks were lit by more than one light source. The same images were copied in *Marooned*, directed by John Sturges in 1969. The film opens with a successful take-off followed by crew checking on-board cameras that will record the mission are working. The disaster that ensues when the space craft has problems re-entering the earth's atmosphere makes for high drama and each segment is filmed and relayed to NASA. Although initially a rescue mission is discounted, it goes ahead because the movie President is aware that under the world's media microscope it is important to be seen to try to save the doomed crew. In the middle of the cold war the rescue attempt includes a joint venture of Russians and Americans. Made only four months after the *Apollo 11* moon landings, the cinematography recalls the lunar mission but Sturges' film accrued added significance when six months after its release, *Apollo 13* suffered an explosion in an oxygen tank and not only did the crew have to abort landing on the moon, but they were also forced to use the lunar module to get back to earth. Disaster in space, a science-fiction staple, had suddenly become real. *Marooned* was followed later by the openly sceptical *Capricorn 1* (1978) in which NASA fakes a mission to Mars.

Cold war fear of radiation was dramatised as a by-product of the space programme and finds its way into episodes of *Star Trek* and the movie *Night of the Living Dead* (1968). Some of the biggest cinema hits emphasise sixties anxieties no matter how distant the setting. *Planet of the Apes* (1968) is a science-fiction fantasy that is also a clever satire on the space race and the arms race and speaks to myriad issues from environmentalism to the rise in popularity of religious fundamentalism. Charlton Heston as the stranded astronaut is, Pauline Kael asserted, 'so absurd a movie-star myth' that he is also 'the perfect American Adam to work off some American guilt'.[20] When his space craft travels 320 light years from earth, Taylor (Heston) realises that the ship and its crew have been away from home for 2,000 years and when they are forced to make a crash landing, he is certain that the planet where apes rule men is not Earth. The final frames of the film see Taylor riding a horse along the coast in a utopian image of a new Eden until the Statue of Liberty comes into view, smashed and broken. Humanity has almost destroyed itself in the years that Taylor has been in space and has made Earth a wasteland, a truth the apes tried to hide from the astronaut.

Figure 2.2 Jane Fonda as Barbarella (1968). Paramount/The Kobal Collection.

Perhaps the most outlandish example of spacefaring is *Barbarella* (1968), a film about a woman exploring her sexual identity in encounters in outer space. The film is gloriously camp and its cultural borrowings, not only from Jean-Claude Forest's comic book for its heroine, but also from French film culture, led Kael to describe Jane Fonda's portrayal as a pornographic version of Henry James' heroines adventuring in Europe.[21] Throughout the 1960s Fonda tried on different identities, not only in acting but also in life. Her films are stepping stones across issues that affected American women: she began the decade as the sixties 'sex kitten' in *Period of Adjustment* (1960) and concluded it by parodying that role as 'space kitten' Barbarella. In the middle of the decade, in her forays into French film, she dared to be nude in *La Ronde* (1964) and Barbarella's ability to beat the machine designed to kill her with an overdose of erotic pleasure is an explicit statement about women's sex drives. *Barbarella* was read as a frothy sci-fi fantasy but it also struck a cultural chord. Sociologists and philosophers such as Herbert Marcuse had argued that US capitalism contributed to sexual repression and reports such as *The Human Sexual Response* (1966) were best-selling. Gender roles were being transformed. *Barbarella* was spirited and tongue-in-cheek and Fonda would make the cover of *Life* for the role in March of 1968. The film would become a cult hit in later decades.

The idea of space travel as a 'crazy blast', a sixties 'trip' in the 'Age of Aquarius', was a final burst of optimism at the end of the decade. In an episode of *Lost in Space* (1965–8), 'spaced-out' hippies turned out to be little green aliens. The screening of the space race has combined satirical spoofs (*Dark Star*) with pioneering special effects (*2001: Space Odyssey*) but little could match *Star Trek*, which ran from 1966–9 and was the most successful and epic exploration of space travel screened during the decade.

Star Trek: Spatial and Racial Frontiers

From the first episode, which aired in September 1966, *Star Trek* was an entertaining, imaginative and often laconic commentary on the times. Its cult status is assured; it made a number of creative interventions into television history. Market spin-offs continue to reinforce the *Star Trek* brand and the phenomenon that is the *Star Trek* franchise. Its cast would become household names. William Shatner has became a populist icon and in her 1994 memoir Nichelle Nichols has stated that Martin Luther King Jr described her as an important role model. Nichols' role as communications officer Lieutenant Uhura conformed to none of the stereotypical roles that African American actresses had historically been expected to fill; a career officer, she is never less than professional or competent and frequently creative in the solutions she finds to problems that beset the *Enterprise*.

Star Trek portrayed the first interracial screen kiss, between Captain Kirk (William Shatner) and Lieutenant Uhura. This kiss is significantly different from the first soap opera, kiss on *Days of our Lives,* which prompted hate letters to actress Tina Andrews in 1976. In 'Plato's Stepchildren' which aired on 22 November 1968, Kirk and Uhura are made to kiss against their will as a form of punishment that forces them to contravene their roles. They are seen straining *not* to kiss each other as their movements are controlled telekinetically. Uhura is only able to utter 'I feel so ashamed' to her captain as their lips meet. On a planet that is a dystopian version of Plato's Republic in which only a slave speaks out against the cruelty of the rulers, the kiss is part of the 'revels' in which captain Kirk and Mr Spock are forced to dance and sing and writhe in agony, that is to 'entertain' in ways that could kill the emotionless Vulcan Spock. The kiss is just one of these revels and while it is possible to argue that popular cultural productions are precisely the sites where radical or oppositional representations critical of the status quo first find place, Kirk's statement that 'Where I come from size, shape, or colour makes no difference' is an ironic byline in an episode that demonstrates so emphatically that an interracial kiss would not yet be represented as the natural consequence of romance or love – even In outer space. Earlier in the year, Harry Belafonte and Petula Clark refused to re-tape the segment of the NBC programme *Petula* in which she held his arm while they sang a duet. It is probable that the timing of the show, two days before Martin Luther King Jr was assassinated, ensured that the controversy passed quickly. The public outcry from sponsors Chysler, however, makes the racist ideology that underpinned broadcasting very visible.

The image of outer-space dystopia was the subject of a February 1969 episode, 'The Way to Eden', in which a group of space hippies recklessly speed across the galaxy until their stolen space ship is at the point of explosion and they are rescued by Kirk and his crew. Their first reaction is to 'sit-in' in the transporter room, chanting, an action which provokes Kirk to behave like a stern parent and them to call him a 'stiff' and a 'Herbert'. Kirk is contrasted with Spock whose sympathies derive, he states, from the fact that 'They regard themselves as aliens in their own world, a condition with which I am somewhat familiar'. The hippies' search for Eden, a planet that many, including Kirk, believe is mythical, is led by Dr Severin, an intellectual and scientist who recalls Timothy Leary but who is not only insane but also the carrier of a deadly bacillus, the dangers of which he hides from his idealistic followers. The hippies are so seductive in their innocence and eroticism that they 'swing' crew members to their cause with only Kirk and Scott holding out against them, Mr Scott worrying on seeing beatific helmsman Sulu and lovesick Chekov, 'I don't know why a young mind has to be an undisciplined one'. When the hippies take over the *Enterprise*, the reality of Severin's monomaniacal plan is revealed when he uses high-frequency ultrasonics to disable the crew. As hippie Adam leads the group in song, the camera pans around their 'dead' bodies in a pastiche of a nuclear holocaust. Having used violence to trick their way to Planet Eden, the hippies find it poisoned: simply to brush against its vegetation is to suffer an acid burn and the fruits of its beautiful garden kill the group's troubadour Adam on first bite of an apple. That Mr Spock should remain sympathetic in his belief that if the survivors do not find Eden, they will make it themselves, is a muted signal that such utopianism had not been completely eradicated by the end of the decade.

Figure 2.3 Captain Kirk (William Shatner) and Lieutenant Uhura (Nichelle Nichols)
Paramount Studios/ Courtesy of the Kobal Collection

Cultural Clashes

The media and culture industries were tuned to the cross-generational tensions that characterised much of the decade. Young Americans for whom sci-fi, horror and titillation at the drive-in could guarantee a great evening out were the target audience for low-budget 'teenpics' and exploitation movies. American International Pictures (AIP) exploited the teenage market with cheap, quickly made movies about youth. Filmmakers had been moving the demographic steadily downwards until by the 1960s the primary audience was eighteen- to twenty-four-year-olds whose new-found consumerism made them lucrative; AIP were 'intuitive demographers' as Thomas Doherty has proved.[22] The nineteen-year-old male, who would be mythologised by the 1970s as the American casualty of the Vietnam War, was AIP's audience as rationalised in the following way:

1. A younger child will watch anything an older child will watch.
2. An older child will not watch anything a younger child will watch.
3. A girl will watch anything a boy will watch.
4. A boy will not watch anything a girl will watch.
5. Therefore, to catch your greatest audience, you zero in on a nineteen-year-old male.[23]

With directors such as Roger Corman in its stable, AIP's businessmen founders Sam Arkoff and James Nicholson successfully exploited the 'Peter Pan syndrome' marketing strategy outlined above. Corman's cycle of adaptations of Edgar Allen Poe's stories lent a kitsch class to the cheaper horror picture but it was the teen flick that was a cultural phenomenon. In *Planet of the Apes* the youngest ape protagonist, Lucius, states that it is important to 'keep flying the flags of discontent. Never trust anyone over 30'. This maxim forms the core narrative of films aimed at a youth market. It was popularly understood that more than half of the US population was under twenty-five years of age, as conveyed through sound bites about 'The Generation Gap', and as represented by *Time* magazine whose 'Man of the Year' cover in 1966 focused only on men aged twenty-five and under. *Wild in the Streets* (1968) and *Gas-s-s-s* (1970) epitomise the trend in which rebellious youth is explored – and exposed. Released in May of election year 1968, *Wild in the Streets* was darkly satirical. Rock star Max Frost is elected President by a large majority with the slogan 'We're fifty-two per cent', decrying any nation that would want a man in his sixties

running it. He is interviewed on television by an uncomfortable Walter
Winchell and Dick Clark and makes thirty the age of mandatory retirement to 'Paradise Camps' in which LSD 'treatment' is used to 'psych-
out' the older generation and render them harmless. By the end of
Wild in the Streets, Russia and America have abandoned their space
programmes. The hippie President has disbanded military forces, dis-
solved the FBI, CIA and all protection services to remain close to the
people, and shipped free grain to the hungry abroad. But he has also
herded those over thirty into camps and given the citizens of Hawaii,
the only state to rebel against his rule, a drug overdose that renders
them catatonic. When in the final frames a sullen child tells him he is
old at twenty-four and that 'We're going to put everybody over ten out
of business', the boy recalls the disturbing image that photographer
Diane Arbus created in 'Child With a Toy Hand Grenade in Central
Park, New York City' (1962). The camera focuses on the President's
face, expressive of belated recognition that in living out one's youth
one should continue to live.

Cold war anxieties underpinned much of AIP's output from *I Was
a Teenage Werewolf* (1957), in which teenagers evolve as a species that
will survive the end of the world, to *Gas-s-s-s* in which gas kills everyone over twenty-five. George Romero's *Night of the Living Dead*
redefined the horror movie for the 1960s with a young hero at its
centre. An epidemic of mass murders is committed across eastern and
midwestern states by men and women who have mutated into flesh-
eating predators. This cold war fantasy shifts the encounter between
human and 'Other' so resonant in science fictions into civil war. It
opens with a white brother and sister visiting their father's grave in
rural Pennsylvania. The man who lurches towards them across the
graveyard is a zombie who kills the brother and chases the sister
(Barbara) to a seemingly deserted house. The black hero (Ben) also
finds shelter there against a mob of living dead encircling the house.
They are joined by a young couple and a family. Frightened and over-
whelmed, the pocket of survivors fails to work co-operatively, the conflicts inside the house overbalancing their focus on defending
themselves against incursions from outside. Internal conflict reaches a
crescendo when the (white) American family is destroyed from within:
the daughter, contaminated when injured by a zombie, hacks her
parents to death and begins to eat one of them. Evincing no humanity,
her actions recall the mechanical killing Raymond Shaw carries out,
brainwashed not by Korean Communists but home-grown politicians
including his own mother, in *The Manchurian Candidate* (1962).

Romero's small-budget movie is, among many other things, a comment on race relations, a clever satire on the nation's defences and communications networks, and a critique of environmental dangers – as engendered by the space race. Experts identify a connection between an exploratory satellite and the 'dead'. The high level of radiation it emits has reactivated their brains and turned them into murderous cannibals preying on their own families. A journalist's plea that 'Somewhere on this planet there has to be something better than man' echoes almost word-for-word lines from *Planet of the Apes*. The quality of the TV on-the-spot interviews is also satirised: 'Beat 'em or burn 'em. They go up pretty easily' says one national guardsman. 'Are they slow moving?' asks the reporter. 'Yeah, they're dead. They're all messed up' is his informative reply. The lone hero, Ben, the only one of the protagonists to respond intelligently to a deadly situation survives to the bitter and ironic end when instead of looking for survivors, a guardsman sees the black man moving in the house and shoots him dead without question.

Filmmakers and TV producers seemed unsure of how to bring stories about changing race relations to the screen and the most illuminating examples are not the most obvious. Independent Melvin Van Peebles is best known for the iconoclastic *Sweet Sweetback's Badaasss Song* (1971) but his first feature was self-financed and shot in France where be believed he would enjoy more artistic freedom than in the US. In *Story of a Three-Day Pass* (1968), an African American soldier's relationship with a white French girl is marred by his fear of racist repercussions and ends in his demotion. Van Peebles and French-born director Michael Roemer could not be more different in background but together they forged powerful and realistic representations of African Americans. Directed by Michael Roemer with cinematographer Robert Young, *Nothing But A Man* (1964) was described by contemporary reviewers as a 'small-town' movie or a 'hicks pic' but the $300,000 project was also described by Donald Bogle as a 'Black Art Film', a term usually reserved for independent filmmakers like Van Peebles but here made to incorporate small-budget films in which white directors explore racism.[24] Young's cinematography elicits a documentary-style drama of black life. Labour relations are foregrounded: picking cotton earns a black worker $2.50 a day in Alabama in 1963 and the most reliable job Second World War veteran Duff Anderson (Ivan Dixon) can find is as a member of a section gang on the railroads. Living on the social periphery without the responsibility of family causes the veteran fewer problems than when he tries to find a position in town that will support a family once he has met and fallen in love with a minister's daughter (jazz singer Abbey Lincoln). Refusing to feel like 'just half a man', he is angered by the resignation of those in whom the threat of violence produces silence but the film makes clear that every aspect of black life in the South is regulated by that threat. When Duff finds a job at a garage and refuses to engage in small talk with the white man whose wrecked car he tows out of a ditch, he is immediately made to pay the price. The man threatens the garage owner with a boycott if Duff isn't sacked. He loses the job. *New York Times* reviewer Bosley Crowther eschewed Roemer's materialist analysis of his protagonist's plight:

> On the surface and in the present climate, it might seem a drama of race relations in the South, and in a couple of sharp exchanges of the hero with arrogant white men, the ugly face of imminent racial conflict shows. But essentially it is a drama of the emotional adjustment of a man to the age-old problem of earning a livelyhood [*sic*], supporting a family and maintaining his dignity'.[25]

In this way, the movie is glossed and carefully enfolded into a safer category than a racist exposé or cinéma-vérité; it becomes an old-fashioned liberal movie: a *Marty* for the South, perhaps.

Nothing But A Man is a far more radical statement about Jim Crow segregation than contemporary reviewers allowed and famously described by Malcolm X as the most important film ever made about the black experience in America. On re-release in 1997, Roger Ebert celebrated it as remarkable for *not* having employed the liberal pieties of its period in an attempt to reassure white audiences that 'all stories have happy endings'.[26] For example, *Guess Who's Coming To Dinner* (1967) tagged as 'a love story of today' is a sop to liberal ideals when viewed in the context of *Loving and Loving* vs *The State of Virginia*, the 1967 Supreme Court ruling that finally made interracial marriage legal after Mildred and Richard Loving's nine-year battle to decriminalise their marriage. Sidney Poitier's role was a safe liberal version of such conflicts. A middle-class and successful doctor whose blackness seems the only bar that his future (Northern) parents-in-law can find against his marrying their white daughter, his safe characterisation represents an unthreatening 'happy ending'. In *In the Heat of the Night* the factors that make Poitier's doctor acceptable to a liberal East Coast family are those which deem him unacceptable in Mississippi as the state is again placed in stark counterpoint to the rest of the nation.

Norman Jewison's *In The Heat of the Night* (1967)

In The Heat of the Night brought together key figures in the 1960s film industry on a movie that would win five Oscars and earn $10,900,000 in domestic rentals. Director Norman Jewison had enjoyed success with Doris Day in romantic comedies *The Thrill of It All* (1963) and *Send Me No Flowers* (1964) and cinematographer Haskell Wexler, renowned for political documentary, had worked with creative success on features including *The Best Man* (1964), adapting Gore Vidal's play, and *Who's Afraid of Virginia Woolf?* (1966) based on Edward Albee's Broadway hit. Rod Steiger was one of the first and finest proponents of Method Acting. Beginning his career in the 1950s, his repertoire by the 1960s included a powerfully intense performance in *On the Waterfront* (1953). His work in *In the Heat of the Night* as Sheriff Gillespie would result in the Best Actor Oscar. Ray Charles, who sings the title track, was already an icon who courted controversy, not only in protesting against segregation but also by finally getting busted for heroin, spending the year before the film was released on parole. Quincy Jones's score of blues and bluegrass is expressive of distinct and supposedly racialised southern musical traditions. That he creates a fusion of these sounds is a reflection of the ambivalence that suffuses the protagonists too: when a white man pits himself against a black man, he discovers much more than his upbringing has led him to expect.

Sidney Poitier was by 1967 an anomaly in American cinema: in *Guess Who's Coming To Dinner* he proved to be *the* black actor functioning at the heart of mainstream American cinema, a box office draw in films such as *To Sir With Love* (1967) and an early indicator of the success that black genre films would enjoy in the 1970s. He was a transitional actor; in *The Defiant Ones* (1958) he had succeeded in conveying a depth of character and a dignity that seemed extra-textual. Although he has been described as the model integrationist hero, and he certainly appealed to whites as well as blacks, Poitier would begin to shift gears with *In the Heat of the Night*.

The film is set in the small-town South, in Mississippi, the state that throughout the 1960s was the nation's strongest example of massive resistance to integration, as immortalised by Nina Simone in the 1963 song 'Mississippi Goddamn'. As Ray Charles sings over the opening credits, a train rolls into the fictional town of Sparta. The murdered body of a Northern entrepreneur whose factories have brought prosperity is discovered just off Main Street. As was becoming ubiquitous in low-budget horrors and murder mysteries, the 'outsider' is eyed with suspicion and therefore the immediate suspect. The criminalisation of Virgil Tibbs (Poitier), arrested by Deputy Sheriff Wood (Warren Oates) simply for being a black man waiting for a train in the middle of the night, recalls the scene in *Sergeant Rutledge* (1960) set a century earlier in 1861. When a railroad stationmaster finds a man dead and runs straight into cavalry sergeant Rutledge (Woody Strode), the black sergeant finds himself on trial, not only for killing his commanding officer but also for raping and murdering his white daughter.

Despite the fact that he is in Sparta to visit his mother – a fact he chooses not to release – Tibbs is no longer recognisable as a southern black man who knows his place. When asked 'What they call you boy?' his reply through clenched teeth, 'They call me *Mr* Tibbs', recalls Sgt Rutledge's protest on the witness stand that 'I am a man'.

James Baldwin described *In the Heat of the Night* as preposterously unrealistic, but almost despite himself, he succeeded in capturing one of its most pressing claims on film history; that it conveys 'the anguish of people trapped in a legend. They cannot live within this legend; neither can they step out of it'.[27] The legend is Jim Crow racism that has poisoned the white man while demeaning the black and is underpinned by a culture clash in which the South battles what it perceives as the North's disdain. It is also a significant portrayal of African American manhood. Therefore, when Tibbs' police-chief boss in the northern city of Philadelphia offers the services of his 'Number 1 homicide expert' to help solve a crime in the South, Gillespie is insulted. However, the film is more than a 'message movie'. It is a thriller whose magisterial comedic touches derive from what was to become a classic plot of the buddy movie by the 1980s, a sub-genre that Poitier was significant in establishing via *The Defiant Ones* (1958) and *Duel at Diablo* (1966).

The most memorable scene in the film begins with a long tracking shot that follows Tibbs and Gillespie as they drive through cotton fields to the Endicott plantation to question the owner. It repeats almost exactly a scene in Roger Corman's *The Intruder* (1961) in which William Shatner's white supremacist character conspires with a local planter to stir up a mob to oppose desegregation. In both cases the image of the bourgeois planta-tion owner reflects Senator James Eastland and his fifty-four-hundred-acre place in Sunflower County, Mississippi. In the film, Mr Endicott compares the orchids he tends to black southerners, 'like the nigra they need care and feeding and cultivation and that takes time', but when he slaps Tibbs, he finds the violence returned swiftly and decisively. It was the first time that a black actor had hit a white with such steely pride in a Hollywood movie.

Locked together, despite Tibbs' defensive pride and anti-white bigotry and Steiger's closed mind and lack of self-worth, the two men discover commonality and mutual respect; that is to say, more than the racial and regional animosity that divided them at the film's beginning. Stirling Silliphant's screenplay is more subtle than most in this genre, even though Pauline Kael described the story as 'a good racial joke about a black Sherlock Holmes and a shuffling, redneck Watson' in a 'Tom and Jerry cartoon of reversals'.[28] Focusing on its popular appeal, Kael captures something of the film's significance in breaking open the stereotype of the corrupt southern sheriff. Marlon Brando's Sheriff Calder in *The Chase* (1966), beaten to a pulp by a southern lynch mob because he protects his prisoner from vigilante 'justice', is a clearer example of a movie in which the stereotype is openly undermined but Haskell Wexler's camera controls the image of the sheriff: close-up shots of Gillespie's incessant gum-chewing make clear that Steiger's performance is also modelled on real southern sheriffs who had become media pariahs by 1967, notably Harold Strider of Mississippi and Alabama's Jim Clark.

Send in the Marines! Looking for America ...

In his ironic song 'Send in the Marines' (1965) Tom Lehrer sang, 'We'll send them all we've got – John Wayne and Randolph Scott/ Remember those exciting fighting scenes?' The Vietnam War as fought by classical Hollywood heroes is also recalled with bitterness in later decades. In his memoir *Born on the Fourth of July* (1977), adapted into a blockbusting film in 1989, paraplegic Ron Kovic laments with cruel irony: 'I gave my dead dick for John Wayne and Howdy Doody'.[29] And Nicolas Cage as veteran Alfonso in *Birdy* (1984) admits, 'In any other war we would have been heroes. Oh man, we didn't know what we were getting into with that John Wayne shit, did we? Boy we are dumb'. John Wayne is also at the centre of a 'mythopathic moment' in Michael Herr's *Dispatches* (1977) in which he is remembered as the veteran fighter in the Western *Fort Apache* (1948) whose advice, had their commander only heeded it, would have prevented a platoon of men from being wiped out. In 'the Marine bunkers of the "frontier"', from which Herr reported in 1967, he judged the Western as paradigmatic of the situation in Vietnam.[30]

Like Disney, John Wayne might seem an odd figure to conjure in the context of the sixties but at the height of the Vietnam War, he used his star image to support America's war. Wayne was a supporter of McCarthy's HUAC witch hunt and President of the Motion Picture Alliance for the Preservation of Ideals, and he supported Goldwater in 1964 and Nixon in 1968. *The Green Berets* (1968), which his son produced and in which he starred, presented America's presence in Vietnam as Hollywood had represented the Second World War: a 'good war', patriotic and righteous. Wayne's persona is satirised to effect in the opening frames of *Gas-s-s-s*. A cartoon of a US general speaks in John Wayne's voice and is made representative of the military industrial complex, upholding the use of chemical warfare with the motto, 'It became necessary to destroy the world in order to save it'. A staunch Republican, Wayne fought the anti-war movement, *The Green Berets* reflecting the tendency for American films to split into two cycles – Left and Right – in the late 1960s. *The Green Berets*

presented the US military as heroes saving the South Vietnamese from
the communists in the North; war correspondents who report otherwise are traitors. Wayne's cinematic intervention into Vietnam vilifies
the Vietcong as baby murderers and village burners and by featuring
Star Trek's George Takei (helmsman Sulu) as commander of South
Vietnamese troops, the film ensures that when he says he longs to
return home to Hanoi but first he has to 'kill all stinking Cong', the
audience is soothed by the familiar (Japanese American) face associated with the USS Enterprise's honourable interventions on another
dangerous 'frontier'. Most importantly, Wayne was still the American
hero at the frontier, wherever it was located, and the moral force of the
'gunfighter nation'.[31]

Within the first few frames, two soldiers – one black, one white,
who have each survived three tours of duty – answer questions posed
by the public touring Fort Bragg. The black soldier is made to voice a
propagandist response to whether the Vietnamese 'really want us
there': 'If this same thing happened here in the United States, every
mayor . . . every teacher . . . every professor, every governor, every
senator, every member of the House of Representatives and their combined families all would be tortured and killed . . . But in spite of this,
there's always some little fella out there willing to stand up. . . They
need us . . . and they want us'. A journalist (David Janssen) stands in
for the sceptical viewer, his experience over the course of the film
intended to reassure even the most disbelieving that America's mission
is both humanitarian and just. Wayne was not alone in committing his
political sympathies to celluloid. Marshall Thompson, friendly veteri-
narian of TV's Daktari (1966–9) directed and starred in two pro-war
films, A Yank in Vietnam (1964) and To the Shores of Hell (1966). But
by 1968 the anti-war movement was challenging government policy on
moral as well as military grounds and in Vietnam morale was at its
lowest, as evidenced by escalating army desertions and 'fraggings', the
murder of officers by their troops. The war had lost media sympathy
but Wayne's star persona ensured The Green Berets would not be
ignored. When it opened in New York in June, its jingoism was subject
to demonstrations, not only by anti-war groups but veterans and
reservists as well.

The Green Berets, produced by Wayne's son Michael, is a rare
instance when the two generations came together in a creative effort in
which they were on the same side ideologically. Instead, the 'generation gap' would be represented at the Oscars. In 1969 Dustin Hoffman
and John Voight were each nominated for the countercultural hit

Midnight Cowboy. While the film was awarded Oscars for Best
Picture and Best Director, they lost the Best Actor battle to an ageing
John Wayne for his role as cowboy Rooster Cogburn in a movie set in
the 1870s: *True Grit*. *Life* magazine pitted 'Dusty' against 'The Duke'
in a 'Choice of Heroes'.[32] Hoffman was acclaimed following his portrayal of a boy trampling the Apollonian house of the father in *The
Graduate*, the top-grossing film of 1968 nominated for seven Oscars.
In *Little Big Man*, his anti-hero Jack Crabb was something of an anti-
dote to Wayne's persona as Western hero. Nevertheless, Wayne hung
on as 'Old Hollywood' even as it lost the pitch battle with the 'New
Hollywood'.

The biggest movie stars of the decade never fought the war on
screen. Paul Newman and Steve McQueen, the faces of the sixties,
played nonconformists in less controversial contexts: Newman
extending the character of the lone rebel as an alienated anti-authority
figure in *The Hustler* (1961), *Hud* (1963) and *Cool Hand Luke* (1967)
and McQueen perfecting the quixotic yet resilient individualist in
The Great Escape (1963), *The Cincinnatti Kid* (1965) and *Bullitt*
(1968). McQueen found fame as bounty-hunting Josh Randall on
CBS's *Wanted – Dead or Alive* which debuted in 1958 and ran for three
seasons and some ninety episodes. In many ways, his is a typical career
path from the 1950s into the 1960s; he parallels Clint Eastwood whose
appearance in *Rawhide* as Rowdy Yates prefigured the iconic sneering
drifter he would become in Sergio Leone's visually operatic *The Good,
the Bad and the Ugly* (1965). From the first, McQueen was celebrated
as the bad-boy-made-good by the movies because he had attended a
school for 'problem' children and spent time in the brig while a marine,
as represented in *Life*'s photomontage of September 1963. McQueen
is photographed playing with his two-year-old son and lounging in a
bath with his wife but the majority of the spread is given over to his
taking part in a gruelling cross-country motorcycle race, camping in
Sierra Madre and visiting Boys' Republic, the school he attended,
donating a $500 Steve McQueen Scholarship to the delinquent boy
who makes the biggest success of himself. *Life* celebrates McQueen's
speech as 'the lingo of the rough world that spawned him – a world of
hipsters, racing-car drivers, beach boys, drifters and carnival barkers.
Steve has been all of these'.[33] McQueen professes to 'dig his old lady',
and to be 'the greatest scammer in the business' because acting is 'a
hard scene'. Wiry and athletic, cool and unbending, he flouts authority and institutions (he will rarely attend a Hollywood premiere), and
youthful vigour is the dominant visual image. Clearly Paul Newman's

long career as an actor and latterly as director has involved far more
twists and turns than McQueen's but his persona in the 1960s was similarly located. A student at Yale who dropped out to be an actor, he personified sixties 'cool' and the classic line he utters in *Cool Hand Luke*
provided a much-quoted synonym for the culture clash: 'What we've
got here is failure to communicate'.

In film and media history, it is important to consider what was *not*
presented on screen and the dearth of images of biological warfare or
close combat signalled a broad culture of censorship. In Haskell
Wexler's *Medium Cool* (1968) there is a brief shot of a poster of
Eddie Adams' Pulitzer Prize-winning 1968 photograph of a South
Vietnamese police chief executing a Viet Cong officer with a shot to the
head. Such images captured the reality the film industry could not yet
represent. International interest in documentary style was the equivalent of the New Journalism epitomised by Tom Wolfe and Norman
Mailer. It was also prompted by the development of lightweight,
portable camera equipment and faster 16mm film which could be syn-
chronised with sound, as shown to effect in Robert Drew's *Primary*
(1960) which followed Kennedy and Hubert Humphrey's election
campaigning, and was in some ways the ur-text of political documentary for the decade. The evolving fly-on-the-wall style of filmmaking
has come to epitomise documentary's privileging of the cinematographer over the director. The act of filmmaking would become a self-
conscious politics in itself when Wexler went to Chicago in 1968 to
find footage that would help to distil images of the era's political
clashes in a new genre. Mainstream hits such as *Butch Cassidy and the
Sundance Kid* (1969) included innovative cinematography, the swift
editing together of hundreds of still shots in this case, and small-budget
and exploitation movies had traditionally used news footage, in *Wild
in the Streets* of the Sunset Strip riots of 1966, for example, in which
West Hollywood police clashed with hippies.

In *Medium Cool* Wexler went a stage further and created an innovative film drama that became a cult as well as a critical hit, a fictional
film of footage of the 1968 Democratic Convention in Chicago and the
demonstrations it engendered with two imaginary characters, a
newsman and an Appalachian woman who has moved to Chicago for
work, at its centre. Wexler's film can be compared to Mailer's *Armies
of the Night* in its facility for capturing the Zeitgeist. When Mayor
Richard J. Daley complained loudly against those who 'have been successful in convincing some people that theatrical protest is rational
dissent',[34] he ordered police to release tear gas on demonstrators and

used the kinds of tactics that had helped him manouevre Martin Luther King Jr out of 'Fort Daley' in 1967, underlining his reputation for political 'bossism' and his renown as an extreme version of the 1950s 'Organization Man'.[35] Wexler prepared for this event and kept the cameras rolling. Traditionally the documentary filmmaker was expected to recede into the background, if not into invisibility, so that the material would speak for itself and Wexler's pugnacious personality, unlike Mailer's, remains in the background except on two occasions when the director uses his persona to effect. In the first, he and another camera operator are tear-gassed when following demonstrators to the edge of police cordons. The line the other man utters – 'Look out Haskell! It's real!' – was added afterwards as a fictional emphasis on what was, in fact, real. The second reference is the final shot when a camera pans to Wexler who turns his own camera on the audience. It is a disquieting distillation of the power of the *camera* to record 'history' and drama as it happens and of the *reporter*'s inability to remain impartial or unaffected by the events he both witnesses and experiences.

Chapter 3

Fiction and Poetry

Interviewed in the 1990s about a novel she set in 1968 called *Mona in the Promised Land*, Chinese American writer Gish Jen stated, 'As soon as you ask the question "Who am I?" you are an American'. She reinforced her observation with the declaration 'to be a citizen is to participate and speak up'.[1] The question 'Who am I?' is the structuring principle and defining question of much writing of the 1960s when speaking up and speaking out became axiomatic. Examples abound in literature, as in comedy and theatre. While the immigrant story may be the quintessential 'American' story, as Gish Jen implies, questions of identity dominated in a plethora of imaginary contexts specific to the 1960s, from the violent existential self-fulfillment Stephen Rojack experiences as the result of killing his wife in Norman Mailer's *An American Dream* (1963), to the passionate intellectualism of Saul Bellow's Moses Herzog, weighed down by the search for peace amidst chaos, and the postmodern subjectivity of young Californian housewife Oedipa Maas in *The Crying of Lot 49* (1966) who asks *'Shall I project a world?'*. First-person narratives, especially those in which teenage anxiety was a major concern, took off in the 1950s, as evidenced by the phenomenal success of J. D. Salinger's *The Catcher in the Rye* (1951), but were legion in the 1960s. American voices, strident in protest, confiding in desperation, or filled with hatred or sexual bravado, distinguished much of the decade's fiction.

In dramatic monologues, confessional poetry, plays in performance, framed narratives and novels as soliloquies, the 'universal third person' was supplanted by an emphasis on individual consciousness. The man 'we all want to be', invented by the nation and embodied in the characters of Stephen Rojack – a US congressman, television personality and professor as well as a murderer – and David Bell, the TV advertising executive of Don DeLillo's *Americana* (1971), was under

attack, not only by feminists but by writers of both genders from racial
and ethnic 'minorities' for whom 'identity politics' became a watch-
word. The emphasis on individual awakening and rebellion is part of
the reason that realist fiction delineating social 'norms' is felt to recede
in the 1960s, despite Richard Yates and John Cheever, and perhaps
because their characters are chronic dreamers who worry less about
social revolution or the spirit of reform than about being tortured by
conformity and deadened by suburbia, concerns that animated the
cold war fifties. In 'Writing American Fiction' (1961), Philip Roth
defined the turn in the literary tide: while it is always, he argued, 'the
tug of reality, its mystery and magnetism, that leads one into the
writing of fiction', a shift is forced when the writer is not mystified but
'stupefied', not drawn to but 'repelled'. Roth's answer was to write as
an active participant in the community or to take refuge in the historical novel.[2] Pynchon set V. (1963) in the 1950s to represent the decade
as frenetic. However, narratives about the 1950s began to feel 'historical' very quickly unless they weighed in with 'sixties' issues. While the
quiet desperation-driven characters in Revolutionary Road (1961)
and Bullet Park (1967) continued to influence writers who began to
publish in the 1960s, such as Joyce Carol Oates, a movement coalesced
around writers for whom alienation became absurdist disaffection, the
'Catch-22' in American life, or for whom runic narratives were a way
of engaging with a society in flux.

James Baldwin argued in Nobody Knows My Name (1961) that US
writers did not have 'a fixed society' to describe: 'The only society they
know is one in which nothing is fixed and in which the individual must
fight for his identity'.[3] The Black Arts Movement would extend this
idea; Larry Neal's reaction to Invisible Man (1952), Ralph Ellison's
novel of racial existentialism, is a case in point: 'We know who we
are, and we are not invisible, at least not to each other. We are not
Kafkaesque creatures stumbling thorough a white light of confusion
and absurdity'.[4] In Give Birth to Brightness (1972), Sherley Ann
Williams described writers of the 1960s such as Baldwin and Neal as
'Neo-Black', defining 'their people in images which grow out of their
individual quests and group expectations' in a literature that centred
on 'a continuing conversation among Black people'.[5] Cultural nationalism was a developing feature of African American writing but across
the board national allegories were predominating as diagnostic of protagonists' outrage and idiosyncrasies and taken to disturbing extremes.
In Thomas Berger's Little Big Man (1964), the 111-year-old sole white
survivor of the Battle of Little Big Horn is condescended to by an

interviewer for whom his life story is merely a 'tall tale'. Berger uses a American literary form familiar from Washington Irving and Mark Twain to create a feisty countercultural hero. Jack Crabb tells the interviewer to turn on his tape recorder, 'Now you jest sit there and you'll learn something', gives the lie to myths of the 'Old West' and presents himself as a cultural force, an agent of change who determines the death of an evil and corrupt General Custer, even as he fails to save his Indian wife and child.

Novels 'about' the decade, its public life and events as well as its 'sensibility', are often large canvasses on which 'reality' seems to be speeding out of control and include Updike's *Rabbit Redux* (1971) and Thomas Berger's *Vital Parts* (1970) as well as Bellow's *Herzog* (1964). Updike's Harry 'Rabbit' Angstrom and Berger's Carlo Reinhart, like Jewish intellectual Moses Herzog, are anti-heroes who nurse every grievance and kick against the American grain in epic narratives that navigate a chaotic cultural landscape. The protagonist's loss of control is represented as social entropy, an idea at the heart of much writing of the 1960s from Pynchon to Edward Albee. As early as 1960 in his play *The American Dream* Albee represented the white middle-class family home as the deceptively benign site in which cruelty and delusion find place. He pinioned the grotesque at the heart of American family – an idea to which Charles Webb turns in *The Graduate* (1963) as does Mailer in *Why Are We in Vietnam?*: 'Does this idyll of family life whet your curiosity, flame your balls, or sour your spit?'[6] Albee infused his subjects with existential angst and anarchy so that he became focal in Martin Esslin's study *The Theatre of the Absurd* (1961), even as he struck with barbed realism at the most traditionally American of themes. A three-time Pulitzer winner who in 1994 was honoured by President Clinton as the playwright in whose rebellion the American theatre was reborn, Albee was castigated throughout the 1960s by reviewers for disguising homosexual love in heterosexual failed marriages. That Albee was open about his homosexuality from his first success with *Zoo Story* (1958) makes such claims typical of the critical prejudice from which Tennessee Williams also suffered when, like Williams, Albee has written powerful roles for women.

American literary culture seemed to be characterised by intellectually polarised factions and gridlocked racial and sexual relations. However, as in music and art, cultural crossovers when they occur are revealing. Malcolm Cowley, having endorsed Faulkner and remade his reputation in the 1950s, turned his attention to Ken Kesey and the publication of *One Flew Over the Cuckoo's Nest* (1962). The established

Marxist literary critic Maxwell Geismar having bemoaned in *American Moderns: From Rebellion to Conformity* (1958) that writers had forsaken politics, recognised the same dramatisation of social turbulence that Cowley valued in Eldridge Cleaver's *Soul on Ice* (1968), describing Cleaver in his Introduction as 'simply one of the best cultural critics now writing . . . an "outside" critic who takes pleasure in dissecting the deepest and most cherished notions of our personal and social behavior'.[7] Cleaver's angry polemic was lauded as one of the best ten books of 1968 by the *New York Times*, his 'outsider' status precisely the characteristic most valued.

There seemed to be a division between Jewish American writing at the centre since the 1950s – 'Zion as Main Street' as Leslie Fiedler put it – and other 'minority' groups writing themselves into the literary mainstream. 1964 saw the rediscovery of Henry Roth's Freudian *Call It Sleep* (1934) and its publication as a paperback original, amidst the upsurge of Jewish American writing by Bellow, Malamud and Roth. Other literary or ethnic groups were still out on the margins in the early 1960s though by the end of the decade African American and American Indian writers would have staked a claim on the literary landscape with N. Scott Momaday's *House Made of Dawn* (1969) winning the Pulitzer Prize. Momaday's protagonist Abel is a conflicted veteran of the Second World War and his efforts to secure a sense of identity dominate the novel. The idea of identity as 'unfixed', open to possibility as well as trauma, underpins the work of Lebanese American writer Vance Bourjaily whose protagonist Quince Quincey values the freedom *not* to belong:

> In the fluid society through which I move there is no . . . community of moral belief; it cannot hold itself nor me its child, to any comprehensive and unquestioned single code. And though there are many groups within this society which guard separate if often overlapping codes, I am in no very unusual position when I say I belong to none of them – I am more or less without class or national origin or locality or regular intellectual persuasion, as is true of many men of my time.[8]

In the 1960s Arab Americans were one of a number of seemingly invisible ethnic minorities. Bourjaily's heritage was scarcely acknowledged by him or by his publisher and in *Confessions of a Spent Youth* (1960) Quince is of mixed heritage: 'a quarter of what is more or less colonial American, of which my mother tried to teach me to be proud. A quarter Welsh, of which no one ever said anything much. Half

Lebanese the largest fraction, pretty well concealed . . .'[9] Quince winds up in his father's birthplace in Lebanon during the Second World War with another soldier who is also 'fractional': half Cherokee and half Arab. The responsibility of the writer to his ethnic and racial group was becoming a subject ripe for debate in the 1960s, with Irving Howe, Philip Roth and Norman Podhoretz, for example, disagreeing about the issue in the pages of the conservative periodical *Commentary*. Ralph Ellison and Irving Howe also debated the 'appropriate' content for 'the Negro novel' in *Dissent* and the *New Leader* and Norman Podheretz threw caution to the critical winds. Reputedly annoyed that James Baldwin, having been asked to write a piece on US race relations, preferred to place it in *The New Yorker*, Podheretz wrote his own position piece with the provocative title, 'My Negro Problem and Ours' (1963). The essay he had 'lost', 'Letter From a Region in My Mind', was re-titled 'Down at the Cross' and published to acclaim in Baldwin's *The Fire Next Time* (1963). Issues in literary culture found their way into novels. In *The Tenants* (1971) Bernard Malamud pitted two writers against each other, African American Willie Spearmint whose pen is his weapon and Jewish Harry Lesser trying to write a literary masterpiece. Gish Jen revisits these politico-literary tensions when her Chinese American characters Mona and Callie discover that publishers in the 1960s are only interested in publishing their African American friend Naomi: 'We're not book material . . . Naomi's experience has an import ours just doesn't'.[10]

Letting Go

Tony Tanner used the title of Philip Roth's 1962 novel to argue in *City of Words* (1971) that 'letting go' was the key metaphor for US fiction in the late 1950s and early 1960s. John Updike's *Couples* (1968) was the first novel by a major writer to celebrate life post-The Pill – the contraceptive pill had been licensed in 1960. His portrait of adulterous marriage and its dissolution struck at the heart not of the counterculture but of the 'ordinary' small-town and the middle-class suburbs. Updike made the cover of *Time*, its legend 'The Adulterous Society', in April 1968. Most often cited, though, in this context is Roth himself. Initially 'black humour' was the term commonly used by reviewers to describe his fiction and Roth compared his aesthetic to that of the outrageously controversial comedian Lenny Bruce, with *Portnoy's Complaint* like Bruce's comedic style 'oscillating between the extremes of unmanageable fable or fantasy and familiar surface realism'.[11] Roth's own description when revisiting the novel in 1975 recalls Jacob Brackman's 1967 definition of 'the put-on', a precursor to more critically defined sixties style: 'It occupies a fuzzy territory between simple leg-pulling and elaborate practical joke, between pointed lampoon and free-floating spoof.'[12] The shock of in-your-face sexual imagery that Roth employed was hardly new in the 1960s. Henry Miller and Anaïs Nin, writing from Paris, were renowned for having pushed erotica to aesthetic extremes, with Miller's *Tropic of Cancer* (1934) only finally un-banned as a result of its Grove Press publication in 1964 and the tenacity of publisher Barney Rosset. Roth's works do not comprise the most sexually risqué of those published in the decade that finally saw D. H. Lawrence's *Lady Chatterley's Lover* (1928) un-banned, Lenny Bruce on trial for obscenity, and exploitation movies developing into the sexploitation and blaxploitation markets. Leslie Fiedler, for example, reviewed Herbert Kubly's *The Whistling Zone* (1967) as 'culminating in a campus orgy dripping with more sperm than has flowed in any American book since *Moby Dick*'.[13] However, such fictions are no longer remembered.

Much 'louder' in resonance is *Portnoy's Complaint* which remains by reputation alone a scandalous masturbatory fantasy that made its author a household name and fulfilled a Jewish fantasy by transgressing the image of quiet and scholarly Jews in the Gentile imagination, in the way that Ross Posnock has described 'the unending struggle of the nice Jewish boy . . . to be a bad man'.[14] However, a novel that was re-issued in paperback each year of the decade in the UK as well as the US was a 'rollicking sexual odyssey' first published in 1960: Vance Bourjaily's *Confessions of A Spent Youth*. Reading them together serves to disabuse us of any assumptions that the sexual 'revolution' was the province of young writers. Neither Bourjaily nor Roth was particularly young nor caught up in countercultural hedonism – Bourjaily began publishing in the 1940s and as a tutor for the Iowa Writers Workshop encouraged younger novelists; Roth was already in his late thirties when *Portnoy's Complaint* was published. Yet, in the persons of their sexually obsessed narrators, they best capture the 'permissive' turn in American fiction that began in the 1950s and was played out in the 1960s. Roth's novel is an entertaining confession by Alexander Portnoy, the thirty-three-year-old Assistant Commissioner of Human Opportunity for New York City to his psychiatrist, who is attempting to cure him of the feeling that he is living in the middle of a Jewish joke, but who is silent throughout Portnoy's hysterical outpouring until he finally speaks at the end of the novel: 'So . . . Now vee may perhaps to begin. Yes?' Sexually obsessed and in Oedipal melt-down, Portnoy is notoriously unreliable, trying on a series of masks or putative identities; riffing on his name – Alton Petersen, Al Parsons and so on – he poses as non-Jewish personae designed to attract non-Jewish girls of whom his mother would disapprove.

In the 'Confession of Intentions' that opens *Confessions of a Spent Youth*, Quince is much less ribald but allows that 'Like most men, I tell a hundred lies a day' and closes his tale of worldwide philandering during the Second World War with a denial of having been a terrible sinner and a request that the reader accept his story not as unusual or exotic, 'but as a specimen account of how a contemporary youth was spent – not misspent nor well-spent, merely spent – exhibiting no special depths of degradation, nor special heights of intellectual or sensual joy, but only such ordinary ones as most youths know'.[15] Inflaming readers as well as enchanting them has always been Roth's way and Boujaily's semi-autobiographical narrator is named, of course, after the English Romantic writer Thomas De Quincey whose *Confessions of an English Opium Eater* was not only a *succès de scandale* in 1822 but also a popular intertext in the 1960s when the war in Vietnam began to be represented as a drugged and torturous night-mare.

In the 1960s the academy was 'letting go' of what has been termed the 'classic' phase of American Studies – involving the so-called 'myth and symbol' critics, from F. O. Matthiessen in *American Renaissance* (1941) and Henry Nash Smith in *Virgin Land* (1950) to Leo Marx in *The Machine in the Garden* (1964). Novelists and critics including Philip Roth, Mary McCarthy, John Barth and Leslie Fiedler were bat-tling over the cultural status of the novel and whether a new kind of postmodern fiction was beginning to be written. In 1967 Barth pub-lished 'The Literature of Exhaustion' in *The Atlantic*. There had been heated literary debates declaring a moratorium on literature, typical of the decade's disquisition on 'the sense of an ending', explored so deli-cately by British critic Frank Kermode in 1968, and summed up by Jacques Hermann in 'The Death of Literature'.[16] However, as Barth pointed out, the idea of 'exhaustion' did not mean the novel was dead but rather that it was reflexive, ripe for experiment and regeneration. Many of the debates about the status of literature took place in uni-versities where the professoriate included the very writers over whom such battles were fought: Saul Bellow (Chicago), John Barth (Penn State and State University of New York at Buffalo), Vance Bourjaily (University of Iowa) and Howard Nemerov (Brandeis University), for example. Of the magazines in which literature and culture were debated, *Partisan Review* and *Commentary* were well established and their editors – like Podheretz – often threw themselves into the literary fray with spiky editorials. 'Little' magazines such as *The Noble Savage* founded by Saul Bellow, *New American Review* (1967–) in which a section of what would become *Portnoy's Complaint* was published and Robert Bly's *The Sixties* sought to capture the Zeitgeist and mark out new literary territory. Literary criticism like fiction often contained within it a personal poesis. Rebellion and revisionism were literary-critical watchwords which coincided in the position pieces of one of the most prolific and outspoken of critics who came to prominence on the crest of the 1960s: Leslie Fiedler.

Leslie Fiedler and Literary Culture

Fiedler was a self-proclaimed literary anthropologist, whose revisionist examination of myth-criticism in *An End To Innocence* (1955) and attacks on New Criticism in essays such as 'Archetype and Signature' (1952) characterised the postwar climate of change in which psychoanalytical concepts began to be applied to images that haunted 'the American psyche' and which were powerfully present in literary discourse, especially after studies of Freud were published in the 1960s. Fiedler's political position underwent a series of changes: his anti-communism and condemnation of Ethel and Julius Rosenberg would be replaced by the end of the decade by his interest in the countercultural turn of events epitomised by the nation's youth.

Fiedler embarked on the kind of interrogation of the literary canon that would characterise the intellectual left during the hot 'culture wars' of the 1980s and 1990s. Fiedler set out to be controversial. For some, notably Morris Dickstein in *Gates of Eden* (1977), Fiedler was writing little more than advocacy criticism and his Freudian re-readings of the canon remained conservative in comparison with the Freudian radicalism of Herbert Marcuse, Norman O. Brown, or even Lionel Trilling. For others, he was groundbreaking. *Love and Death in the American Novel* (1960, revised in 1966), *Waiting for the End* (1964) and *The Return of the Vanishing American* (1968) comprise a trilogy in which Fiedler's key motifs are evident. The national status quo in race relations, challenged as it was in the 1950s and 1960s by civil rights and anti-colonial struggles around the world, had produced, in Fiedler's view, a peculiarly American nightmare experience which he began to articulate in 1948 in an article published in *Partisan Review*. 'Come Back To the Raft Ag'in, Huck Honey!' may be read as a preface to *Love and Death* in that Fiedler argues: 'It is perhaps to be expected that the Negro and the homosexual should become stock literary themes in a period when the exploration of responsibility and failure has become again a primary concern of our literature'.[17] The failure of love – specifically heterosexual love – is at the centre of Fiedler's thesis that in nineteenth-century American literature, there is an archetypal and sentimental image in which 'two lonely men, one dark-skinned, one white . . . have forsaken all others for the sake of the austere, almost inarticulate, but unquestioned love which binds them to each other'.[18] The buddy formula so beloved of Hollywood in the 1960s and epitomised by *In the Heat of the Night* (1967) derives from the model of intimacy that Fiedler examined in its literary manifestations. The paradigm of 'the white and colored American male [who] flee from civilisation into each other's arms' formed a central plank in his assessment of the fiction of the 1960s in the second edition of *Love and Death*, in which footnotes to contemporary fiction provide a lively commentary on classic American literature. In 1968, Fiedler argued that texts as different as *One Flew Over the Cuckoo's Nest* and *In Cold Blood* were equally obsessed by the alliance, homosexual or otherwise, of the maverick white man and the Indian as they set themselves against 'the respectable White world'.[19] While attention to the socio-cultural context of race, gender and sexuality would become the basic co-ordinates against which all literary merit would be measured by the 1980s, Fiedler was instrumental in using the preoccupations of 1960s identity politics as a lens through which to re-read the canon. Literary critics continue to return to Fiedler's thesis: Nina Baym recalls Fiedler in her formulation of the American critics' 'drama of beset manhood', which excluded women writers from the canon.[20]

Fiedler championed genre fiction. He examined the melodrama at the heart of American literature, declaring most tellingly that, 'Our literature as a whole, at times seems a chamber of horrors disguised as an amusement park "fun house", where we pay to play at terror and are confronted in the innermost chamber with a series of inter-reflecting mirrors which present us with a thousand versions of our own face'.[21] He tackled the aesthetics of pornography in a short story that prefigured *Portnoy's Complaint* and caused a ripple when published as 'Nude Croquet' in *Esquire* in 1957. Like Philip Roth, a fellow Jewish writer also from Newark, New Jersey, Fiedler was a literary rebel or 'bad boy' and in a short story called 'The Last Jew in America' played to that reputation. He achieved a countercultural notoriety when small quantities of soft drugs were found in his home and a legal trial ensued but Fiedler turned the experience he described as a Keystone comedy into the best-selling *Being Busted*, published in 1969 when Fiedler was fifty.[22]

In 'Cross the Border-Close That Gap: Postmodernism' published in *Playboy* in 1969, Fiedler argued that a new generation of writers was entering the 'madhouse' to produce the 'anti-madhouse' novel and his criticism demonstrated the gap between 'high' and 'mass' culture that modernist aesthetics had cleaved open but many critics still kept separate.[23] His hope was that a postmodernist practice would not only re-examine but also reshape aesthetics and epistemology; the substance as well as the style of cultural productions.

Following the paperback revolution of the 1950s and the escalation of the 'two-bit culture', the paperback book had become ubiquitous, with Dell Pocket Books and Fawcett's Gold Medal among many other imprints staking out market space for popular fiction, 'true stories' and risqué confessions. However, during the 1960s, publishers such as Grove Press also successfully extended the paperback's commercial appeal to provide new and good 'quality' literature and modern classics at competitive prices. Jay Parini remembers that university students of the late 1960s 'would not be caught in a café without a copy of Walter Kauffman's *Existentialism: From Dostoevsky to Sartre*. We all wrestled with our finitude . . . and were aware that we must act to define ourselves' and youth activists Tom and Casey Hayden read Camus to each other as part of their wedding ceremony.[24] Even in the small-budget radical film *Greetings* a student reads *Hitchcock by Truffaut*. The 'scriptures for a new generation', to borrow Philip D. Biedler's phrase, were logged by *The Chronicle of Higher Education* which ran a feature called 'What They're Reading on the Campuses'. Campus reading was both eclectic and indicative. Key texts included, for example, the 1968 English translation of Martinique psychiatrist Frantz Fanon's *The Wretched of the Earth* (1966) with a preface by Jean-Paul Sartre. Extrapolating from Fanon's colonial Algerian context, the Black Power movement celebrated this as a manifesto. Students also returned to classic English poetry by William Blake and Lord Byron, because Blake's mystic vision of the 'doors of perception' lent a cultish credence to the Beats' experimentation with drugs (and, later, Jim Morrison of The Doors), while the vedic and the vatic would underpin Carlos Castaneda's rendition of Byron's Don Juan as a Yaqui medicine man, written while Castenada was a student at UCLA. While students in the 1960s revisited classic texts, new books were the most popular best-sellers in paperback, not least those which spoke to present concerns.

Allegories for America at War

Ken Kesey uses the insane asylum as a metaphor for American society's failure of logic and sanity in *One Flew Over the Cuckoo's Nest*, an inmate of mixed American Indian heritage disclosing the 'humming hate and death and other hospital secrets' that are 'too awful to be the truth' but are the truth of what is hidden.[25] In the provocative documentary *Hearts and Minds* (1974), high-school football is used as a metaphor for a violent America and a nation of competitive and compulsive winners. The prevalence for such analogies in and about the 1960s is evident whether allegory is purposefully outlandish, as in John Barth's *Giles Goat-Boy* (1966), or sustained as a speculative fiction of 'other worlds', as when Kurt Vonnegut's Billy Pilgrim comes 'unstuck in time'. The Second World War on which Vonnegut's allegory turns in *Slaughterhouse-Five* (1969) and to which Joseph Heller's *Catch-22* (1961) returned readers was re-worked through a scrim of distracting images which forced the war in Vietnam to the imaginative surface. 'If World War II was like *Catch-22*, this war will be like *Naked Lunch*', Norman Mailer declared in *Partisan Review* in 1965.[26] However, the Second World War was already merely the backdrop to the novel in which the neologism 'Catch-22' in all its anarchic absurdity reflected the postwar political impasse into which the American government had pushed the nation, in Korea in the 1950s and again in the escalating foreign conflicts of the 1960s, notably Vietnam.

Mailer said *Why Are We in Vietnam?* was neither planned nor written as a book 'about' the war. Supposedly the hunting trip at its centre – a motif that would be returned to in the movie *The Deerhunter* (1978) – was to form only a prelude to the novel's real setting: the tip of Cape Cod or the end of the world 'where the land runs out' and the sand dunes bear a resemblance to the desert where bikers and hippies could live 'in the wild'.[27] If Puritan 'America' is seen to begin in this landscape with the Pilgrim Fathers landing here before docking in Plymouth, the apocalyptic vision of landscape as dystopian textures Mailer's novel as it would other cultural forms, such as the California desert 'Death Valley' in Antonioni's movie *Zabriskie Point* (1970) and Peter Watkins's film documentary *Punishment Park* (1971). Mailer's novel is entirely set in Alaska during a hunting trip, a male bastion of rugged competition just like the field of war, and the voice that describes events is made deliberately ambiguous. Is DJ a white teenage boy sent to military school whose Texan slang is a nod to his southern roots, or is his hip talk the key to his 'real' identity as a black disk jockey hipster from Harlem? DJ is both southern and northern, white and black, at times quixotic and at others cruel, the kind of protagonist recognised early by literary critics as vital to sixties fiction.[28]

The very youth of the child protagonist was an important mechanism for cultural critique. As Joyce Carol Oates has pointed out, adolescents are vehicles for adult writers like Mailer who feel 'they must go back in order to possess the freedom to tell what they see of the truth'.[29] The idea of a generation 'gap' was an issue that preoccupied many cultural commentators in the 1960s (a theme to which this book

returns) distinguishing the Boomers' sixties from the decade as lived
by their parents. But Mailer, recalling perhaps Robert Kennedy's paean
to a youthful spirit discussed in the Introduction, described himself as
carrying 'different ages within him like different models of his experience'.[30] Never having fought there, Mailer's *Why Are We in Vietnam?*
chipped away at the expectation that the young veteran of Vietnam
would be the 'authentic' or final arbiter of Vietnam fiction. In this
respect the novel compares with *the* American war story against which
others have been measured. Stephen Crane became the internationally
acclaimed writer of *The Red Badge of Courage* (1895), a witness-
participant's account of the American Civil War, a war in which he had
not served. Nevertheless, 'The Youth', or Henry Fleming as he is once
named in Crane's text, is the archetypal lone individual tossed around
in the chaos of war, battling internal conflicts: fear and cowardice. John
Carlos Rowe and other critics have argued that an over-privileging of
a 'personalist epistemology' is a reflection of a specifically American
'mythologizing of the special value of direct experience and displaces
the serious political and historical analysis necessary to understand the
Vietnam War'.[31]

Looking Backward

The influence of classic American literature was discernible in pastiche
and parody. John Berryman wrote a homage to Puritan poet Anne
Bradstreet in *77 Dream Songs* (1964) and Adrienne Rich returned to
Emily Dickinson. Wallace Stevens was a significant influence on John
Ashbery and in Hunter S. Thompson's *Fear and Loathing in Las Vegas*
(1972), a drug-fuelled, misogynistic road trip is likened to pursuing the
American Dream in 'a classic affirmation of everything right and true
and decent in the national character'. Thompson's parody winds up
with: 'I felt like a monster reincarnation of Horatio Alger. . .' [32] Even
writers trying to forge new and radical myths of selfhood and self-
annihilation returned to the American literary canon to ground them
in what remained the most enduring of myths: the American frontier
as it informed ideas of American exceptionalism.

Other writers had more personal reasons to look back to the literary past. The publication of Robert Lowell's *Collected Poems* in 2003
was a significant step towards re-evaluating the son of America's 'first'
aristocratic family of New England poets. A prize-winner in the 1940s,
interest in him was renewed by Beat writers in the 1950s. He was
labelled the 'first' confessional poet in M. L. Rosenthal's review of *Life*

Studies (1959), a *volte face* against modernist symbolism in which Lowell's depression and mental illness found philosophical and poetic place. The autobiographical traits in his verse encompass his mental breakdowns and three marriages but are transformed in ways that both prefigure Sylvia Plath and act as a contrast to her poetic anger. Lowell was a historically conscious poetic voice of 1960s America in whom the nation's past was conserved and via whose images it might be re-envisioned. From the European-influenced free translations of *Imitations* (1961) to *For the Union Dead* (1964), there is a seismic shift in focus to the contemporary United States. Therefore, the label 'confessional' as it epitomises his work in the 1950s fails to account for a poet who was at the height of his powers as a commentator on the 1960s. Lowell created masks and characters to tell of the 'savage servility' of the 1960s, while making clear his own stand against America's war in Vietnam: he refused an invitation to Lyndon Johnson's White House in 1965 to protest against the escalation of the war. In 'Waking Sunday Morning', the most famous poem in his collection *Near the Ocean* (1967), he protested the Vietnam War and, along with fellow poets Denise Levertov and Allen Ginsberg, who marched with Lowell on the Pentagon, he used 'war' as a potent mobile metaphor for the decade.

The title poem in *For the Union Dead* (1964) is written at the bloody crossroads of at least two wars. It is a poem that speaks at once to the unsettled historical moment that produced it, as it revisits the 1860s and the Civil War that pitted American against American in a national cauldron of hate. The poem is 'about' the Civil War and at first sight acts as a commemoration like 'Ode to the Confederate Dead' (1926, rev. 1930), in which Allen Tate's narrator attaches memories to monuments commemorating dead soldiers erected in the South. Lowell dedicated his poem to (white) Colonel Robert Gould Shaw (1837–63), commander of the first black regiment in the North who died fighting in South Carolina and whose memorial is in Boston. Shaw's monument 'sticks like a fishbone/in the city's throat' and the poem asks whether there is a point to such monuments when black soldiers have the right to die in war but not to enjoy full citizenship even a century later. Both Muhammad Ali and Stokely Carmichael would very publicly refuse to fight 'the yellow man in Vietnam who ain't never called us nigger' and Lowell's own refusal to fight in the Second World War involved his imprisonment in 1943 as a conscientious objector. In *For the Union Dead*, he displaces the act of war in the poem's commemoration of neglected heroes with the radical patriotism of the Colonel who 'cannot bend his back' as he leads his men to their deaths:

Shaw's father wanted no monument
Except the ditch,
Where his son's body was thrown
And lost with his 'niggers'.

Most significantly in this context, like Angus Wilson whose *Patriotic Gore* (1962), a study of the literature of the Civil War, was published against a backdrop of the Civil Rights Movement, Lowell shows that the legacy of American slavery haunted civil rights struggles. He writes, 'When I crouch to my television set/ the drained faces of Negro school-children rise like balloons'. In this way, a reference to civil rights demonstrations played out on TV screens across the nation occurs in the middle of a poem about the Civil War written on the eve of that war's centenary. Previous wars would infiltrate the most bitter poetic distillations of war such as Bob Kaufman's 'War Memoir' (1965), which returns to the Second World War and asks with bitter irony:

What one-hundred-percent red-blooded savage
Wastes precious time listening to jazz
With so much more important killing to do?
Silence the drums, that we may hear the burning
Of Japanese in atomic color-cinemascope
And remember the stereophonic screaming.[33]

The dramatic monologue is a form that 'takes possession of the speaker', as Mississippian Eudora Welty described most succinctly in *One Writer's Beginnings* (1984). The form can allow a character enough rope to hang herself simply by virtue of her own words, as in Ellen Douglas's barbed short story 'I Just Love Carrie Lee' (1963) in which a privileged white lady describes her black retainer Carrie Lee as if she were a clever family pet: capable, discerning – and almost human. The framed narrative has traditionally confined African American literary subjects since ex-slave narrators were contained by white amanuenses who mediated the slave's presence as abolitionist (as black messages in white envelopes, to borrow John Sekora's phrase). The white narrators deployed to subversive effect by black writers such as Charles Chesnutt in the 1890s allowed black characters a space within a dominant white literary tradition. In the 1960s, the first-person and/or framed narrative began a new lease of life and is used to effect in fictions as different as *One Flew Over the Cuckoo's Nest, The Confessions of Nat Turner* (1967) and one of Welty's own stories.

'Where Is The Voice Coming From?': Eudora Welty and the Murder of Medgar Evers

One of the most resonant first-person narratives was begun the night on which a courageous civil rights activist was murdered by a Klansman. Medgar Evers was the leader of the NAACP in Jackson, Mississippi, Welty's and Evers' birthplace and home town, and under surveillance by the State Sovereignty Commission which tagged him a 'race agitator'. On 12 June 1963 he was shot in the back with a single bullet which cut through his body, ricocheting through the window of his home and into the kitchen where it lodged itself as evidence. Evers died in front of his wife and three children still clutching his house key. His murder took place on the night President Kennedy broadcast his breakthrough speech on the 'moral crisis' of race relations and first called for a civil rights bill and reforms: 'If an American, because his skin is black, cannot enjoy the full and free life all of us want, then who among us would be content to have the color of his skin changed and stand in his place?'

Late that night as news broke of Evers' death, Welty sat down to write 'Where Is The Voice Coming From?' The story's title bespeaks the anguished plea that his murderer be found:

> I thought with overwhelming directness: Whoever his murderer is I know him: not his identity, but his coming about, in this time and place. That is, I ought to have learned by now, from here, what such a man, intent on such a deed had going on in his mind . . . I felt, through my shock and revolt, I could make no mistake.[34]

Her story was accepted for publication in *The New Yorker* but she was asked to edit it once Byron De La Beckwith was arrested; some of the details Welty had imagined resembled facts becoming clear in the case. It was even feared that the short story might be prejudicial against the man on trial.

Eudora Welty has not traditionally been read as a political writer and often described herself as living a sheltered life but in the 1960s she joined her literary voice with black Mississippians clamouring for change. What is probably her most openly political statement remains unpublished:

> Heroism and shame have lightened or darkened the pages of [Mississippi history]. It is filled with extremes – some of it is tragic, some is ugly beyond bearing. But in order to be good writers, we need to face and encompass all we are – no human action is too good or too bad to forgo being understood.[35]

Controlled by the first-person narrative form, Welty's story begins *in medias res* with a comment that confuses white bigotry with freedom of speech: 'I says to my wife "You can reach and turn it off. You don't have to set and look at a black nigger face no longer than you want to, or listen to what you don't want to hear. It's still a free country." ' The speaker makes the reader complicit, 'Ain't that right?' Immediately, the reader is made aware of the role of the media in the civil rights era, as discussed in Chapter 2, and in Evers' murder. The programme to which the speaker alludes was Evers' first televised speech as a leader of the Jackson movement in answer to charges from mayor Allen C. Thompson that black people in Mississippi were stirred up by outside agitators. On 20 May he recorded the speech that made him seem the most dangerous man in Mississippi to those who were violent as well as vehement in opposition to black civil rights. Evers was as concrete as he was unequivocal:

> Tonight the Negro knows from his radio and television . . . about the new free nations in Africa, and knows that a Congo native can be a locomotive engineer. But in Jackson he cannot even drive a garbage truck . . . there is not a single Negro policemen or policewoman, school crossing guard, fireman, clerk, stenographer, or supervisor employed in the city department.

Jackson had a population of around 50,000 blacks in the 1960s but was one of the most racially conservative towns in the South. People who had not known what Evers looked like would be able to recognise him after that night's television. Welty's fictionalised murderer says: 'I could find right exactly where in Thermopylae that nigger's living that's asking for equal time . . .' and heads up Nathan B. Forrest Road, named after the founder of the Ku Klux Klan, to find his victim and shoot him into silence.

The key structural and interpretative direction of the story is inwards to a twisted psyche: the segregationist ideology which governs the murder and determines the social conditions in which it may be committed but not considered a crime. In 1964 James W. Silver would publish *Mississippi: A Closed Society* and it is to the 'closed mind' of a cold-blooded killer that Welty turned her creative attention in 'Where Is The Voice Coming From?' Welty makes vivid the reactionary individual supported by the prevailing discourse of white racial superiority; racism remains resolved in the mind of the racist who never questions. Importantly and emphatically, the murderer knows nothing of his subject personally but he is consumed by jealousy: the black man's street and his driveway are paved and he has a 'new white car'. When he returns home, the killer's wife points out that he 'might could have got you somebody better' since the NAACP office run by Evers will soon be fully staffed. Her endorsement of his crime is simple and stark: a chilling end to the story that would not find any moral resolution until Beckwith, not quite the poor white Welty had imagined, was finally convicted of the murder in 1994. When journalist Rick Bragg covered the trial he observed that 'The story of Mr. Evers and Mr. Beckwith is almost too profound to be real . . . as if it were pulled straight from Eudora Welty's short stories instead of being the inspiration for one of them'.

Figure 3.1 Medgar Evers' grave site in Arlington Cemetery, Washington DC. Courtesy Francisca Fuentes.

Writing Race and the Controversy It Makes

Equally disturbing in its exposé of segregationist ideology is James Baldwin's 1965 story 'Going to Meet the Man'. Baldwin enters the consciousness of Jesse, a white deputy sheriff twisted with race hatred who uses a cattle prod and a club on activists campaigning for voter registration and almost kills a boy he has jailed. The man Baldwin imagines has been hardened by hate nurtured in a loving white family, as becomes apparent when Jesse recalls attending his first lynching 'picnic' and remembers his mother had never seemed more beautiful than in the moment she watches the lynching of a black man, and that he has never loved his father more. He stokes his hatred; the memory of the lynching and the castration he witnessed so visceral that he is brought to the edge of orgasm and the sex he has with his ironically named wife Grace is torrid. Like Welty, Baldwin bears witness to a racist crime and the mindset that made this crime possible.

In 1964 Shirley Ann Grau won the Pulitzer Prize for *Keepers of the House*, a family saga full of secrets, family curses and gloomy wrongs. Grau writes out of New Orleans, a city which remained distinctive, an Africanised and Caribbean city, heavily Catholic in a predominantly Protestant South, until devastated by Hurricane Katrina in 2005. The machinations of entangled racial relationships and racist crimes dominate the lives of Grau's protagonists. That such a novel should be awarded the Pulitzer Prize in the mid-1960s may be read as testament to a cultural fascination with the lives of black and white southerners at the height of the Civil Rights Movement. Grau was acclaimed for her moral toughness as the teller of a tale in which the keepers of the segregated southern 'house' are brought trembling to their knees. However, three years later another white writer who wrestled with the legacy of the slave South found himself at the centre of one of the most heated literary and ideological battles of the decade.

William Styron's *The Confessions of Nat Turner* (1967)

In August 1965, while working on a new novel, the white Virginian writer William Styron asserted that 'to break down the old law, to come to know the Negro, has become the moral imperative for every white Southerner'.[36] In 1967 *The Confessions of Nat Turner* won the Pulitzer Prize and became the number one best-selling fiction. Dr King chose it along with the Bible and Galbraith's *The New Industrial State* as his reading while in jail in Birmingham in November 1967 for having violated a law against demonstrations in the city in 1963. But Styron was also vilified as an unreconstructed southern racist for violating historical truths and presenting Turner as sexually obsessed with a white woman. The impetus toward integrationist politics was losing ground by mid-decade and African American intellectuals, historians and novelists calling themselves 'Ten Black Writers' published a polemical volume in which they excoriated Styron for betraying the memory of Turner, who in August 1831 in Southampton County, Virginia was hanged after his army of slaves (twenty-eight in all) killed fifty-seven whites.

In his 'confession', Turner had claimed that the whites were killed in the name of justice; in retaliation, at least 100 blacks were murdered and Turner reputedly skinned and souvenir money pouches made of his skin. Turner's *Confessions* of 1831 were elicited and published by Thomas R. Gray, a white Virginian lawyer but also a slave owner fallen on hard times, who interviewed Turner in jail. Gray asserted his aim was to tease out the motives for the rebellion but he named the act 'insurrection' from the first page of his pamphlet and his language is loaded with pro-slavery rhetoric. He speaks of 'diabolical actors' in a plot, 'a ferocious band' of 'remorseless murderers' and of Turner as a 'gloomy fanatic'. When Turner's 'voice' is first recorded, he discounts the term insurrection: 'Sir, you have asked me to give a history of the motives which induced me to undertake the late insurrection, *as you call it*' (my emphasis).[37] Despite his actions being framed in Gray's terms, Turner authorises his own words; he pleaded not guilty after all. Both he and his aide de camp, Will Francis, were Christians who felt bitterly the scourge of slavery yet, Styron's dissenters complained, he made Turner and Francis demented rather than determined. Styron's novel reworked Gray but focuses on the murder of Margaret Whitehead, the only person Turner was known to have slain during the rebellion and includes Freudian dreams in which Turner fantasises about white women, although apart from a homosexual encounter with another slave, Styron's Turner is sexually inexperienced. Styron was attacked for pandering to pernicious racial stereotypes about pathological blacks, while he asserted he had created a psychologically complex individual.

The framing of a slave's life in 1831 and again in 1967 by white authors was read as a clear signal of the extent to which black lives remained at the mercy of white assessors – in fiction as in politics – and the Black Anti-Defamation Association successfully thwarted attempts to make the novel into a film in 1968. In interviews Styron made comparisons between the slave revolution he described and Black Panthers like H. Rap Brown and Stokeley Carmichael, who following Martin Luther King Jr's assassination and riots in American cities had called for change by any means necessary; Styron's comments added fuel to the fire.

The critical impasse has not yet been bridged largely because Styron in the introductory note to the novel professed to have 'rarely departed from the known facts' declaring 'What there is to know about Nat Turner can be gleaned in a single day's reading'.[38] His detractors marshalled what facts were known against him and the novel remains caught in cultural crossfire over revisionist vs culturally conservative histories of slavery that characterised the era. Styron had reviewed white Marxist historian Herbert Aptheker's *American Negro Slave Revolts* (1943) when it was finally published in 1963. Styron's main criticism was that Aptheker's thesis in which slave insurrection was a prevalent form of resistance – he details some 250 revolts in his study – was revisionist and Styron leant on Stanley Elkins' *Slavery: A Problem in American Institutional and Intellectual Life* (1959) to argue that the totalitarian ideology of slavery infantilised slaves.[39] Aptheker was one of few white commentators to join African Americans protesting Styron's image of Turner. The controversy was debated in a forum on 'The Uses of History in Fiction' at the Southern Historical Association conference in November 1968 where Styron observed that facts 'don't really mean anything' and Ralph Ellison retorted: 'They *mean* something. That's why you're in trouble'.[40]

Controversy continues beyond Styron's death in November 2006. In 1999 Tony Horwitz had called for a re-evaluation of the furore that surrounded *The Confessions of Nat Turner* and Henry Louis Gates Jr and Spike Lee reopened the controversy when plans for a feature film based on Turner were mooted. However, to date, the only film about Turner is Charles Burnett's 2003 documentary *Nat Turner: A Troublesome Property*. James Baldwin's refusal to segregate his imagination by entering the minds of white racists in stories such as 'Going to Meet the Man' was, Styron said, an inspiration, but, like Ralph Ellison, Baldwin had warned his friend of the culture wars his portrayal could evoke. Ironically, in 'This Quiet Dust' (1965) Styron had taken for granted that the problem of race and representation had 'long since resolved itself into an aesthetic one'.[41] However, as he discovered in the 1960s, the ideological nexus at which racism and representation coincided was fraught with implications that would continue to matter down the decades.

Black nationalist thought coalesced in the Black Arts Movement of which Styron fell foul, as epitomised in anthologies such as Larry Neal and Amiri Baraka's *Black Fire* (1968) which combined a black aesthetic with Beat and Be-Bop culture, or what Baraka summarised later as the attempt to put distance between themselves and 'the mindless gibberish of "square"; i.e. the commercial maximum-profit minimum-consciousness values that run the United States'.[42] It is an aesthetic to which hip-hop returned in the 1990s and to which rappers such as Mos Def have expressed allegiance. In the 1960s and early 1970s, in poetry and stories, slaves – historical or fictional – were presented as neither benign nor long-suffering. Julian Mayfield's *Ten Times Black* (1972), for example, a collection of short stories dedicated to 'Sister Angela Davis', includes Barbara Woods' 'The Last Supper', a story set in 1862 in which slave Rosa Lee poisons a white family and slits the throat of the master of the house who abuses her.

The controversy over Styron's prize-winning fiction was a direct reflection of the 'neo-abolitionist' principles that had entered literature and history by the mid-1960s. In Margaret Walker's Reconstruction-set novel *Jubilee* (1966) and Ernest Gaines' *The Autobiography of Miss Jane Pittman* (1971), former slaves are represented as important ancestors, their stories resonant for the sixties. A largely forgotten but incisive narrative about the ongoing impact of slavery is especially representative: Ronald L. Fair's *Many Thousand Gone* (1965) subtitled 'An American Fable'. It is the story of a Mississippi county in the 1960s where 'the clock has stopped' and 'the old way of life' has been preserved, the sheriff ensuring that plantation slavery continues unchecked until the oldest slave, 'Granny', and the elderly slave preacher write to the President. Reflecting a very contemporary anxiety, the old folk are as concerned by the rift developing between the generations as by slavocracy itself: 'The young colored folks are mad down here. The young people say you forgot all about us down here. I say you don't know about us . . . if you don't come down here or send that army down to do something to free my people they is going to kill every white man and every white woman and every white child in Jacobs County'.[43] When the President sends federal marshals to investigate, they are outwitted by the wily white sheriff and his

Figure 3.2 'A Study in Black'. A display in Memphis State University bookstore photographed by Vernon Matthews, *Memphis Commercial Appeal*, 29 April 1969. Courtesy the Mississippi Valley Collection.

deputies who, supported by the state Governor, lock the marshals in the county jail. It is left to precisely the young black people the older generation is sceptical about to resist the corrupt forces of the law and to set their 'emancipators' free. In the same year that Fair published his fable, Martin Luther King Jr visiting an Alabama plantation was shocked to discover that sharecroppers had never seen US currency because their commissary still traded only in 'scrip' or credit so they would remain perpetually in debt.[44] These were the 'long shocks' of slavery that Richard Wright had described in *12 Million Black Voices* (1941) and which endured into the 1960s.

In 1964 President Johnson declared war on poverty and in 1965 instituted the Great Society programmes. Johnson's vision of a Great Society was intended to bring about 'a society of success without squalor, beauty without barrenness, works of genius without the wretchedness of poverty'.[45] In his internal report 'The Negro Family: The Case for National Action' (1965), Daniel P. Moynihan, Assistant Secretary for Labor, a conservative pessimist with a liberal belief in the federal government's ability to address social disorder, caused a furore. His report was leaked as the fires in Watts, Los Angeles burned with the cynicism of the black poor who had for too long been regarded as an excess population: in the rural South agricultural labourers were replaced by machines and when they moved to northern and western cities, they were regarded as an alien subculture, the black ghetto a problem for which they were responsible rather than the result of *de facto* segregation. Brian Ward has argued that songs such as Lee Dorsey's 'Workin' in a Coalmine' or The Impressions' 'I'm a Telling You' expressed the difficulties and disaffection of African American men in the labour market and the symbolic presence of James Brown and Ray Charles lent credence to their effort: 'Charles' struggle against crushing poverty and discrimination, compounded by the fact of his blindness and his personal wrestling with the demons of drugs and alcohol, was the black community's struggle against disadvantage and prejudice writ large'.[46] However, in Moynihan's Report, a 'tangle of pathology' was presented as the inevitable by-product of black poverty, and single-parent families the major cause of 'family break-down', an assumption that would enrage critics. White fear of a black subculture was satirised in Ed Bullins' play *It Bees That Way* (1970), in which black slum-dwellers turn on a white audience, and Toni Cade Bambara's 'Blues Ain't No Mockin Bird' (1971) in which filmmakers producing a documentary about the food-stamp programme march into a black family's yard and begin to film without permission until outwitted by canny grandparents, the grandfather 'tall and silent like a king'.[47] Black writers challenged what Stephen Steinberg describes as the stock morality tale in sociological texts about race: 'In the master narrative of this tale, civic virtue, moral principle, and social ideals are all imperilled by an array of (literally) dark and sinister forces'.[48] Like

Styron, Moynihan returned to Elkins in his thesis and, rather than social deprivation and political neglect, emphasised cultural pathologies. The report's cultural impact would include the blocking of subsequent studies that might have covered similar ground. Like Styron, Moynihan was reviled as a racist, although black militants including Malcolm X also warned that female-headed households demanded a re-assertion of black manhood. Moynihan wrote to a friend, 'If my head were sticking on a pike at the South West gate to the White House grounds the impression would hardly be greater'.[49]

Creating a sense of 'the black family' whose tragedies are borne if not overcome was salient in forging a countervailing argument as part of what African American historian Lerone Bennett determined in 1970 would need to be an 'intellectual offensive' against 'the false universality of white concepts whether they are expressed by William Styron or Daniel Patrick Moynihan'.[50] Dick Gregory's *Nigger* (1963), for example, is an exposé that can be compared in content, though not intricacies of style, to works by Richard Wright and James Baldwin. Gregory's life story is that of 'a welfare boy' and contains the ironic preface, 'Dear Momma – wherever you are, if you ever hear the word "nigger" again, remember they are advertising my book'. The image and memory of his mother frames Gregory's published work; his mother forms the closing image of *Callus on My Soul* published almost forty years after *Nigger*: 'Poor Momma would walk miles in the snow . . . to feed her children. She simply would not give up . . . I understand the calluses on your soul, because now I have my own'. [51] The celebration of the resilience of the black mother in the face of poverty and racism is powerful refrain in African American writing in the 1960s.

Sarah E. Wright's novel *This Child's Gonna Live* (1969) may be read as a critique of what Eldridge Cleaver called 'The Allegory of Black Eunuchs' whereby the strong black woman is demonised and love between black men and women reduced to a battle of wills. The Upshur family lives 'in the shadow of the plantation' to borrow Charles S. Johnson's title for his 1934 sociological study.[52] Focusing on Moynihan's thesis and borrowing from black nationalist discourse, Wright's 'folk novel' is a powerful critique of what African American cultural critic Albert Murray called 'the fakelore of black pathology'.[53] At first, the narrative seems similar to Gwendolyn Brooks' long poem 'In the Mecca' (1968) for its focus on a twenty-three-year-old black mother's desperate love for her children. The Upshur children are dying of TB, and suffering from malnutrition, pellagra and hookworm as their mother shucks oysters, digs potatoes, and skins tomatoes in order to support them. Brooks' Sallie Smith, a poor single mother of nine children who works as a domestic, becomes frantic when she discovers a child missing. The residents of the run-down Chicago tenement band together until they find her murdered. However, Wright's graphic fiction also challenges ideas of black deviance and criminality and of matrifocal black families as fatherless. The Kerner Commission had warned in 1968 that despite reforms, white racism ensured the nation was moving inexorably toward 'two societies, one black, one white – separate but unequal'. In Wright's novel the black family adapts and survives: mother and father, Mariah and Jacob, end the novel together at the head of an extended family that includes orphans and children born of one or the other parent's affairs, as well as their own living children, united in their hopes to break the thrall of poverty and to 'build up something for the coming of the black nations of the world'.[54]

Rebuttals to Moynihan's thesis would continue to be published across disciplines. One of the earliest was sociologist Joyce Ladner's *Tomorrow's Tomorrow* (1971) in which she states, 'the Black community is a product of American social policy, not the cause of it . . . practices of institutional racism [are] designed to create the alleged "pathology" of the community, to perpetuate the "social disorganization" model of Black life'.[55] Ladner, who grew up in rural Mississippi and pursued her study of African American girls in Chicago, derived a sense of family resilience and support from the former and a sense of cautious hope for future generations in the latter. She was followed by cultural anthropologist Carol Stack's study *All Our Kin* (1974) and historian Herbert Gutman's *The Black Family in Slavery and Freedom* (1976). The coming together of politics in fiction – or as fiction – presupposes that individuals live as closely with public facts – news and history – as personal feelings. In the 1960s the doubling of the political point in slogans such as 'The personal is political' was taken up in writing across the genres. Adrienne Rich's poem 'The Burning of Paper Instead of Children' (1968), for example, is inspired by the Catonsville Nine who burned draft files to protest the Vietnam War and the observation that 'In America we have only the present tense' which closes the poem, a pointed reminder that if the fictions of the 1960s and the issues with which they grapple do not continue to exercise readers, their significance will disappear.

Chapter 4

Art and Photography

Art historians have mapped a genealogy from Abstract Expressionism as symbolic of 'free' expression during the cold war to the Minimalist movement's emphasis on art in 'real' space that continues to dominate critical discussion. Minimalism's decrying of painting as illusion and its emphasis on paring down both its conceptual framework and the artwork to its elemental core began to be evident at the end of the 1950s in Frank Stella's black paintings and Robert Ryman's white paintings. The influence of Abstract Expressionists such as Jackson Pollock would be taken to 'extremes' in 'radical' painting limited to a single colour field where the canvas itself is textured so that the sole 'composition' in the frame is the effect of brushstrokes or the graininess of the canvas itself. One interpretation was that such art would be impossible to market or commodify and Ad Reinhart used that philosophy to protest the capitalist corruption of the art world as he saw it.

Kirk Varnedoe, a former curator of the Museum of Modern Art (MoMA) delivering his Mellon Lectures in 2003 as a defence of so-called 'pictures of nothing', argued that the less you have to look at, 'the more you have to look, the more you have to be in the picture' and that 'one of the valuable things it does more fiercely than a lot of other art is to make us think and read what others think'.[1] The viewer's sensibility is the intellectual pivot on which the work may find place.

Roland Barthes' essay 'The Death of the Author' published in the US in 1967 followed a structuralist line of critique whereby the creator's 'text' is only completed by its audience. At the same time, the spectator's central role was, inevitably, ripe for artistic critique: performance artist Bruce Naumann performed without an audience and the physical location of one of Robert Smithson's best known earthworks, *Spiral Jetty* (1970), ensured that it was inaccessible to viewings. Both artists reconstituted their art in film and photograph and in written

narratives. The very material of production was challenged as was its
ability to transcend the social, through the literality of Warhol's objects
and the abstraction of Cy Twombly's paintings, often annotated with
dates, places or notes, which functioned as formal questions that could
derive as easily from architecture as from modernist painting.

Tastemakers changed as hybrid forms of art required cultural channels though which to discuss the styles and techniques. Journals,
notably *Artforum* (inaugurated in 1962) and *Art in America* (1913–)
situated sixties art within critical discourse, publishing some of the
most controversial of articles, such as critic Michael Fried's 'Art and
Objecthood' and artist Sol LeWitt's 'Paragraphs on Conceptual Art'
(both in *Artforum*, June 1967). *Artforum* kept pace largely because
artists and critics held an ongoing conversation in its pages. As one
reader and art historian remembers, 'You read it because it told you
what was going on partly because so much of what was going on was
not to be seen in the galleries'.[2] However, the circulation of such journals was inevitably small, emphasising the self-referentiality of art
culture. What *Artforum* and the Smithsonians' s *Archives of American
Art* (1965–) made clear was that the aspiration to break free of art
history was a tautology; art's vanguard signalled its own disappearance
in Guy Debord's thesis of spectacular consumption.[3] The most experimental forms and critiques become hardened into new orthodoxies
and parodied. Kitsch Day-Glo brightness, for example, an artistic
cliché of the 1950s, was parodied by artist Philip Guston[4] and Pollock's
painting *Convergence* (1952) was manufactured as a 340-piece jigsaw
puzzle in 1963.

Tastemakers' sanctioning of commercial and consumerist reproduction styles as 'worthy' of critical attention might not have been new
in the 1960s – Duchamp and Dada may easily be cited as precedents[5] –
but it constituted a sea change in the way that art was publicised,
debated and monumentalised. The transition from mechanical to elec-
tronic culture is central in tracing the cult values of art. Walter
Benjamin's essay 'Art in the Age of Mechanical Reproduction' (1936)
was translated into English for the first time and published in the
US in 1968. Read alongside Marshall McLuhan's work, especially
Understanding Media: The Extensions of Man (1963), the idea of art
media extending human sensibility is foregrounded. In his examination of the proliferation of televisual images, McLuhan depicted the
viewer's relationship to television as tactile and kinetic, as the 'inter-
play of the senses', the imagery he chose mirroring descriptions of the
individual's response to sculpture and art installations. In *Nothing*

Personal (1964) Richard Avedon's photographic image of James Baldwin lying in bed surfing the channels with an early remote control adds an ironic footnote.[6]

It is tempting in a book about American cultural forms to focus on those images that are overtly referential, and to read them as cultural artefacts, set against the 'ready-made' object or Pop Art simulacrum. However, as art critics such as Thomas Crowe, Hal Foster and Kirk Varnedoe have successfully argued, a keen social critique underlies Andy Warhol's 'Death and Disasters' series of prints, and Jasper Johns and Cy Twombly may have debunked Abstract Expressionism but they also reworked each of its tenets, with Johns, Varnedoe asserts, 'at the vanguard of a new counterpoint to abstraction'.[7] Objects can emote as in Danny Lyon's photograph of a 'Whites Only' water fountain next to a broken water bowl for blacks. Robert Rauschenberg's 'combines' of the mid-1950s are an early indication that describing art and photography in the 1960s according to a set of neat oppositions would be entirely spurious. It would be possible to concentrate solely on countercultural values evident in artworks and celebrate an anti-establishment visual revolution paying particular attention to, for example, psychedelic art as it derived from hippie values and expressed changes in musical styles. Album covers of the era epitomise this repeatedly, none more so than *The Velvet Underground and Nico* (1966); an Andy Warhol banana screen print could be 'peeled' from the album. However, there is a much more promiscuous bank of archival images than such concentrations allow and countercultural values about nature and the environment and the influences of the anti-war movement infused all kinds of art, from conceptual or 'process works' to earthworks.

Most significantly, the decade saw the democratisation of the visual arts to include an emphasis on public art and performance designed to engage a broad demographic rather than solely an art-educated gallery elite. The Romantic idea of the artist as a cultural outsider, an inspirational bohemian genius, neglected and impoverished, even mad (epitomised by Gaughin and Van Gogh, and in the US context by 'characters' such as 'action painter' Pollock or rebel Guston), would all but disappear in the 1960s as the artist's relation to the market improved in material terms.[8] Democratisation of the arts involved the inauguration of a series of programmes to foster them, including the National Endowment of the Arts (NEA) founded in 1965 and the Art in Public Places Program, established by the NEA in 1967. In 1959 Philadelphia had established its 'Percent-for-Art' programme in order to explore the interrelationship of art and urban spaces. This oddly named programme derived its name from a new city law whereby one per cent of the total cost of a new public building was put towards art that would illuminate it to best effect. Other cities followed and new and often avant-garde art works commissioned for squares and fore-courts and the foyers of buildings began to change the city space – though not without controversy.

While government-funded grants helped to ensure the expansion of the arts, individual and business enterprise also underwrote the pro-fessionalisation of the art market. The Foundation for Contemporary Arts was established by Jasper Johns and John Cage in 1963 and David Rockefeller funded the Business Committee on the Arts in 1967. By Howard Brick's calculation, between 1962 and 1969, 170 municipal arts centres were established in 69 US cities.[9] Individual galleries and areas became associated with the entrepreneurial promotion of con-temporary artists, Leo Castelli's Gallery in New York City and Ferus Gallery in Los Angeles, unsurprisingly, gaining most media attention, along with Greenwich Village and Venice Beach in the same cities. Castelli offered many artists their first solo exhibitions and promoted Warhol and Lichtenstein as 'New Realists'; in turn, he was immor-talised by Warhol. Patrons and promoters such as Castelli and Robert and Ethel Scull (also painted by Warhol in *Ethel Scull 36 Times*) were instrumental in ensuring that the New York scene would remain focal. Virginia Dwan was more unusual in that she succeeded in maintaining a bicoastal influence with a Dwan Gallery in LA from 1959 and in New York from 1965. The Wadsworth Atheneum, America's oldest public art museum, founded in 1842, successfully changed with the times and although art museums such as the Charles H. Wright Museum founded in Detroit in 1965 by the eponymous African American entrepreneur had a more difficult task in breaking into art culture, it survived and houses permanent exhibitions of art of the African Diaspora that narrate a cultural legacy.

By the end of the decade, cultural workers such as the Art Workers Coalition (AWC) and Women Artists in Revolution (WAR) were cam-paigning to ensure the diversification of the artists chosen to exhibit in galleries and collected in museums to include women and all ethnic minorities. They also fought to extend the spaces in which art could be accessed beyond the formal settings of galleries and museums to small and informal neighbourhood venues. While the most radical use of space outside of institutional spaces was seen in Land Art, the nexus at which art and politics meet was evident in surprising places. In 1964, for example, the Mississippi Freedom Democratic Party delegation to the Democratic Convention in Atlantic City used the boardwalk to display photographs as evidence of racist murders and exhibited a burned-out Ford car as a reminder of the one from which civil rights activists James Chaney, Michael Schwerner and Andrew Goodman were dragged to their deaths. The Artists' Tower of Protest in Los Angeles was the site of protest art by some 418 collaborating artists and dedicated in February 1966 at a ceremony at which Susan Sontag, artist Irving Petlin and a former Green Beret delivered speeches about peace at home and abroad. The tower was protected by young men from Watts. Creative expression was made evident outside the formal process that had traditionally legitimated art as culture.

It is impossible – nor is it desirable in the context of this study – to extricate the visual arts from other cultural forms. Rauschenberg began his career painting Disney's Mickey Mouse for his son; and Andy Warhol made silk screens celebrating Rauschenberg. Musician John Cage wrote essays on artist Jasper Johns and was himself the subject of artwork by Claes Oldenburg and Walter De Maria. Art was seen as the visual equivalent to music, especially jazz styles on which visuals might riff as in Bob Thompson's *Gardens of Music* (1960). Poet Frank O'Hara was also curator of MoMA until his death in 1966 and Sylvia Plath, Anne Sexton and Allen Ginsberg all produced artwork. William Demby's novel *The Catacombs* (1965) is a cubist collage studded with allusions to sculptures and art and Bernard Malamud's story 'Pictures of Fidelman' (1968) is based on Oldenburg's conceptual sculpture 'The Hole' – or more formally *Placid Civic Monument,* a grave-shaped hole dug in Central Park on the morning of 1 October 1967 and filled in that afternoon. Gwendolyn Brooks wrote poetry about Chicago's 'Wall of Respect' (1967), a mural at the corner of 43rd Street and Langley designed to celebrate African American heritage and cultural resilience. Artist Joe Overstreet designed the sets for Amiri Baraka's *The Dutchman* for its first staging in Harlem and collaborated with writer Ishmael Reed. Artists were also filmmakers, not only Warhol but also Oldenburg, filming their artwork or reactions to it as well as using film *as* art, as the graphic designer Saul Bass did in the credit sequence that opens the movie *Psycho* (1960). Stanley Kubrick and Arthur C. Clarke chose to open *2001: A Space Odyssey* (1968) with the image of a monolith based on John McCracken's Minimalist sculpture *Blue Column* of 1967.[10]

This chapter bears such cultural crossovers in mind as it considers the significance of art and photography in the 1960s while maintaining an emphasis on the photographer in particular as a witness to history. Realism and trauma made photo-journalism a very significant form in the communication of struggles for civil rights and against poverty and in bringing images of wars fought abroad back home. Other and sometimes contradictory trends and nuances are explored for the extent to which they represent the heterogeneity of US art in the 1960s. Of those critics who succeeded in popularising critical debates, Susan Sontag sought to define the new sensibility.

Susan Sontag: Self and Sensibility

Susan Sontag had the courage of her aesthetic convictions, adding a scholarly gravitas to any and all subjects. Like Simone de Beauvoir, she cited the character Jo March in Louisa May Alcott's *Little Women* (1869) as an influence and like de Beauvoir, she would personify Platonic, Socratic and also erotic responses to contemporary culture. She was described as the intellectuals' 'darling' at the time and it has been argued since that Sontag brought 'a certain histrionic (i.e. Parisian) quality' into American intellectual culture that one critic calls 'position-taking as existential drama'.[11] The same quality would be cited by Griel Marcus in *The Dustbin of History* (1995) as evidence of her inability to celebrate quintessentially 'American' culture and even described as anti-American. For her critics, Sontag was never less than controversial and often elliptical.

To begin with Sontag's critical position could be read as an extension of the New York Intellectuals but it soon became a reaction to them. Just at the moment that they feared the end of classic modernism, she advanced a thesis in which 'high' and 'low' art required no such distinction. Her kind of adversarial cultural engagement which began in 1961 would probably have been noticed in any decade of American culture. It is therefore possible to compare her to other modernist innovators whatever their politics. Her 'Notes on Camp' initially published in *Partisan Review* in 1964 was her version of Ezra Pound's modernist slogan 'Make It New' or Gertrude Stein's essays. 'Many things in the world have not been named; and many things, even if they have been named, have never been described', Sontag writes, recalling Stein's 'Tender Buttons' (1914).[12] Even if a Camp aesthetic was already being explored by others in art and criticism, she situated herself as breaking new ground. Sontag would advance the theory that 'Being-as-Playing-a-Role' or 'the metaphor of life as theatre' was Camp and that 'Camp' was 'the consistently aesthetic experience of the world'. Any attempt to distil an age is subject to catechresis but that was precisely Sontag's point. She emphasised eclecticism, and her own – and the culture's – style embodied its critique, as made manifest in her declaration that 'the very nature of thinking is *but*', an idea that is reminiscent of philosopher Hannah Arendt's metaphor of 'thinking without banisters'; Arendt would praise Sontag's first novel *The Benefactor* (1963).[13]

Sontag set out to define a new cultural sensibility that she saw in sixties cultural crossovers, the same radicalism of style that characterised the performance politics of the new social movements as it infused art and photography. She compared a Rauschenberg painting to a song by the Supremes and stated that a Jasper Johns painting was accessible in the way of a Beatles record. Her essays in *Against Interpretation* (1966), written between 1961 and 1965, including 'On Style' (1965) and 'One Culture and the New Sensibility' (1965), are influenced by McLuhan's idea that the 'model arts of our time' are the 'cooler' arts of less content. Contrasting McLuhan with Matthew Arnold's idea of culture, she argues that the new sixties sensibility understands art as an extension of life. Sontag may be read as prefiguring later studies such as Debord or Baudrillard's ideas of simulation and reproduction. Her own style is variously described as spare, modernist and Puritan, her voice as either passive or dominating; Sontag maddened some critics who thought her snippy and elitist but the superlatives far outweighed the cant. She is celebrated by Craig Seligman, for example, as a 'prototype of the intellectual' for the reading public of the 1960s, 'a scout bringing back news from territories we would all (she was sure) eventually visit'.[14] Her willingness to deal with alternative cultural contexts is evident in her trip to Hanoi in 1968 and throughout her discussion of politically seductive images of the Vietcong, or of Cuba, as in her 'Introduction' to Dugald Stermer's study of poster art, *The Art of Revolution* (1970).

When considering hortatory prose elsewhere in this book it has been possible to read elements of such cultural criticism as autobiography – or at least as self-presentation and self-scrutiny. Sontag is ostensibly harder to 'find' in her work. She was a cultural analyst and an art critic but her scholarly elitism also contributed to her intellectual struggle with fame, in contrast to Norman Mailer or Pauline Kael. Even in her most 'autobiographical' writings in early journals, she is analytical about the egotistical self, as when she notes that it is 'superficial to understand the journal as just a receptacle for one's private, secret thoughts – like a confidante who is deaf, dumb and illiterate. In the journal I do not just express myself more openly than I could to any person; I create myself'. For Sontag writing was 'a vehicle for my sense of selfhood'.[15] She attempted to hold herself above the trappings of mass cultural celebrity while simultaneously flirting with the cultural connotations of fame. She did a screen test for Andy Warhol in 1964, was photographed by *Vogue*, *Vanity Fair* and by Diane Arbus for *Esquire* in 1965, and later appeared in Woody Allen's movie *Zelig* (1983), providing intellectual commentary on his shape-shifting protagonist. Visually iconic, especially as a result of the white streak that shot through her dark hair, in her final years her private life was photographed by partner Annie Leibovitz. That Sontag kept her sexuality out of the sixties limelight may be read as a significant comment on the fear that the complex persona she had cultivated might be seen to be unlocked or explained away by reference to her lesbianism.

Her quest to understand the ethical quandary involved in viewing images that shock or appal exercised her from early essays such her study of pornography in *Styles of Radical Will* (1969) to *On Photography* (1977), and *Regarding the Pain of Others* (2003). Her idea of photographs as '*memento mori*' revealing the subject's mortality and mutability underpins many critical studies and while Sontag felt that photographic images always require their 'story' to be provided as written text, examples discussed below indicate that this is not inevitable. Sontag contributed much to ongoing debates about representation, narrative and authenticity.

In the 1960s art and design became audacious as artists and critics including Sontag endeavoured to break the cultural hierarchies according to which the 'popular' in popular culture had been distinguished from 'art'. This intellectual endeavour may be compared to the evolving mode of the postmodern in the critical production of fiction, in the work of writers such as Robert Coover and Donald Barthelme, whereby reality was contingent, meaning contested, and what Debord called the 'commodity society' became a source of imaginative critique. The shift from a modernist aesthetic and the sixties reaction against what was perceived as Abstract Expressionism's antinomian individualism is explored in John Updike's novel *Seek My Face* (2002) in which the elderly former wife of two famous artists, the first based on Pollock and the second a composite of Pop artists, is interviewed over a single day in 2001 and her memories map the shifts in mid-twentieth-century US art.

In *The Society of the Spectacle* (1968), Debord declared that 'our time prefers the image to the thing, the copy to the original, fancy to reality . . . appearance to essence'.[16] While Debord's context was primarily the Situationists in France, his assertion echoes Sontag's 'Camp' which is equally descriptive of the image as artists such as Warhol, a successful commercial artist with a moralist's eye, sought to project it, as mediated by capitalism and as mechanised by production – dematerialised, to borrow Lucy Lippard's term. Pop Art was a movement that posited with exuberance that there was beauty to be found in everyday objects that had been thought of as 'the crass excreta of the Eisenhower Age'.[17] The term originally found its cultural provenance in the UK where Lawrence Alloway celebrated work by Richard Hamilton and because, as Thomas Crowe summarises, 'American artists were slow to capitalise on their own vernacular culture of advertising, film and mass consumer production'.[18] Pop Art and Op Art – the latter initiated by British artist Bridget Riley in 1964, deriving from

Figure 4.1 Andy Warhol in 1968. The Kobal Collection.

modernist works in which optical intensity was achieved through repeated geometrical shapes – were quickly adapted to consumerist cliché, especially in fashion where Op Art patterns were reproduced on dresses and kitchenware. Irony of a different colour and texture can be seen in the work of nun Sister Mary Corita (Frances Elizabeth Kent) for whom the silk screen with which Warhol had become associated proved to be a liberating form. Her *enriched bread* (1965) plays on the ironically if ubiquitously named Wonder Bread and its packaging in order to represent the holy sacrament of communion. Soup cans, cereal packets, pink cows or, much more disturbingly, images of state-sanctioned violence from police brutality in Birmingham, Alabama to the atom bomb and the electric chair, were reproduced seemingly *ad infinitum* so that Barthes could argue that 'nothing is more identifiable than [Warhol's] Marilyn, the electric chair, a telegram or a dress as seen by pop art'.[19]

Pop artists were bricoleurs. They relocated significant cultural objects already understood within social discourse in different contexts to create a new message in an altered discourse, as Roland Barthes explained in relation to a photograph of J. F. Kennedy 'praying' in 1960 or Caryl Chessman's cell door prior to his execution in 1960 as it contributed to a movement to ban capital punishment.[20] Like Elvis and Dylan, discussed in Chapter 1, Warhol changed direction in ways that animated his art; building on the aesthetics of danger and death, he produced some of his most powerful images of American society. His art also exhibited a queer aestheticism hidden by the art world even at the height of his fame. As Sontag veiled her sexuality, the queerness infusing Warhol's Camp artistry was largely hidden, even in Alice Neel's uncompromising portrait of Warhol of 1970. His torso is naked and disfiguring scars from Valerie Solanas' assassination attempt are visible, as is the corset he wore to combat some of the effects of the shooting. His eyes are closed. Even in this most 'naked' of portraits, by a self-proclaimed 'collector of souls' who gloried in sexual and political exposé, much is hidden even as much is revealed.

What is 'American' about US Art? The South and the West

Museums from MoMA to the Whitney and the Los Angeles County Museum of Art have asked the question in their exhibition titles 'What is "American" about US art?' Critics repeatedly grapple with the same: Maurice Tuchman emphasised the 'anti-traditional' as peculiarly American in *American Sculpture of the Sixties* (1967) and Donald Judd hoped that his identical plexiglass boxes would help put an end to European influences on an anti-accommodationist American art. Cross-generational debates shed light on areas of tension in art, such as the symposium 'The Black Artist in America' (1969) during which Romare Bearden and Tom Lloyd clashed over whether there is a cultural form called 'Black Art' and over the need for a separate black aesthetic.[21]

When we examine politically charged interventionist artworks and seek to use them as cultural markers, it is important to recall that prescient art and photographic works are sometimes also 'lost' or neglected pieces, or were created by amateurs or came about incidentally. Wally Hedrik's crumpled American flag 'vandalised' by the word 'Peace' (1953) is a reminder that sixties dissenters were neither new nor young; his 1959 painting *Madame Nhu's Bar-B-Q* is also explicit in its critique of US support of a corrupt regime in Vietnam. Prescient artworks may also make visible what federal, state or municipal authorities might prefer hidden, as in Ron Haeberle's secretly shot photographs of the My Lai massacre, or the artistic turn towards the avant-garde that Los Angeles civic authorities fought to suppress through the 1950s and into the 1960s. Photographer Matt Heron feared that the work of the Southern Documentary Project recording southern culture in the 1960s had been lost until Black Star returned some six thousand negatives shot by photographers including Danny Lyon that had been 'unused, unsold and unutilized' for twenty-five years.[22]

Photographs may be representative of American culture in the 1960s but not necessarily as art. On 14 October 1962 a U2 spy plane took photographs of Soviet missiles in Cuba and brought the US to the brink of war. The flying cameras could function from 70,000 feet and shoot miles of film but photographic interpreters within the intelligence services were required to authenticate the images. The CIA deemed them sufficiently reliable for President Kennedy to order the blockade of Cuba and for the United Nations to organise the televised hearing in which the USSR was questioned about agreement with Castro to site nuclear missiles on Cuba, only 90 miles off the coast of Florida. The Super-8 film shot by Abraham Zapruder is noted in Chapter 2 but once the rights were secured by *Life* it was turned into still photography, first published in 1963 in small black-and-white frames to offset charges of *Life* sensationalising Kennedy's murder. However, the images appeared in a large colour display on 25 November 1966 to coincide with the Warren Commission report that included Zapruder's film in its review of 'forensic' evidence.

Photographs may be art precisely because they form the sole record of another ephemeral artwork, such as Oldenburg's 'Hole', Dennis Oppenheim's snow projects of 1968 or Robert Barry's wire installations of 1969. Art was transient rather than kinetic and artworks a metaphor for the precariousness of life. In 2004, for instance, John Rockwell asked 'Preserve Performance Art? Can You Preserve the Wind?'[23] Art critic Lucy R. Lippard's *Six Years* (1973) takes the form of the art it records; a postmodern collage of conceptual art over six years in the art object's 'dematerialisation'. Artworks are sometimes also works of the imagination only; if never completed by the artist, it is their conception of American culture that is revealing, as in Diane Arbus' idea for a 'Family Album', or the book that would have been scholar and curator Kirk Varnedoe's critical assessment of the influence of Southern-born artists on American art, still in planning on his death in 2003.

As far as it may be understood, Varnedoe's project sought to inject a regional cross-current into the history of 'American' art that Clement Greenberg and Harold Rosenberg had centred on the East Coast and in Manhattan most particularly. His book would have contributed significantly to a reappraisal of the regional as it helps define the national and addressed regional disaffection and dissidence as it informs national culture. Nancy Marmer, for example, exploring Californian Pop Art, notes 'the "separate but equal" positions taken by West Coast practitioners of the style'.[24] Despite figures such as

Edward Kienholz and Ed Ruscha whose work was prototypically Pop Art, critics and artists in the West often saw themselves as members of artistic sub-cultures, even though this was the decade in which the West Coast art scene came to national prominence. Marmer notes that by 1966 Pop Art functioned as 'an opening wedge' through which new forms could enter, such as assemblage, junk art and the 'finish-fetish' style that honed industrial techniques.[25] The West was asserting radical new forms. The journal *Artforum* founded in San Francisco in 1962 remained located in the West until 1967 when it moved its base to New York. It would initially foreground art in the West; in fact, its original editor had planned to call the journal 'Art West' in recognition of the sensibility of a beleaguered art community, so far away from New York's metropolitan centre. Roy Lichtenstein's *Masterpiece* (1962) is a stark satire of this sensibility. The speech bubble reads, 'Why, Brad darling, this painting is a MASTERPIECE! My, soon you'll have all of NEW YORK clamoring for your work!' The canvas disappearing off the edge of the frame is unseen, the viewer discerning no more than a white border over which the New York art world might clamour. In the South, most particularly, the beleaguered sense of 'regional curse' was so acute that even as recently as 2005 Hal Crowther discussing the Ogden Museum of Southern Art in New Orleans could opine that 'Art news is no news unless New York notices'.[26]

Cy Twombly may be taken as a case study of what Varnedoe's study might have begun to elucidate: a Southern-born US artist he has remained outside New York for most of his career and is readily associated with Europe since moving to Rome in 1957, via his 'Roman Paintings' of the early 1960s, and on through to his Golden Lion at the Venice Biennale in 2003. While his 'Southern-ness' seems to matter to art critics, it is rarely analysed as an influence. Simon Schama writes of 'the courtly gracefulness of the Virginian translated to Italy' only to smash any hint of the neo-classical in his argument that this quintessentially 'American' artist succeeded in 'tearing a strip off the tendency of abstract painting to its own monumentalism'.[27] Jonathan Jones, celebrating Twombly as 'the last great American artist', implies one reason for neglect of the mythology of place as a critical influence on the work but without actually arguing the case. He asserts that the artist's passion is the past: 'He was born in the Old South where history throttles the present like weeds overgrowing a plantation house'. He also notes that Twombly was born in Stonewall Jackson hospital in Lexington, Virginia. Immediately afterwards, though, he states that the US that emerged out of the Civil War 'tells its history as progress and that includes the history of art'. To locate Twombly as significant in the history of American art since the Civil War, or as representative of the 'new' American art of the 1950s and 1960s, is to push his passion for the Southern past to the background – or to elide it. Jones compares Pollock to Virginia based Edgar Allen Poe and, by extension, likens his abstract paintings to those Roderick Usher paints in Poe's short story 'The Fall of the House of Usher' (1840). He situates Twombly as Pollock's heir precisely for the gothic qualities he believes form part of a tragic and pessimistic 'Southern story' but he goes no further in elucidating it.[28]

To see this story as a narrative influence both on Abstract Expressionism and Minimalism in art of the era would be to explore ideas of southern gothic excess and heightened personal and site-specific memory as it flows into US art. Kirk Varnedoe was born in Savannah, Georgia and his university study of modern art took place between 1963 and 1972. To read the significance of the South in the work of Southern-born painters Jasper Johns, Robert Rauschenberg and Cy Twombly (Varnedoe's primary subjects) would have presumably returned to the significance of Black Mountain College in Asheville, North Carolina as the nation's most progressive and experimental art centre, which despite its close in 1957, had already launched the key avant-garde figures of the 1960s. A glance across the teachers and students at Black Mountain reveals the interdisciplinary cultural forces that came together there and John Cage recalled that before their friendship foundered in 1961, Jasper Johns and Robert Rauchenberg, both former students, were referred to as the 'Southern Renaissance'.[29] Outside of Black Mountain, individual southern artists who were initially outsiders to the New York City scene would also make their mark upon it. The saxophonist turned painter Tennessean Robert Ryman was marginal insofar as he worked at the edges of the New York art scene as a guard at the Museum of Modern Art and as a self-taught artist in an era when most were academically trained. But his highly textured canvases, such as his white paintings of 1957 to 1964, would influence painters at the centre of 1960s visual arts, from Reinhardt to Rothko.

Francis Frascina and Suzaan Boettger have contributed much to the study of West Coast art. Frascina notes the idea raised in the Introduction to this book: that US 'regions' enjoy a cultural history of non-conforming to national ideals. His study of Los Angeles foregrounds those elements of sixties visual culture that are countercultural in expression such as 66 Signs of Neon (1966) built by Noah Purifoy and Judson Powell out of found objects after the Watts disturbances. For Judy Baca the Chicana artist, the city is central to her vision of ethnic diversity. *The Great Wall of LA*, a mural painted inside the Tujunga drainage canal and created between 1978 and 1983, includes significant sections on community organising by ethnic minorities that was a salient feature of social networks put in place in the 1960s. Suzaan Boettger argues for the 'exuberant brashness' of West coast 'Funk Art' as compared to a more aestheticised East Coast Minimalism.[30] She also examines earth sculptures of the late 1960s. The latter were not entirely new: Frederick Law Olmstead in the 1850s may be cited as a key precedent and Rauschenberg's *Nature Paintings* and *Dirt Paintings for John Cage* could be read as part of Marcuse's 'Great Refusal' as it began to inform Land Art.

Sublime Western landscapes inspired pioneering radical ventures, from The Sierra Club founded in California in 1892 to the Wilderness Act (1964), designed to preserve landscape as symbolic of the national character. The earthworks that engaged with that landscape may be read as quintessentially 'American' because of the frontier's significance as history and myth, and for their engagement with American intellectual culture from the Puritans through Emerson and Thoreau and their non-conformity of style, scale and execution. The rise of the environmental movement, explored in Chapter 5, coincided with the proliferation of earthworks that represent 'the consciousness of America in trauma' by the 1960s.[31] West Coast-based artists sympathetic to the environmental and anti-war movements, including Dennis Oppenheim, Michael Heizer and Robert Smithson, contended with ideas of violence and destruction, reclamation and regeneration. The Nature vs Civilisation dichotomy was reconceptualised on a new artistic frontier. By 1970 Smithson would declare, 'There's no going back to Paradise or nineteenth-century landscape which is basically what the conservationist attitude is'.[32] The quiet pastoral heritage Leo Marx examined in *The Machine in the Garden: Technology and the Pastoral Ideal in America* (1964) was giving way to an active protectionist environmentalism. Smithson worked with industry, including mining and engineering companies, to reclaim land for sculpture, and also produced art of environmental catastrophe such as *Tar Pool and Gravel Pit* (1966). By the 1970s earthworks would to a great extent be absorbed into the American mainstream, even institutionalised, as Suzaan Boettger claims, as Land Art.[33] They would inform national monuments such as Maya Lin's Vietnam Memorial which recalls 1960s earthworks in its conceptualisation of a gaping wound in the earth.

Nothing Personal? Sixties Portraiture and 'The American Family'

In 1964 fashion photographer Richard Avedon and James Baldwin collaborated on a photo-essay collection called *Nothing Personal* intended to portray 'the heart, mind and soul of a troubled nation' by combining pitiless portraits of iconic Americans with a biting if elliptical commentary. The collection was never reprinted and was panned by contemporary reviewers like *Time* who famously asserted that Avedon's camera was 'a crueler instrument of distortion than any caricaturist's pencil'. The images may be compared to Diane Arbus' portraits from her earliest shots of New Yorkers in *Esquire* (1960) which included a nameless corpse in the city's morgue. Portraiture in whatever form it takes, from Avedon and Arbus to Johns, Lichenstein and Warhol, is often stark; idolatry, crucial in mythologising the era, and the Romantic fascination with the individual is both evident and exploded. American Nazi Party leader George Lincoln Rockwell recognised the importance of portrait photographs when he commissioned Presidential portrait experts Harris & Ewing.

Eve Arnold's candid but sympathetic portraits of celebrities contrast markedly with Richard Galella's invasive paparazzo-style shots. By the 1970s, Jackie Kennedy would take out an injunction against Galella for stalking her for pictures. Jackie Kennedy credited fashion photographer Mark Shaw with becoming her 'family photographer' for the images he took of Kennedy's Camelot in the run-up to the 1960 election, including Kennedy's favourite picture which seems an unlikely snapshot of the senator walking off into the sand dunes at Hyannis Port, Massachusetts. *Look*'s four-day 'photographic binge' entitled 'The President and His Son' was taken a short time before Kennedy's assassination. Stanley Tretick's photographs begin with three-year-old John-John watching the helicopter that brings his father home and Laura Berquist's prose follows the images to narrate a typical day – rocking in Lincoln's chair, clambering on to the table in the Cabinet Room: 'A boy is absolutely not allowed to yell Gromyko! to get daddy's attention'.[34] No mention is made of the President's death; instead a perfect picturing of the father–son bond acts as an elegy. However, *Life* would feature Bill Eppridge's exposé of white middle-class husband and wife John and Karen, heroin addicts, in February 1965. It featured shots of him shooting up and her prostituting and pushing drugs, their private life an exposé of the nation's underside.

Diane Arbus called a project of 1968 'Family Album'. It would combine commissioned portraits with the images with which she is most famously aligned – the bizarre, uncanny and even frightening subjects of her unflinching gaze, some of which were collected in the exhibition *Untitled* in 1970–1. Arbus found the strange and grotesque in 'the American family' but did not publish her subjects under such a loaded descriptor. A very different dystopian variation on the 'family' theme is apparent in Lee Friedlander's ironic photographs of television sets in family homes around the country (*Philadelphia* in 1960, *Washington DC* in 1962 and *Florida* in

1963) which forced viewers to confront the human subject on the screen in distorting and even frightening close-ups that seem to render the television itself an alien interloper at the heart of American family life.

Finding one's way onto a magazine cover may be read as a measure of popular cultural credence but Carl Fischer's photographs on the cover of *Esquire* magazine blasted conventions time and again. His Christmas 1963 cover featured heavyweight boxer Sonny Liston, whose association with organised crime had just broken in the news, in a red-and-white Santa hat ('Had me enough of this mother-fuckin' crap'). It is reported that it cost the magazine around $750,000 in lost advertising.[35] Nevertheless, managing editor Harold Hayes and art director George Lois continued to collaborate on some of the most controversial images of the decade. Fischer photographed Muhammad Ali in 1967, while protesting his vilification as a draft dodger and the stripping of his championship title, as St Sebastian, based on Casagno's famous painting. His body pierced with arrows, Fischer created an iconic image of Ali as martyr to his own image and to the nation's need for scapegoats.[36] More comically, he featured Andy Warhol drowning in a can of the Campbell's soup he reputedly ate every day for lunch as well as commemorating it in Pop Art.[37]

Self-portraits could take surprising if revealing shapes, as in Jasper Johns' emblem of the Savarin coffee can filled with paint brushes that he used as a signifier of himself, and Rauschenberg's *Autobiography* (1968) which includes the text 'Began silk screen paintings to escape familiarity of objects and collage' as a signal that art and biography are inextricable for the artist. Avedon discussed his portraits in 1959 in ways that prefigure *Nothing Personal* and illuminate his juxtaposition of 1960s celebrity figures such as Truman Capote and Andy Warhol with the marginalised citizens who drift at the liminal edges of US culture. He confided in Capote that 'Sometimes I think all my pictures are just pictures of me . . . the human predicament may be simply my own'.[38]

In Photo Veritas: Photographers as Cultural Shock Troops

At the beginning of the decade photography remained marginal in status in critical discourse. But as the photo-journalism in *Life* magazine (explored in the Introduction) and exhibitions such as the Whitney Museum of American Art's 'Evidence of Impact: Art and Photography 1963–1978' demonstrate, by 1977 Susan Sontag could go so far as to argue that 'all art aspires to the condition of photography' insofar as it is an aesthetic form that turns all subjects into art.[39] The camera's propensity for disclosing reality to be an aesthetic form was central to sixties culture, uncovering what might otherwise remain unnoticed, whether so familiar as to be passed over or too extraordinary to be believed. Soon-to-be-actor Dennis Hopper's beautifully staged and laconic *Double Standard* (1961) incorporates Standard Oil as represented in a petrol station's sign viewed through a car window whose rear-view mirror reflects traffic waiting to cross a junction. Such images would be explored as a cliché and made into 'art-photography' by the 'myth maker of LA' Ed Ruscha in *Twenty six Gasoline Stations* (1962). The extraordinary could be seen in Fritz Goro's scientific photo-essays in *Life* such as his exploration of a pre-natal foetus (10 September 1965). William Anders' photograph *Earthrise* taken on 25 December 1961 came about accidentally insofar as he was photographing possible lunar landing sites as *Apollo 8* orbited the moon but his image of earth as viewed from the moon and reproduced in *Life* was iconoclastic. For the first time earth was seen from another world.

Among the shock troops dealing very much with the world as it was were civil rights photographers Ernest Withers, Charles Moore, Danny Lyon and others who aimed to captured the quotidian as well as the extraordinary movement event and to bring them together as news. Withers had begun covering the civil rights 'beat' in the late 1940s and would photograph its end in the iconic images of the Memphis sanitation workers' strike that brought King to the city where he met his death. Images of the Movement are imprinted in collective memory, from the news footage in which water cannons and police dogs were turned on children in Birmingham in 1963 and non-violent demonstrators beaten by club-wielding Alabama state troopers during the 1965 'Bloody Sunday' attacks in Selma, to James Meredith, shot at during his 'March Against Fear' in 1966. Photographing such events was both defiant and dangerous. Alabama-born Vernon Merritt, a staff photographer for *Life*, describes Sheriff Jim Clark assaulting him: 'I had a couple of Nikons around my neck, and he snatched them off and whacked me with a cattle prod. I was shocked a few times and hit a couple of times and then thrown out [of a bus] on to the street. I wound up in jail'.[40] Tom Langston of the Birmingham *Post-Herald* was attacked along with Freedom Riders on 14 May 1961 but not before photographing the beating of James Peck that almost killed him, while Danny Lyon took a shocking photograph of SNNC photographer Clifford Vaughs almost literally pulled apart by police 'arresting' him for taking pictures of a 1964 demonstration in Cambridge, Maryland.

Sontag argued that even those photographs that shock and emote 'are not much here if the task is to understand' because narratives are what provoke understanding.[41] In fact, the most cataclysmic clashes were often the most quotidian, narrating the flashpoints of the sixties,

Figure 4.2 Vietnam Victory Parade, 13 June 1970, Sam Melhorn for *Memphis Commercial Appeal*. Courtesy the Mississippi Valley Collection.

as in the image that Sam Melhorn, staff photographer for the *Commercial Appeal*, captures of a Vietnam Victory Parade marching through downtown Memphis as anti-war protestors march alongside (see Figure 4.2). While the pro-war – or pro-victory – demonstrators outnumber the protestors, the placards the protestors carry are by far the most prominent in the photographer's frame.

Similarly, Garry Winogrand's visual skit in a 1967 photograph of an interracial couple carrying pet monkeys is simultaneously a narrative and a critique of US race relations while Howie Epstein's photograph of Nixon's inauguration ceremony in 1969, a ghostly black-and-white shot of spectators wearing Nixon masks, is an apocalyptic pantomime of the election story. On other occasions, the precise context is the meaning, as in Ernest Withers' shots of the Staple Singers standing on the balcony of the Lorraine Motel mourning Dr King, surrounded by wreaths, and his photograph of a tearful Aretha Franklin with Coretta Scott King beside her at the SCLC (Southern Christian Leadership Conference) Convention Club in Memphis. The musicians Withers usually photographed in the act of performing are still, shocked and muted by King's death.

In the documentary *Hearts and Minds* (1975), a Vietnamese coffin-maker, who has lost seven children himself, makes between 700 and 800 coffins a week, and when interviewed is planing coffins that will contain poisoned children. While pictures of death are seemingly ubiquitous in war, artists found many ways of focusing the spectator's attention. On 27 June 1969 *Life* carried 242 photographs, a portrait-by-portrait reproduction of 'One Week's Dead' in Vietnam. Men in uniform, or in college year books, smiled at readers and their ghosts brought home that US casualties in the war were approaching 37,000. However, when Robert Hughes went to live and work in the US in 1970 and became art critic for *Time*, he bemoaned the dearth of images of the war: 'Here was America, riven to the point of utter desolation over the most bitterly resented conflict it had embarked on since the Civil War. Vietnam was tearing the country apart, and where was the art that recorded America's anguish?'[42] He does single out Leon Golub as an 'honourable exception' to a general rule; Golub's studies *Napalm I, II* and *III* (1969) would be followed by *Vietnam II* in 1973. But the lack of an 'art of anguish' that Hughes observed is revealing. It is at once an omission of painters who were not yet vogue – and indeed of anguish associated with other facets of US culture aside from war – and a recognition that the photographic arts rather than the painting or sculpture that was Hughes' primary subject were in the foreground when picturing death. African American artist Joe Overstreet is overlooked although he successfully combined abstract techniques with protest politics, as in his critique of the practice of lynching, *Strange Fruit* (1965), and most expressively in Robert Hughes' context, of the Vietnam War in *Agent Orange* (1967).

News services ensured that photo-journalists would be at the forefront of the 'art of anguish'. It is estimated that 135 photographers died while covering the wars in Vietnam and Indochina, beginning with Dickey Chappelle in 1965, one of the few women photojournalists and who had arrived in Southeast Asia as early as 1961. Roger Mattingly's photographic portrait of Larry Burrows on the Laotian border in the days before Burrows was killed in a helicopter crash along with fellow photographer Henri Huet depicts him as war-weary, aged by the proximity to death.

The helicopter would prove a central image in Vietnam photography. Fredric Jameson argues that it invokes 'the essential "motion" of the war' and Vietnam fictions such as Joseph McElroy's *Lookout Cartridge* (1974) and Stephen Wright's *Meditations in Green* (1983) engage in postmodernist fashion with the role and responsibility of the

Figure 4.3 US Army helicopters providing support for US ground troops fly into a staging area fifty miles northeast of Saigon, Vietnam, 1966. Henri Huet /AP Photos. Courtesy PA Photos.

photographer.[43] Any understanding of combat photography owes much to past masters such a Matthew Brady during the American Civil War and Robert Capa in the Second World War but the photo-essay and televised footage came together as never before and while explorations of Vietnam as the 'first television war' are ubiquitous in studies of the 1960s,[44] still photography was, I would argue, far more effective in ensuring a war 'story' would be told and its salient images memorised.

Larry Burrows had begun shooting images of the war in Vietnam in 1962 after having covered crises from Suez to Cyprus. He was a British citizen whose identity may have allowed him a certain detachment from debates about the 'rightness' of US intervention but he described himself as something of a 'hawk' to begin with. He had worked with *Life* since the age of 17 and was therefore enfolded into that magazine's middle-American ethos. Free from the adherence to deadlines that characterised TV's breaking news, however, he was able to explore the war as a correspondent, and his changing relationship to Vietnam may be read as shadowing the nation's. The photograph sometimes called 'Reaching Out' and alternatively referred to as 'Purdie' after the gunnery sergeant at its centre was taken on 5 October 1966 during the battle of Mutter Ridge but was not viewed by the public until 1971. This image for which Burrows would become best known

posthumously was one *Life* had never previously selected for publication. The shot is of some ten or so soldiers caught in chaos in the midst
of a bombardment. One casualty lies in the mud and another – Purdie
with a bandage around his head – is reaching out to him. In 1971,
located among the images selected for *Life's* elegy for Burrows, it
could be read as symbolic of his own and *Life's* recognition that in this
thwarted *pietà* of black and white American wounded lies the visual
epitome of a tragic, twisted and unwinnable war.

Pictures of war drill deep into the US's democratic ideals of self and
nationhood, as in Philip Jones Griffiths' *Agent Orange: Collateral
Damage in Vietnam* (2004) which photographs the grandchildren of
Vietnamese people exposed to Agent Orange to uncover the legacy of
1960s chemical warfare. That exposé began with William F. Pepper's
'The Children of Vietnam' published in *Ramparts Magazine* (1967),
with a preface by the long-acknowledged cultural expert on American
childhood, and anti-war protestor, Dr Benjamin Spock. It has been
cited as the trigger for Dr King's public denouncement of the war. The
devastating effects of carpet-bombing and chemical warfare on the
Vietnamese were first captured by Magnum photographer Griffiths in
Vietnam Inc. which was ground-breaking in 1971. It was published
just as the Pentagon Papers leaked to the *New York Times* the extent
of the US's military commitment in Vietnam and the government's
deception of the nation over the depth it had reached in the quagmire.
Where Burrows steadily came to despise the effects of war, Griffiths
exhibited no reservations: alongside victims of napalm, he includes
women waiting on an army base for soldiers to pay for sex and a
picture of a married soldier sexually taunting a young Vietnamese
woman as another soldier encourages him.[45]

In a milieu of burgeoning criticism over the war, Griffiths juxtaposed
a blurred image of Vietnam war hero George S. Patton who, Griffiths'
caption reports, carried a skull around as a gruesome souvenir, with a
clear picture of a Vietnamese mother's desperate weeping over the grave
of her son. The paired photographs give the lie to the safety of the
'strategic hamlet' and question the commander whose soldier father was
immortalised in President Nixon's favourite film: *Patton* (1970). A
similar juxtaposition occurs in a single image of a meditative soldier
standing over a Vietnamese woman and child, who Griffiths reports are
shortly to be killed by GI artillery fire.[46] Even the most banal images are
contextualised with a sharp and sometimes scathing irony: a river of
garbage that Griffiths explains would not exist without the Americans
and a child being bathed by a GI before an audience of women:

Every American seemed quite convinced the people were somehow 'unhygienic'. On the other hand, the Vietnamese who found it necessary to bathe three times a day could never understand why Americans restricted themselves to once-daily washing. The marine was demonstrating to bored mothers how to bathe a child. One mother realised the marine was using her vegetable dish to stand the boy in and . . . grabbed the dish and strode off, cursing such disregard for the basics of cleanliness.[47]

Griffiths uses captions forcefully; the dehumanising forces at work in war are highlighted in each visceral image. Notably, there is one image he fails to include as pictorial evidence of the horrors of war but alludes to only in written text: 'the sight of a father, convulsed with tears, retching in the gutter, clasping the money he's just earned for spending half an hour in an American's hotel room'.[48]

At home one of the most tragic images of the era was taken in 1970 at Kent State University when the Ohio national guard shot dead four students. Its precursor is less well known. Nacio Jan Brown captured an anxious police officer, night stick in hand, looking into the camera as he crouches over a bludgeoned student whose eyes stare out of a blood-streaked face. Ronald Reagan's infamous comment on student demonstrations at San Francisco State College in 1968, 'If it takes a bloodbath, let's get it over with. No more appeasement', is a fitting caption.[49] Student John Filo was one of few photographers on Kent State campus two years later when chaos erupted. The iconic image the amateur took of the dead body of Jeffrey Miller, a girl kneeling over him, her agonised face caught mid-scream and her arms wide in a gesture of tragic hopelessness, won a Pulitzer Prize and became a poster called 'The Cost of Freedom'. President Nixon's comments on the tragedy echoed Reagan's when he asserted 'bums is perhaps too kind a word' to be applied to students who 'burn buildings . . . terrorise other students and terrorise faculty'. Dean Kahler, shot and paralysed on the day he was curious to see his first student demonstration, describes waking up in hospital to receive letters including one which read, 'Dear communist hippie radical, Hope by the time you read this, you're dead'.[50]

Honouring the dead in artistic terms remained controversial throughout the era not least because of assassinations of actual or putative political leaders. Oldenburg's idea for a memorial called 'Kennedy Tomb' which would have been a metal casting of Kennedy based on the Statue of Liberty was never made.[51] In 1971 Leonard Bernstein would throw himself into a commission from Jackie Kennedy to inaugurate the already controversial Kennedy Center and compose his most controversial piece of music, a requiem called *Mass* which shocked some members of the Catholic Church into banning its performance. A hectic, cacophonous, multi-faith explosion of sound overwhelms the 'Simple Song' of the lone celebrant whose faith is tested at each phase of Bernstein's composition. The artistic depiction of death and assassination tested the shifting boundaries of taste in each genre, as with Carl Fischer's 'Three Assassinations' (1968) which graced the cover of *Esquire* magazine and in which the figures of John F. and Robert Kennedy and Martin Luther King Jr in funereal suits and ties are 'cut and pasted' together standing in the graveyard at Farmingdale, New York, a line of grave stones receding into the distance.

Robert Kennedy, brother of the most telegenic President was, like any other politician of the 1960s, supremely aware of the importance of the camera. It is well known, for example, that Kennedy made at least two closely photographed visits to his brother's grave around Lyndon Johnson's inauguration. Still photographs and moving images were equally insistent reminders of political hopes dashed. The assassination of Robert Kennedy occurred immediately after he won the Democratic Primary in California, after eighty-five days of campaigning for nomination. It followed hard on the murder of Martin Luther King Jr in April. Arthur Schlesinger Jr concluded his 1979 biography by asserting that Kennedy could have been a new Franklin Roosevelt but the long-term effect of Kennedy's late entry into the race – whether indeed he would have won a Democratic nomination – will never be known, as signalled by the title of David Halberstam's book, written after accompanying Kennedy on the campaign trail, *The Unfinished Odyssey of Robert Kennedy* (1968). Nevertheless, he has been mythologised as the last powerful liberal standing, his death the only way that he could have been prevented from beating Nixon in 1968.

The manner of his murder, shot to death in the kitchen of the Ambassador Hotel, captures the violence that Charles Moore said he tried to escape when he left America for the best part of 1966. Paul Fusco's photographs of America mourning Kennedy's death contribute a very different image of the public performance of mourning. In a decade when the state or public funeral was becoming ubiquitous, Fusco's photo-essay contributes significantly to an understanding of the faith that even at the end of the 1960s many Americans could still place in political leaders, especially one as symbolically central as Robert Kennedy.

RFK: Funeral Train (1968/2000)

When Robert Kennedy was shot on 5 June 1968, Norman Mailer claimed, 'Our country started to fall apart that day'. After his funeral was held in St Patrick's Cathedral in New York City, Kennedy's coffin was taken aboard the train that would transport his coffin, his family, friends and news and television crews to Washington DC for the burial. The train made slow progress south because people lined the track to pay their respects. Two mourners were killed by an oncoming train and the train had to slow when others neared to pay their respects to the coffin, elevated so that it could be seen in the last of twenty carriages. In this way, the journey to Arlington cemetery that could have taken around four hours took almost nine and the burial did not begin until 10 p.m., lit by floodlights and television lighting.[52]

Life photographer Bill Eppridge captured the most devastating picture of the slain senator, on the Ambassador Hotel kitchen floor as busboy Juan Romero held him and stared with shock into the camera: 'I made that picture and suddenly the whole situation closed in again. And it became bedlam'.[53] He shot scenes of bedlam on the streets that night too. Magnum photographer Paul Fusco, however, reveals the quiet and solemn aftershocks. It is ironic that the first of Fusco's pictures to be published were collected in a special memorial edition of *Look* magazine (*RFK: The Bob Kennedy We Knew By the Editors of Look*) but that the photographic collection he would entitle *RFK: Funeral Train* would not be published until 2000, a year after Mailer's *A Time of Our Time* (1999) included the essay in which he described the scene.[54] While the memorialisation of Senator Kennedy began in the week of his death, and would include the documentary *Robert Kennedy Remembered* put together in four weeks in order to ensure its release by the Democratic Party Convention in Chicago, it would take until 2000 for more than a handful of the images to be viewed by the public. When *Look* ceased publishing in 1970, its photograph collections were housed in the Library of Congress, where most of Fusco's pictures remain.

It also seems ironic that *Look* chose to reproduce five of the photographs that Fusco took in monochrome in an issue that predominantly features colour photography of the Kennedy family. While it is axiomatic to note the Kennedys' iconic status as the 'First' family, it is odd that photographic 'evidence' of the nation's mourning should be made auxiliary. In his assessment of the day, Michael Harrington notes that the funeral train would inevitably pass through 'the other America' because 'the affluent never live in sight of the tracks but the poor do' and he underlines what has become part of the legend of Kennedy as the last liberal hope when he asserts that the American poor were 'mourning their own aspirations along with the man who had spoken for them'.[55] As the funeral train left New York, Fusco was shocked to see the crowds amassing and his short 'Afterword' to the collection recalls Harrington: 'those most in need of hope crowded the tracks of Bobby's last train, stunned into disbelief, and watched that hope trapped in a coffin pass and disappear from their lives'.[56] His photographs record the grief of so-called 'ordinary' Americans and yet some of the images he chose for *RFK: Funeral Train* contradict popular consensus about the racially polarised 'end' of the sixties as described in the Kerner Commission's report of 1968. Some of the most memorable shots are those in which black and white Americans stand together. In one a black woman's arm is draped across a white woman's shoulders in a gesture of comfort. Another is married with the legend on the facing page in which RFK declared that 'as long as people are not free, the American Revolution will not be finished'. Fusco's photographs are testimony to the allure that Kennedy's family held in the national imagination but this is a very different kind of 'family album'; standing in family formation in order of height, still and ramrod straight, a young family – parents casually dressed and children, boys and girls alike, wearing only swimming trunks – stands with heads lowered to the passing train (see Figure 4.4b).

In this portrayal of collective grief, a woman prays on her knees, another holds a handkerchief to her tearful face; others stand with hands on hearts or holding flowers, waving or saluting. In one shot a man holds his box Brownie at waist height and in another a young boy points a Kodak Instamatic, ubiquitous since 1963, to record the funeral train as a snapshot. The dead Kennedy is the absent centre around whom the images gather; neither RFK nor his coffin is present in any of the shots selected for *RFK: Funeral Train*. Rather, the book's paratexts allude to his tragic death via Senator Edward Kennedy's eulogy reproduced as 'A Tribute', Mailer's observations as 'The Promise', an extract from Evan Thomas' biography that emphasises the small plain cross to contrast with Kennedy's memorial at Arlington,[57] and quotations from RFK's speeches in which his words to the poor and to 'outsiders' resonate poignantly.

RFK: Funeral Train is a photographic event as memorial and the act of memorialisation seems to be taking place in a continuous present tense. Fusco's use of colour (elided by *Look*) contributes to a mood of timelessless; 'typically' sixties fashion prints mingle with 'ageless' classic clothes and seem less typical when viewed against the mêlée of fashions that characterises the collection's moment of publication in 2000. The mourners are caught mid-wave and often in a blur. By slowing the speed of the film and keeping the light low, Fusco caught the blur of movement in almost every frame so that the images register as moving pictures, keeping pace as it were with the funeral train. Those images which close the collection are completely blurred giving both the impression of movement and speed and seeming to gather up the moment in a memory loop in swathes of grey and purple, fantasy colours. More generally throughout the collection, onlookers are colourfully and casually dressed as if caught *in medias res*, their decision to pay their respects natural, as in the case of a girl in a pink bikini whose sombre pose is strikingly incongruous and members of a family rising from lawn chairs as the train passes the end of their garden. However, portable chairs set along the track belie the organisational prowess of others, as do home-made signs stating 'So Long Bobby' and 'RFK We Love You' and the presence of a boy scout troop or a group of World War II veterans.

Figure 4.4a Paul Fusco's *RFK: Funeral Train* (1968/2000). Courtesy Paul Fusco/Magnum Photos.

Figure 4.4b Paul Fusco's *RFK: Funeral Train* (1968/2000). Courtesy Paul Fusco/Magnum Photos.

Disillusion is evident in artwork produced late in the decade as in John Filo's iconic photograph at Kent State, Rauschenberg's *Currents* print series (1970) and, in the aftermath of the War on Poverty, Bruce Davidson's photographs of the urban poverty of Spanish Harlem, and Bob Adelman's photographic portrait of rural poverty in Alabama in *Down Home* (1972). Photography continues to be entangled in ideological debates about what it reveals and how it commemorates, an idea to which the Conclusion returns in its exploration of Birmingham, Alabama's continued association with the violence of 1963. Artistic reproduction of an event can also turn it into a market phenomenon that distances it from the event itself. Boomer interest in art of the 1960s has ensured that it remains buoyant in the art market and in 2004 Warhol's *Mustard Race Riot* (1963), based on a *Life* magazine photograph of police attacking demonstrators in Birmingham, achieved $15.1 million (then around £8.1 million).

How secure one may be in reading artworks in and out of context and across time is illustrated by Yoko Ono's performances of *Cut Piece* (1964–), at once a disturbing performance of abuse and an overt critique of scopophilia as she invited members of the audience to cut sections of clothing from her body. Preserved only in the memories of participants and in photography, in 2003, aged seventy, Ono performed *Cut Piece* again in Paris. On the one hand, there is a paradox at the heart of any reclamation of an artwork that was conceived to exist in its moment of production; it will neither be the same work, nor will it necessarily escape becoming a parody of itself or of its original intent. However, in 1995 Faith Wilding was asked to recreate her 1972 installation *Womb Room (Crocheted Environment)* for an exhibition history of women's art and, on the other hand, as Miwon Kwon notes, to decline such an invitation would have been 'an act of self-marginalization, contributing to a self-silencing that would write Wilding and an aspect of feminist art out of the dominant account of art history (again)'.[58]

Contemporary cultural critics continue to engage with images of the 1960s as made by artists. In a story-essay in *Polaroids From the Dead* (1996), for example, Douglas Coupland explores James Rosenquist's collage *F-111* (1965), a painting that 'blew up' the jet fighter-plane ubiquitous in Vietnam to gigantic proportions, and in the opening frames to the movie *Lost Highway* (1997), David Lynch reprises Allen D'Arcangelo's *US Highway 1* (1962) in which the viewer's gaze is pulled via the cat's eyes in the middle of the night-dark road toward the horizon.

Chapter 5

New Social Movements and Creative Dissent

Cultural critic George Lipsitz has repeatedly referred to the era as 'The Age of the Civil Rights Movement', Gary Wills argues that 'the Kennedy era was really the age of Dr. King' and in Alice Walker's first published essay she described it as iconoclastic: 'a call to life' for people who did not exist 'either in books or in films or in the government of their own lives'.[1] The Civil Rights Movement should be read as proto-typical because its principles and strategies in the shape of mass demonstrations and direct action protest were revised to fit other political platforms and are integral to the new social movement as a cultural form and because it is representative of the 'Great Refusal' that Herbert Marcuse described as the root of ideological change. It was revolutionary and reformist, realist and utopian, and in endeavouring to combine multiple ideologies, it would inevitably break into factions. The movement's demise was underscored by COINTELPRO (Counter Intelligence Program), according to which the combined forces of the FBI, CIA and military intelligence sought to destroy 'radical' organisations and undermine or indict movement leaders, from Dr Martin Luther King Jr and Malcolm X to Huey Newton of the Black Panthers, and by local initiatives such as Mississippi's State Sovereignty Commission which spied on 'subversive' citizens and vetted juries. However, across the first half of the decade the Civil Rights Movement stayed in the media spotlight, publicising racial violence in the South and the de facto racially segregated norms whose traditions blocked black progress, North or South.

To begin with, it was customary for historians to investigate social movements as a national phenomenon in order to elucidate the extent to which legislation they fought for operated as a force of social change. More recently, historians have been assiduous in uncovering the stories of grass-roots activists overlooked in scholarly studies whose focus is celebrated leaders. Bringing oral histories and memoirs into historical account has revealed the significance of women, the elderly and of a white minority of activists. Political dissent was not only the province of youth: Jim Lawson's workshops on non-violence underpinned the beginnings of the Nashville movement and Ella Baker of the SCLC and NAACP has been acknowledged as 'midwife' to the Student Non-violent Co-ordinating Committee (SNCC). Nor did so-called radicals always begin their activism on the fringes. Abbie Hoffman, one of the most outlandish of countercultural organisers, was a member of the NAACP and his Yippie philosophy was also informed by his organising experience with SNCC during Freedom Summer. Consensus history had it that the political trend turned from the integrationist politics of the Civil Rights Movement, epitomised by Martin Luther King Jr and the SCLC (Southern Christian Leadership Conference), to the black separatist position encapsulated in the slogan 'Black Power' while sixties histories tend to privilege Students for a Democratic Society (SDS) in movement culture. However, SNCC, founded in 1960, is significant not only because it was in the vanguard of student-led political groups, but also because its vision of an American pluralistic democracy as *interracial* in character demanded a much more radical conceptual shift for the nation than the tenets of SDS which developed out of historically Old Left concerns, or the racial separatism of the Nation of Islam or Black Panther Party, both traditionally read as much the more 'radical' groups. The Deacons for Defense were also pushed to the background of surveys of the era because their armed defence against the Klan contradicted the dominant image of non-violent resistance as consensual. Similarly, the Mississippi Sovereignty Commission papers that began to be released in 1989 reveal conspiracies that ensured post-*Brown* vs *Board* retaliatory violence would receive public approbation, such as Byron De La Beckwith's acquittal for murdering Medgar Evers, explored in its literary context in Chapter 3. While it was not surprising to learn that the Commission vetted the jury, proof of the fact also served to problematise the popular assumption that *any* white southern jury would have refused to convict for a racist crime. Only recently have we come to explore in detail the make-up of a supposedly 'Solid South' and its supposedly unbroken wall of resistance to racial change.

'An attempt to put the movement on wheels', as James Farmer described the Freedom Rides, reveals the heterogeneity of participants. The Commission on Interracial Cooperation (CORE) founded in Chicago in 1942 was mobilised to organise the Freedom Rides of 1961, reworking the Journey of Reconciliation it co-sponsored with the Fellowship of Reconciliation in 1947 after the Supreme Court first made segregation on interstate public transport illegal. Volunteers came from across the US and sometimes travelled internationally to participate, as Ray Arsenault's epic study proves. James Peck had been on the 1947 Ride and in 1961 suffered fifty-three stitches in the face as a result of being beaten in Birmingham. He wrote his story almost immediately. Novelist Lillian Smith's introduction to his account acts as a validation of on-the-spot historiography: 'this thoughtful participant in ideas and acts' has written 'factual stuff, valid for historians of the age' and Peck acknowledges the power of the media for the movement when he notes Bayard Rustin watched him on TV in London, a friend teaching in Hiroshima sent Japanese news clippings and *The New Age* in South Africa carried the story.[2]

The New Abolitionists

SNCC and SDS built ideological platforms on the precepts of the Abolition and Labor movements, contributing to a long tradition of resistance. The political heritage of older participants, like Peck, was often long and complicated. Daniel Horowitz has emphasised Betty Friedan's beginnings in the Old Left and Popular Front feminism, and Bayard Rustin, one of Dr King's key advisors, had been defining and redefining techniques of peaceful protest since the 1930s. Writer Lorraine Hansberry's commentary on images in the photographic text *The Movement* (1964), prepared with SNCC's assistance, stresses that the movement began in the seventeenth century when Africans mutinied on ships transporting them to slavery: 'In strong contradiction to the myth of Negro passivity . . . the "New" Negro has merely brought to the Movement new methods and fresh determination'.[3] Charles Payne's study of Mississippi and Adam Fairclough's delineation of the movement in Louisiana demonstrate a long history of organising at the local level. The 1960s saw continual reinvention of strategies for reform in an effort to counter federal laxity in tackling social injustice, a problem which psychologist Kenneth Clarke described as 'a kind of Alice in Wonderland . . . the same analysis, the same recommendations, the same inaction'.[4]

What was new about the new social movements of the 1960s was that racial, feminist and environmental reforms came together in a political Zeitgeist that united civil disobedience with the performance style discussed in Chapter 1. Direct action in a new media culture

forged new ways of making old demands. Tom Hayden believes that
the new movements were also 'communities of martyrs' that came
about in 'a time of apocalypse'; his rhetoric is overblown but captures
the spirit of the times and serves as a reminder that organisations were
not bureaucracies – or even very organised – and to make them seem
so would be 'like trying to turn a volcano into a skyscraper'.[5] The
tenets to which the Civil Rights Movement held disturbed national
mores. James Baldwin argued that 'the black and the white, deeply
need each other here if we are to become a nation' and King's idea of a
'network of mutuality' was more threatening than calls for a 'separate
but equal' society.[6] John F. Kennedy admired *Finian's Rainbow* (1947),
the play that premiered the year of the first interracial Freedom Rides
and that Francis Ford Coppola adapted into a musical film. At its heart
is the interracial southern community of 'Rainbow Valley' that sits-in
and sings its protests to the sheriff. A non-violent liberal nation was an
impossibility in the 1940s and equally impossible to sustain in the
1960s; released in the year of King's assassination, Coppola's film was
a poignant coda to a utopian dream. The interracial coalition failed not
only because of segregationist fears of 'race mixing' but also because
of liberal qualms according to which a 'beloved community' remained
an abstraction. When King warned that, 'Negroes hold only one key
to the double lock of peaceful change. The other is in the hands of the
white community', he recognised this fact. As one historian allows,
school integration was 'a different kind of Woodstock'.[7]

   Nevertheless, grass-roots activism caught fire across the South and
students were the fire-starters. In February 1960, four black students
at the Agricultural and Technical College in Greensboro, North
Carolina sought to smash Jim Crow etiquette in its quotidian forms by
refusing to leave a lunch counter where they knew they would be
denied service. Their protest would impact on southern custom to the
extent that only two months later it was estimated that 50,000 people
had protested at lunch counters across 100 towns and cities. Their
direct action would develop into the student movement represented by
SNCC and CORE. To begin with, though, their impact would be
underestimated. Julius Lester who would join SNCC, remembers that
he read the news of the sit-in on the back page of his newspaper 'with
less interest than I did the evening's television listings'.[8] As a method
of protest, the sit-in was not new; in 1943 CORE activists had occupied a Chicago restaurant for similar reasons. There were occasional
demonstrations across the South in the 1950s and a sit-in initiated by
the NAACP Youth Council in Wichita, Kansas in 1958 was followed

by another in Oklahoma. However, established organizations such as the NAACP typically organised through focused and cumulative law suits rather than direct action. Spearheaded by the students, action as theatre ensured demonstrations would be covered by the media and memorialised as events. Martin Luther King Jr defined non-violent direct action as seeking 'to create such a crisis and foster such a tension that a community which has constantly refused to negotiate is forced to confront the issue. It seeks so to dramatise the issue that it can no longer be ignored' and David Dellinger, one of the Chicago Seven prosecuted for disrupting the Democratic Convention in 1968, could refer to the peace movement as 'a creative synthesis of Gandhi and guerrilla'.[9]

Figure 5.1 Freedom Summer Murders marker, Mount Zion Church, Longdale, outside Philadephia, Mississippi. © Sharon Monteith.

SNCC and Freedom Summer

The Student Non-Violent Co-Ordinatating Committee's philosophy encouraged affiliations between groups including NAACP and SCLC, CORE, SDS and Nonviolent Action Group (NAG) as symbolised in their coming together as the Council of Federated Organizations (COFO) to campaign for voter registration during 'Freedom Summer' of 1964. They would 'take Mississippi to the nation'.[10] SNCC emphasised a 'redemptive community' that 'supersedes immoral social systems', a civic community in which 'each act or phase of our corporate effort must reflect a genuine spirit of love and good-will'. In 1960 student leaders met with Ella Baker who guided them in the formation of their own distinctive group – not a youth branch of the SCLC or an offshoot of the NAACP.

SNCC was courageously heterogeneous in political make-up, whereas other organisations would not openly support Communism, for example, SNCC made no exclusions and its history traces intellectual and political shifts across the decade: from existentialism to Marxism, from integrationist to separatist conceptions of society, and from ballot to bullet. Oral histories demonstrate that its policies followed the system of Field Secretaries carrying out supportive fieldwork in small southern towns – from McComb, Mississippi to Albany, Georgia – and focused on action over administration. The formal staff base was small and dynamic and while it is invidious to name only a few, Bob Moses is cited by other SNCC workers as inspirational, as is Mrs Hamer, and SNCC staffers became renowned political figures down the decades, among them former NAACP Chairman Julian Bond and Congressman John Lewis. Their courage in facing down white supremacists is memorable: Sam Block in Greenwood, Bob Zellner and Mendy Samstein in McComb, Hollis Watkins and Curtis Hayes in Hattiesburg and Anne Moody in Canton. The Freedom Houses in which they lived were frequently bombed, *The Student Voice*, SNCC's magazine until 1965, endeavouring to record the extent of violent attacks.

SNCC's voter registration and education strategies had to evolve to combat massive resistance. The Freedom Ballot (1963), a mock election, demonstrated that despite white authority's spurious rejection of those seeking to register, a 'Freedom Vote' would elect an interracial coalition: the Mississippi Freedom Democratic Party (MFDP). In 1964 this hands-on organisation experienced an influx of volunteers as a result of what SNCC cannily described as a 'peace corps operation' to help voter registration, set up Freedom Schools and community centres and develop special projects. SNCC even envisaged a project to help poor whites with literacy and civic education because 'in many ways Mississippi has imprisoned her white people along with her blacks'.[11] The symbolic importance of Freedom Summer was far more significant than the relatively small number of participants (700 volunteers buttressed by lawyers, ministers and doctors). The insertion of a northern middle class – 'red diaper babies' and students from schools such as Yale and Stanford – into the 'savage' South was a media dream. Nevertheless, communications secretary Julian Bond remembers the resentment he and other black SNCC workers felt when the press was more interested in 'what Susie Smith from Vassar was doing and whether she had stubbed her toe in the middle of a demonstration in which fifty Negroes were beaten'.[12] The biggest media event was also the most tragic. Fifteen activists and demonstrators lost their lives in 1964 but the murder that dominated headlines like no other during Freedom Summer was that memorialised in Figure 5.1.

The murder by Klansmen and police officers of two northern volunteers, Schwerner, established in Mississippi, and Goodman during his very first days on the Summer Project, alongside local black activist Chaney, hit headlines around the world when their bodies were discovered hidden in an earthen dam and the conspiracy unravelled. The conviction of their murderers would be pursued down the decades. Despite the murders and due to the media attention they generated but mostly because of workers' tenacity, the Summer Project was an enormous success, hence Howard Zinn's celebration of 'The New Abolitionists' and Mrs Hamer's saluting Freedom Summer volunteers as 'strangers who were the best friends we ever met': 'They want to make democracy a reality in the whole country – if it is not already too late'.[13] However, as Bob Moses has said, a concomitant challenge was 'whether SNCC could integrate itself . . . and live as sort of island of integration in a sea of separation'.[14] Established staff worried that the presence of whites in the struggle would lead white southerners both to retrench and to assume that the white volunteers had initiated the programmes of a predominantly black movement. They also feared that after Freedom Summer, SNCC would have to rebuild. SNCC did institute many changes, the most controversial its break from integrated reconciliation as an ideology. Charles Marsh notes with regret that the SNCC 'society' became paranoid and closed and in many ways, SNCC foundered on its possible alliance with nationalist movements that leaders Stokely Carmichael, H. Rap Brown and others took in 1966, specifically by joining with the Black Panthers. There was, however, earlier evidence of a developing impatience in the speech John Lewis prepared but did not deliver at the March on Washington because its bellicose language was considered too combative for the occasion: 'We will march through the South, through the Heart of Dixie, the way Sherman did. We will pursue our own "scorched earth" policy and burn Jim Crow to the ground – nonviolently . . .'[15]

SNCC was the fulcrum for an evolving movement culture. It provided the context for the feminist position paper co-written by Casey Hayden and Mary King in 1964 questioning procedures whereby men were fieldworkers and women administrators: 'Assumptions of male superiority are as widespread and deep-rooted and every much as crippling to the woman as the assumptions of white supremacy are to the Negro'.[16] That the paper was believed to be the work of Ruby Doris Smith Robinson is testament to her strength of character as the only woman executive member but also a disturbing indication that gender stereotypes remained racialised within the most egalitarian of groups; it was assumed white women would toe the line of gender division while black women would speak out. However, in November 1965, Hayden and King sent a memo entitled 'Sex and Caste' to women working across the freedom and peace movements to open up dialogue and out of SNCC's structure emerged chapters of the student, Black Power, feminist, Free Speech and anti-war movements.

Mario Savio, who founded the Free Speech Movement (FSM) at Berkeley and spent Freedom Summer in Mississippi, described it as 'the seminal event of the twentieth century that created a cadre of activists for the nation'.[17] The movement he founded would encompass a communist society, The DuBois Club, and Young Republicans for Barry Goldwater. Despite Savio's words, in 1981 Clayborne Carson wrote a history of SNCC in order to preserve the 'shock troops' of the Civil Rights Movement from 'the fate of obscurity' in a period of declension.[18] It is telling that SNCC history was vulnerable, especially since its short and long-term successes are evidenced in the Voting Rights Act of 1965 and its extension in 1982 and in the fact that by 1980, 75 per cent of African Americans in Mississippi were registered to vote, more than in any other southern state. However, in 1980 Ronald Reagan chose the Neshoba County Fair in Philadelphia as the site of his anti-statist campaign for President in a shrewd move to persuade the southern bloc of voters that states' rights would be respected. Rural Mississippi had come to symbolise the place where a conservative counter-revolution would begin. In 1987 SNCC began to return to public notice when its first reunion was organised and Raleigh City Museum, North Carolina would celebrate the fortieth anniversary of SNCC's founding in 2000. The SNCC Freedom Singers continue as the group Sweet Honey in the Rock and in a moment that speaks specifically to Carson's concern that their efforts not be forgotten, SNCC veterans petitioned for a Justice Department investigation into the voting irregularities in Florida that prevented registered African Americans from participating in the 2000 Presidential election.

'Other Americans': Black Power and Red Power

SNCC workers cite Mrs Fannie Lou Hamer as inspirational. The granddaughter of slaves and one of twenty children in a sharecropper family, she had limited schooling because she was expected to till the fields whenever the weather made that possible. Growing up in the plantation environment that Ronald L. Fair explores in *Many Thousand Gone*, discussed in Chapter 3, Hamer remained unaware that black Mississippians had the right to vote: 'When the people would get out of the fields, if they had a radio they'd be too tired to play it. So we didn't know what was going on in the rest of the state even; much less in other places'.[19] But in August 1962 she rallied to SNCC's cause. Unable to persuade her not to continue her politicisation, Mrs Hamer's

Figure 5.2 Mrs Fannie Lou Hamer's grave, Ruleville, Mississippi. The gravestone situated on co-operatively held African American-owned land reads 'Fannie Lou Hamer, Oct 6 1917-March 14 1977' and the inscription is 'I am sick and tired of being sick and tired'. © Sharon Monteith.

landlord evicted her from his plantation after eighteen years; she was no longer suitable labour material. While many agricultural workers were forced into 'Tent Cities' once turned off farms for similar reasons, Mrs Hamer became a field secretary for Sunflower County and an example to the Freedom Summer volunteers she inducted in Oxford, Ohio. She had suffered fighting for the rights she emphasised to the students she trained. In June 1963 she was jailed for attempting to desegregate a lunch counter and two black prisoners coerced to beat her with a blackjack damaged a kidney and caused a blood clot. She remained steadfast and student volunteer Sally Belfrage closes her memoir with the memory of Mrs Hamer singing 'We Shall Overcome' immediately before the crashing blow that was the Democrat Party rejection of the Mississippi Freedom Democratic Party (MFDP).

In 1964 the Democratic National Convention refused to seat representatives of the MFDP, Mrs Hamer among them, in place of the segregationist delegation. It would take until 1968 for black delegates to be seated. If SNCC's strategy had been to shame the liberal establishment into confronting social inequalities, it failed in Atlantic City which signalled the demise of integrationist liberal principles as the movement's underpinning. At the 1948 Convention in the city of Philadelphia the black Progressive Democratic Party had tried to challenge the all-white South Carolinian representatives but failed. Twenty years on, the liberal impasse could not be assailed.

The push to racially desegregate was by no means unanimous, though, and calls to strengthen separatist facilities or to bear arms against white supremacists echoed through each year of the decade. To review the period in terms of a dichotomous black leadership of Martin Luther King Jr vs Malcolm X is to imply that African Americans were caught in a double bind, contained by allegiance to one or the other model for social progress. The 'integration' of 'Martin and Malcolm' has usually occurred only as wish-fulfilment or regret in cultural productions that return to the era. At the end of Spike Lee's *Do The Right Thing* (1989), for example, a photograph of Martin Luther King Jr and Malcolm X is silently pinned to the 'Wall of Fame' and in Steve Earle's 'Christmas in Washington' (1997) he sings, 'Come back to us Malcolm and MLK/ We're marching in to Selma as the bells of Freedom ring'. To set up a dichotomy between two conflicting approaches to the fight for equal rights is to elide the complex relationship between non-violent and armed protest that galvanised legislation. Even in its overtly non-violent phase the movement was underpinned by self-defence and by the will to violence. When Medgar Evers was murdered, enraged protestors demanding 'we want the murderer' threw rocks at white businesses in Jackson and twenty-seven were arrested.[20] Dr King was always aware that the threat of violence was a powerful tool, as when he warned in May 1963 as African Americans protested in Birmingham that the city threatened to be the site of 'the worst racial holocaust the nation has ever seen', an idea returned to in the Conclusion. Daisy Bates used armed guards to protect her activism and E. D. Nixon, Rev. Fred Shuttlesworth and Charles Sims recognised self-defence and argued in movement meetings that segregation yielded to force more than to moral suasion designed to appeal to conscience and character. Even Mrs Hamer confided that 'Sometimes I get so disgusted I feel like getting my gun after some of these chicken eatin' preachers . . . selling out to the white power structure'.[21]

In Monroe, North Carolina, Robert Williams, formerly head of the local NAACP chapter, agitated for armed defence and Ronnie Moore of CORE also made public statements in support. The Deacons for Justice and Self-Defense became very visible in the fight against violent intimidation from white supremacists such as the Ku Klux Klan in a return to Reconstruction-era racial terrorism. The Deacons were an independent working-class group that came into being to fight on the local front but who made the nation face the fact that civil rights legislation would have no impact on the segregated status quo if sheriffs were derelict in law-enforcement with regard to black residents in their counties. Similarly, the beginnings of the Black Power Movement occurred in the South: in Greenwood, Mississippi during James Meredith's March Against Fear in 1966. After Meredith was shot and wounded, organisations rallied to complete his march in anger fuelled by factors including the evidence that the Civil Rights and the Voting Rights Acts had failed to stem violence. Stokely Carmichel and Willie Ricks changed the phrase coined by Richard Wright and others into a call for militant action. 'Black Power' was a sign of disaffection, a signal that nomenclature such as 'Negro' would be superseded in a new identity politics and that Black pride had found an ideological outlet. 'Black Power' functioned like the 'X' The Nation of Islam took to replace a 'slave name', as a powerful way to signal Afrocentric community. It was an ethnic model based on 'closing ranks' to enter American polity as a distinct minority, and a strategy that other minorities would revisit. Dr King described 'Black Power' as a 'psychological call to manhood' in an effort to understand the cultural shift towards separatism and it pre-empted James Forman's 'Black Manifesto' (1969), the beginning of the debate over what the nation owes African Americans as reparations for having held them in slavery that continues today. Grounded in a material analysis of the making of an African American underclass and the church's complicity in its formation, the reparations debate began with Forman's call for white religious institutions to pay $500 million in recognition of black oppression.

Addressing problems of ghettoisation and poor housing had been indirect goals of the Civil Rights Movement but Black Muslims paid attention to the poor and to prisoners, delivering street-corner speeches like those for which Malcolm X was renowned in Harlem, and visiting prisons. Dr King had argued that 'riot' was too often 'the language of the unheard' and while King sought to cross the chasms of suspicion class created, it was not until the mid-1960s that he turned the movement spotlight to poverty. The Nation of Islam looked precisely to those most oppressed economically who feared their needs had gone unrepresented by civil rights organisations. Gordon Parks cites a New York taxi driver protesting that although he was too busy surviving to join a movement, 'these Muslims . . . make more sense than the NAACP and Urban League and all the rest of 'em put together. They're down on the good earth with the brother'.[22] The 'ghetto' was the prison James Baldwin argued African Americans had been expected to perish in 'by never being allowed to go behind the white man's definitions'[23] and Black Power ideology would be crucial in situating the racially dispossessed in global context.

In his 1969 revision of *The Other America* (1962), Michael Harrington stated his regret that, 'quite wrongly', he had omitted American Indians from his study of poverty when they were probably 'the poorest of all'.[24] Harrington's declaration accrues larger meaning when it is remembered that he was a member of the government's task force defining the parameters of the 'War on Poverty'. The late 1960s saw the production of a number of counter-histories in the form of a new politics of 'minorities'. This contributed to the belated recognition of the significance of Indians in movement politics, especially after the Indian Rights Movement seized the media spotlight in the symbolic occupation of Alcatraz Island in San Francisco Bay, first in 1964, demanding the land for an Indian University and then over some eighteen months between 1969 and 1971 demanding both land and rights. In 1970 Dee Brown published *Bury My Heart at Wounded Knee* and Harold E. Fey revised his 1959 book *Indians and Other Americans* to take account of political struggles of the intervening decade. As Dave Murray has demonstrated, revising earlier histories of American Indians and returning to critiques of government policy towards Indians often involved looking backward.[25] But a change in stance and style was evident in the work of Vine Deloria. In 1970 Deloria confided: 'Sometimes when people ask what tribe I belong to, I am tempted to answer "Others" . . . I have yet to attend a conference on poverty, race relations, social problems, civil rights, or pollution without being tagged an "other" '.[26]

Vine Deloria and the Indian Rights Movement

Deloria, a Sioux Indian, former marine, student of religion and latterly lawyer was best known as a human rights activist. Appointed Executive Director of the National Congress of American Indians (NCAI) in 1964, his 1965 editorial 'Now Is the Time' was a call to revitalise the NCAI to catch the movement Zeitgeist. Like other writers and intellectuals discussed in this book, he was influenced by Marshall McLuhan's ideas of communication, criticising strategies such as students taking over university buildings which failed to move student politics beyond the campus gates. He championed education as self- and group-determination, and analysed the 'liberal problem' of a people who with 54 million acres of land worth $3 billion should be neither poor nor benighted yet were treated like a 'conglomerate slum population'.[27] His caustic and witty social critique in over twenty books over three decades is exemplified in *Spirit and Reason* (1999) and Deloria's spirit was countercultural as well as religious. He published in *Playboy*, an album by Floyd Red Crow Westerman took its title from his first and most controversial book, *Custer Died For Your Sins* (1969), and, among other prizes, Deloria was recipient of the Wallace Stegner Award in 2002 for his writings on the land-use philosophy of Indians. He argued in 1970 that the 'white man's conception of nature' was 'obscene' and he was criticised himself for deploying fundamentalist creationist models and, like the conservative leader of the Nation of Islam whose notion of Islam bore little resemblance to the religion, for aligning himself with conspiracy science fiction. Deloria's politics reflect the complexities of the era rather than a superficially 'liberal' or 'conservative' agenda.

In 'The Red and the Black', Deloria argued that Civil Rights was the most important but also the 'least understood movement of our generation' and that the equation of 'race' with 'black' as the signifier of civil rights initiatives risked eliding the presence of Indians. He argued that a typically 'liberal' embarrassment over lack of knowledge about Indian history and communities exacerbated their erasure, the assumption being that all minority groups suffered identical 'problems'.[28] As had psychologist Kenneth Clarke testifying before the National Commission on Civil Disorders, Deloria critiqued government inertia: after the preliminary publicity whitewash, each new administration failed to address Indian policy. Only when the Special Subcommittee on Indian Education chaired by Edward Kennedy published its report *Indian Education: A National Tragedy – A National Challenge* (1969) would its sixty recommendations lead to the Indian Education Act of 1972.[29]

That he has been compared to Martin Luther King Jr is both an accolade and an indication that the Indian Rights Movement would inevitably be measured against the Civil Rights Movement. However, Deloria is missing in most accounts of the ways in which identity politics in the 1960s have informed 'multicultural' culture wars in subsequent decades, despite his essays on the rise of Ethnic Studies at UCLA in the 1960s and his scathing criticism that Indians and Mexicans had never been considered part of the culture the Kerner Report (1968) sought to describe and address. Deloria consistently criticised theoreticians for their unwillingness to address concrete realities: 'The massive amount of useless knowledge produced by anthropologists attempting to capture real Indians in a network of theories has contributed substantially to the invisibility of Indian people today'. Straight-talking and provocative, he made no attempt to soften the history of oppression as he saw it: 'Negroes . . . were considered draft animals, Indians wild animals . . . Orientals . . . domestic animals and Mexicans humorous lazy animals'.[30] DeLoria was keenly aware of the cultural impact

of deleterious stereotypes. He recognised, not without courting controversy, that consigning elder statesmen to the caricature of 'Uncle Tom'
risked destroying 'the entire fabric of accumulated wisdom and experience
of the older generation of minority groups' and left young people underes-
timating social inequities as a betrayal of leadership, especially when
Indian tribal governments had been loath to risk their special relationship
with the federal government during the expansion of social programmes in
the 1960s.[31] In this way, Deloria's Indian-specific cultural commentary also
situated new movements in comparative context. He reiterated that the
failure to teach American Indian history to young people risked a terrible
loss. At the end of the decade his *We Talk You Listen: New Tribes, New Turf*
(1970) provided the intellectual context through which acts such as the
occupation of Alcatraz could be understood in context of what he saw as
the strangulating 'liberal thought-world'. Deloria's critique of liberalism was
scathing and Hubert Humphrey was at its centre; a man with a consistent
record on human rights had played safe with power but 'killed the liberal
image' in Chicago when he watched himself elected as 'Democratic standard bearer' amidst brutality.[32] The end of liberalism was, Deloria argued,
bound up in moral, religious and cultural conflicts and by situating Indian
Rights at the heart of ideological splits between conservatives and pro-
gressives, he also highlighted their long history.

A Time to Break Silence: The Mystique of Gender and the Geography of Hope

Betty Friedan's *The Feminine Mystique* (1963) was a widely publicised
retort to the demonisation of the working woman in such Freudian texts
as Ferdinand Lundberg and Marynia Farnham's *The Modern Woman*
(1947) in which feminism was aligned with Communist conspiracy. Her
book was a catalyst for the burgeoning cultural discourse that would later
be termed second-wave feminism but which was known as 'women's liberation'. Although Michael Klein in *The Turbulent Decade* went so far as
to describe Friedan's as one of the first oppositional texts of the New Left,
it was rather a conservative book in many ways. Friedan's worrying
about 'the alarming passivity' of teenage girls whose lives were stopped
short by motherhood is more representative of the 1950s when she began
work on her book than the 1960s when she published it. Furthermore,
her assertion that the (white) housewife-mother had been rendered the
'model for all women' and forced to subsume her interests to her feminine role has a long feminist history that returns us to the writings of
Charotte Perkins Gilman and Thorstein Veblen at the very beginning
of the twentieth century. Friedan's study was in some ways ground-
breaking but in others not entirely unexpected.

Across different cultural forms the role of women was being examined by men as well as women. In *Love and Death in the American
Novel* (1960) Leslie Fiedler argued that a central theme of American
literature had always been the male protagonist's flight from women
and their association with domesticity as a civilising force. In *The
Crying of Lot 49*, Pynchon's housewife Oedipa Maas is caught up in a
paranoid fantasy that may be the result of alcohol or prescription
drugs, fast becoming recognised as crutches for women trapped in a
suburban hinterland. Novelist Richard Yates' exploration of tragic
suburbanites in *Revolutionary Road* (1961) included April Wheeler
whose husband accuses her in an alcohol-fuelled argument of being
like Flaubert's Madame Bovary. Driven to the verge of madness by the
responsibilities of her delimiting role and broken dreams, April dies
when she attempts to abort an unwanted child. Despite her claims not
to write of her times in anything other than 'sidelong' glances, the cold
war and the 'war between the sexes' also texture *The Bell Jar* (1963)
and Plath's exposé of college sororities' initiating young women into
'the nil of belonging' presages Friedan's 'New Life Plan' according to
which women will resist the patriarchal pressure 'taking a far greater
toll on the physical and mental health of our country than any known
disease'.[33] Like Friedan, Plath was a graduate of Smith College and in
her description, the white middle-class feminine norm is first revealed
in college when the 'picked buds of American womanhood' succumb
to 'the pressure of being everybody; ergo, no one'.[34]

In 1959 Stanley M. Elkins had made a loaded comparison between
the Nazi death camps of the Holocaust and the plantation system,
arguing that the inevitable consequence was the dehumanisation of
slaves. Plath deployed the simile of the Holocaust to narrate a woman's
suicide in 'Lady Lazarus' and, as Marianne DeKoven has argued,
poetry by women in the 1960s 'often served as the most powerful, rich,
galvanizing movement statements'.[35] Friedan followed suit, describing
the home as a 'comfortable concentration camp', and her target audience was hooked. 'Women's Studies' was not yet a publishing category
when *The Feminine Mystique* came out in paperback but women's colleges such as Vassar bought copies to include in welcome packs for
incoming students.[36] Criticism of her work began early though, as in
Sylvia Fleis Fava's 1963 review arguing mother-of-three Friedan set
up an equally damaging 'counter-mystique' whereby women were
expected to pursue career ambitions outside the home.[37] Journalist and
novelist Robert Lipsyte sent up Friedan in *The Masculine Mystique*
(1966) while in *The Stepford Wives* (1972), Ira Levin's satire on the

male backlash, Friedan is the feminist speaker who visits small-town Stepford and stirs up docile housewives so that the Men's Association feels forced to crush the movement by killing the community's wives to reproduce them as robotic exaggerations of femininity. While Friedan ignored the ways in which race and ethnicity complicate her model, and the fact that in working-class experience staying at home was an impossible luxury rather than a suffocating bell jar, she did succeed in galvanising a key segment of the female population. However, *The Second Stage* (1981) would signal a conservative return to family values at the expense of what was after all an original contribution to the struggle for feminist autonomy in the era.

The Feminine Mystique should be remembered as a pivotal text that exemplifies a pivotal moment when fifties models of femininity were challenged. However, in the 1990s, Lynn Spigel undertook a television reception study and interviews with undergraduate students revealed they still traced the development of feminism in postwar America according to *I Love Lucy* (the re-runs they watched in their childhood) and similar shows.[38] The close relationship between their popular memory and television emphasised the persistence of those 'exemplary fictions' of a fifties-style 'feminism' that Friedan sought to change. While organisations such as Veteran Feminists of America celebrate such challenges, contemparary cultural productions sometimes return to the era to question the extent of women's liberation. In Todd Haynes's movie *Safe* (1995), for example, a California housewife suffers non-specific 'symptoms' which recall the problem with no name and her privileged environment is proved noxious and dangerous; ABC show *Desperate Housewives* dramatises similar caveats.

In 1966 the National Organization for Women (NOW) issued a 'Bill of Rights' to institute federal change by building an Equal Rights Amendment (ERA) into the Constitution, the continuation of a struggle that began in the 1920s. The shift from pockets of protest seen at local and university levels to a national and legislative struggle for change was subject to a severe backlash from those who stereotyped women's liberation as the province of man-hating feminists 'burning their bras', even though NOW and ERA activists described their position as liberal and presented civil rights reforms as socially beneficial in the widest terms. As the Civil Rights Movement had split into factions, so feminist claims for recognition led to the splintering into groups of women who labelled themselves 'liberal feminists' or socialist or Marxist feminists, and the idea of a separate female culture was advanced by groups of 'radical feminists'. Multiple feminist groups organised against the Miss America pageant of 1968 outside the Democratic Convention in Atlantic City, where MFDP supporters had demonstrated in 1964 for official recognition. United in a Ten-Point Protest against a 'consumer con-game', they argued that Miss America was little more than a 'military death mascot' on cheerleader tours around Vietnam.[39] Much that the feminist movement achieved in the 1960s would be made manifest in the 1970s and 1980s in the writings of Gloria Steinem, Robin Morgan, Charlotte Bunch and Shulamith Firestone among others. Their definitions of (white) female culture would be a spur to more racially nuanced debate and a source of black feminist contention throughout ensuing decades.

John d'Emilio has stated, 'if you press me to talk about "the sixties", almost every one of the stories that would spontaneously erupt from my memory is about events that occurred in the 1970s': stories of the gay liberation movement.[40] Gays and lesbians were involved across new social movements, most notably in the persons of Bayard Rustin and Robin Morgan, but the symbolic demonstration of gay culture did not take place until New York City police raided Stonewall Inn in Greenwich Village in 1969. The reaction precipitated the most famous protest against the suppression of gay civil rights.

In resistance that recalled agitation for civil liberties in the South, especially the taking to the streets of black southerners in Birmingham in 1963, individuals refused arrest and were beaten by police using night sticks. The 'riot' that ensued was treated in the same way as anti-Vietnam war protests, with Tactical Patrol Force Units sent to quell the disturbance. The chant 'Gay Power' was heard and *The Village Voice*[41] described the scene as 'something from a William Burroughs novel'.[42] Stonewall was reported as an all-male fracas, with no reference to the race or ethnicity of participants, but later accounts emphasise the role lesbians played and the significance of the Inn as the focus of a police raid precisely because regulars were African American and Hispanic. The story of Stonewall on 27–8 June 1969 means more than the sum of its parts. In the supposedly dead-end days of Movement politics, a multiracial and multi-ethnic group sent a sharp message that this 'non-vanilla mix' of people would no longer accept criminalisation.[43] The Civil Rights model of public protest was deployed by a group for whom invisibility had afforded a kind of protection but whose existence had been systematically mediated through pseudo-medical discourse in which homosexuality was a cold war disease.

The sexuality of federal employees in the civil service and the Department of Defense was monitored, with known homosexuals

Figure 5.3 Stonewall memorial statues, Greenwich Village, New York City. Courtesy Tina Galloway.

dismissed. Such undercurrents found their way into popular culture. Otto Preminger's film *Advise and Consent* (1962), for example, depicts a Senate confirmation battle during which a closet homosexual is blackmailed, finally killing himself, and in *Greetings* a young man's friends make him into a 'fag' when he is drafted to fight in Vietnam in a pantomime of the most unacceptable of army recruits. In 1964, *Life* published a special investigation of homosexuality subtitled 'A secret world grows open and bolder. Society is forced to look at it – and try to understand it'. Paul Welch's investigative journalism described undercover police operations to trap soliciting homosexuals. Despite a pose of objectivity, it exemplifies the discourse in which homosexuals were trapped: 'discarding their furtive ways and openly admitting, even flaunting, their deviation . . . For every obvious homosexual, there are probably nine nearly impossible to detect'.[44] Cold war fears of invasion, contagion and conspiracy rendered homosexuality pathological as in previous decades. Keeping gay activism outside the movement narrative of the sixties relegates the gay liberation movement to the fringes. It also restricts the scope of the decade by delimiting its close to 1970 when the effects of Stonewall were rebounding and the controversy that was *Roe* vs *Wade* (1973) was building. Both are evidence that sexual politics was on the cultural agenda in different ways throughout the 1960s – as was the environment.

In *Walden* (1845) Henry Thoreau advanced the symbolic importance of water in the environment: 'A lake is the landscape's most beautiful and expressive feature. It is earth's eye; looking into which the beholder measures the depth of his own nature'.[45] A century later in Kurt Vonnegut's novel *Cat's Cradle* (1963), ice-nine is a scientific breakthrough that goes horribly wrong when all the water on earth freezes, destroying the world's ecology, and in the paranoid fantasy *Dr Strangelove* (1964) a US General fears his sexual impotence is the result of a communist plot to destroy American manhood by polluting the water with sperm-destroying fluorides. W. S. Merwin's poem 'For A Coming Extinction' (1967) imagined a dead future and in *Soylent Green* (1973), a movie set in a dystopian future, the failure to sustain natural resources leads to synthetic food made from cadavers feeding the mass population to conserve what little food remains for the elite. The fear that the world's natural resources would be used up, squandered or corrupted prompted concerned individuals to call for a shift from conservation to legislation in the 1960s.

Rachel Carson's *Silent Spring* (1962)

In the early 1960s, marine biologist Carson shifted the imperative of reform from natural history and conservation to ecology and environmentalism in a book that has never been out of print. *Silent Spring*'s publication coincided with the tragic scandal over fertility drug Thalidomide and battles over consumer safety championed by Ralph Nader, as well as pervasive anxieties over the threat of nuclear fallout. Carson was influenced by sociological studies of the power of advertising and of complacent consumerism as critiqued by David Riesman, C. Wright Mills and Vance Packard: 'Lulled by the soft sell and the hidden persuader, the average citizen is seldom aware of the deadly materials with which he is surrounding himself'.[46] Carson charged that the public 'is fed little tranquilizing pills of half truth' about the danger of pesticides[47] and she took agri-business to task for its failure to act responsibly with the environment. Her emphasis on chemicals as 'elixirs of death', and her recitation of resultant conditions from cancer to genetic mutation, made for a powerful exposé; chemical companies put together a 'war chest' of $250,000 to counter negative publicity.[48]

Silent Spring would be a Book of the Month Selection and a Fawcett paperback by 1964 but even before its publication in September 1962, press coverage was vast due to the June serialisation of extracts in *The New Yorker*, Carson's appearance on *CBS Reports* and because President Kennedy cited *Silent Spring* as a reason for requiring his Science Advisory Committee to investigate the dangers of pesticides. Before anyone had even read the book, its contents were known, exemplifying Marshall McLuhan's thesis that to understand the new media was to apprehend the ways in which news in one medium was carried and transformed by another. In June 1963 Carson was asked to present her findings at Congressional hearings on pollution. She was prescient in her concern about what are now all-too-commonly cited environmental crises such as the greenhouse effect. However, Carson was a surprising champion of social change. The books she published in the 1950s did not presage the furore she would create. *The Sea Around Us* (1951) won the National Book Award, *The Edge of the Sea* (1955) was a celebration of the seashore and Carson was a regular contributor to *Ladies Home Journal* and *Women's Home Companion*, casting her readership net wide. However, she would be hailed as a revolutionary prophet by some and her training in science dismissed and ridiculed by others on the publication of *Silent Spring*

Eugene P. Odum's *The Fundamentals of Ecology* (1953) first identified the ecosystem and Carson's approach may not have been wholly original. A 1946 *New Republic* article on the dangers of DDT for example, cited the ominous silence of birds as its key motif[49] and poets from Keats to Whitman deploy the image of a deathly silence in which no birds sing. But when Carson uses the same trope of silence, it is revealing in the context of a scientist who as a woman was not expected to speak out with such authority. Carson's real success lay in her facility for translating scientific information into accessible prose. William Shawn, Editor of *The New Yorker*, wrote of his admiration of *Silent Spring* in a letter: 'You have made it literature full of beauty and loveliness and depth of feeling'.[50] Her literary strategies include the opening fable of a town in which spring begins without birdsong because a chemical powder like nuclear dust has killed all the birds. In a series of powerful, even sensationalist, analogies, Carson's literary non-fiction pushes her point home. In a chapter entitled 'Beyond the Dreams of the Borgias', she argues that contaminated food holds similar dangers to those experienced by guests at a meal hosted by the infamous Renaissance poisoners.

For her biographer Linda Lear, Carson was a 'Witness for Nature' and in her study of the reception of *Silent Spring*, Priscilla Coit Murphy describes it as a 'perfect storm', a landmark in literary as well as environmental history.[51] But Carson had surprising detractors too: the Sierra Club was sceptical and for others she displayed the advocacy typical of an investigative journalist rather than an objective scientist. Her situation was made more difficult because throughout the period of writing and publicising the book, Carson was dangerously ill. She died of breast cancer in 1964 having undergone a catalogue of ancillary illnesses including temporary blindness, all of which she hid from the press, aware that detractors might use the information to argue that *Silent Spring* was the work of bitterness. In the event, however, her work led to the creation of the Environmental Protection Agency and prefigured various pieces of legislation. Carson's was not a lone voice by any means: Wallace Stegner's 'Wilderness Letter' (1960) had argued that the wilderness was the 'scientific yardstick' against which the world would be measured. However, Carson's was the 'loudest' voice raised from middle America's heartland on the issue in the 1960s and mythologising this middle-class, middle-aged woman has contributed to her importance. Senator Ribicoff introduced her to Congress as 'the lady who started this' in a deliberate echo of President Lincoln's comments to Harriet Beecher Stowe during the Civil War and it is with the cultural phenomenon of *Uncle Tom's Cabin* that *Silent Spring* is often compared.

Federal legislation quickly followed the environmental movement, from the Wilderness Act (1964) to the Clean Air Act (1970). Membership of the Sierra Club (1892–) increased and of the National Wildlife Federation. New organisations were formed including The Environmental Defense Fund (1967) and Friends of the Earth (1969). Senator Gaylord Nelson campaigned in 1968 for a national 'Environmental Teach-In' based on the anti-war Teach-Ins taking place in universities and John McConnell harnessed such initiatives as a platform for Earth Day. The first 'Earth Day' took place on the same endangered frontier over which Wallace Stegner had campaigned, in San Francisco on 21 March 1970, and was repeated with bases around the country the following year when around 20 million people took part in Earth Day on 22 April. The US Senate unanimously passed the Clean Water Act (1970), as a result of such events during which pollution, nuclear power and environmental health were firmly on the nation's agenda with President Nixon declaring 1970 'the year of the beginning' for federal environmental regulation. Ralph Nader began campaigning for alternative and 'soft' energy and in 1977 President Carter issued a National Energy Plan although it failed to win votes in Senate. Almost forty years on, however, indifference to environmentalism – such as pulling out of the Kyoto treaty on global warming – has characterised the George W. Bush administration and led to its being described by Gregory Wetstone of the National Resource Defense Council as 'the most anti-environmental Presidential

Administration ever'. 'Every president has left more of America's landscape protected than they inherited', declared Carl Pope director of the Sierra Club in 2004, 'Bush has gone in the opposite direction'.[52]

Such concerns were already evident in Dr King's speech of 4 April 1967 in which he protested the Vietnam war: 'They watch as we poison their water, as we kill a million acres of their crops. They must weep as the bulldozers roar through their areas preparing to destroy the precious trees . . .'[53] King's speech was called 'A Time to Break Silence' and Elmo Zumwalt Sr, the commanding officer of the in-country navy whose veteran son died in 1988 from chemically induced cancers, broke silence when he campaigned that Centers for Disease Control had failed to point out the dangers of defoliant Agent Orange, the chemical that had been praised as a 'miracle juice' to help US swift boats battle through the 'verdant hell' of Vietnam waterways.[54] That Zumwalt Sr had been commanded to spray Agent Orange and that his son, a swift-boat commander, had died from its effects went to the tragic heart of the American family's relationship with chemical warfare. The Pentagon's belief in Agent Orange's safety was an ironic addendum to the decade's environmental movement especially once the effects of the deleterious chemical warfare programme were revealed to the nation in the 1980s and the Zumwalt story was told in soap-opera style as *My Father, My Son* (1988). The TV movie is typically the genre in which personally tragic responses to controversial social issues first find representation.

A novel which encapsulates many of the issues that saturate the era is environmentalist Wallace Stegner's *All The Little Live Things* (1967). Ruth and Joe Allston find a retirees' haven in rural California but in this anti-pastoral novel of the American West, Stegner leaves its protagonist raw and exposed. As Joe opines in the Epilogue, 'Peace was not anything I saw or smelled or felt. The bell jar that had protected our retirement was smashed . . .' [55] The widening generation gap renders Joe unsure of his cultural footing when a free-falling hippie guru who purports to follow the philosophy of ahimsa becomes his nemesis as soon as he breaches the western frontier Joe has staked as his claim:

> Spacemen, kook, barefoot saint, seeker, searcher, rebel, lush, pothead, idealist, bughouse intellectual, Modern Youth, whatever he was, he looked at me in the eyes for a second that contained our mutual recognition and abhorrence.[56]

Joe turns to Crevècoeur's *Letters from an American Farmer* and to *Huckleberry Finn*, in an attempt to resurrect a frontier credo. The

Allstons' garden carved out of wilderness is a valiant endeavour to cultivate peace but the hippie's freedom to find himself in the land is portrayed as the demolition of Joe's hopes for serenity. In his 'Wilderness Letter', Stegner had first voiced his 'geography of hope' as set against the fear that if American wilderness as reality and idea was insufficiently valued, 'never again will Americans be free in their country from the noise, the exhausts, the stinks of human and automotive waste'.[57]

The hippie movement, often an understudy in surveys of social movements, is important for its ongoing relationship to land and ecology and because, as Alice Erchols argues, 'More people passed through "love ghettos" like Haight-Ashbury than took part in SDS'.[58] A 1967 news report wondered whether hippies were 'fading into the landscape',[59] so successful were they at putting down ecological roots. For example, 250 'flower children' set out from California in a wagon train of 63 psychedelic buses. Arriving in rural Tennessee in March 1971, they set up an organic farming commune that would sell its produce via a health store. By 1981, The Farm was a collective of 1,300 hippies on a 1,750-acre spread and its cottage industries included a school, radio station, publishing company and international hippie news service, a free clinic and their own version of the peace corps – a kind of hippie Camelot – which organised free ambulances as far away as the South Bronx and reforestation projects in Guatemala and Bangladesh.[60] Unlike the internecine struggles that Stegner describes in his novel, the Tennessee hill folk helped the hippies and enjoyed access to their facilities in return. In 2008, The Farm is an eco-village and includes a Hippie Museum and a history of its own development on its web site.[61]

A gathering conservatism began to be apparent in interpreting even the most countercultural of movements from the very beginning which speaks to the hippie movement's complexity. Warren Hickle in the ironic 'Social History of the Hippies' (1970) described hippie young who 'sounded for all the world like young Republicans'.[62] Their utopian ideal of American individualism and their de-emphasising of government controls and central leadership models referred back to utopian experiments such as Brooke Farm. Similarly, in celebrating *Easy Rider* as the first 'above-ground' movie to explore hippie culture, Paul Warshow could already see that its (traditional) virtues were inseparable from its faults: 'gentleness, tolerance, grace, openness to experience; disconnectedness, disengagement, monotony, an emotional and intellectual vacuousness.'[63] The litany of ideals/failings is

Figure 5.4 A hippie walks by the intersection of Haight and Ashbury in San Francisco, California, 10 October 1970. (AP Photo) Courtesy PA Photos.

typical of the way in which newspaper reports vacillated between features on 'graduate hippies' carving out a drugless new world and virulent attacks on their supposed social pathology. 'The year of the hippie', 1967, began with the San Francisco Human Be-In on 14 January but also saw its 'ending' in a three-day wake, 'Death of the

Hippie', on 6 October, a reaction to the violence, exploitative drug scene and 'bad vibrations' in the formerly peaceful Haight-Ashbury district. Ironically, 'Taps', composed during the Civil War and traditionally played at military burial services, was played at the symbolic hippie 'funeral'

The 'end' of the hippies was summed up by a Haight-Ashbury shopkeeper: 'Now we've got lots of troublemaker types. Pseudo-hippies I call them . . . They don't care about anybody else but themselves'.[64] Distinguishing between 'true' hippies who were friendly to everybody and opportunists selling drugs and chasing trouble became a professional occupation for journalists, as Joan Didion explores in her essay 'Slouching Toward Bethlehem' (1967), especially once the 'scene' crumpled and hippies dispersed. On 21 October 1967, for example, the Associated Press reported that Atlanta, the southern city that had designated itself 'too busy to hate', was the 'New Mecca' for flower children and that the Peachtree/14th Street district, a traditionally residential middle-class neighbourhood that included Piedmont Park, was the hippie centre. Hippies were, the press was pleased to report, children of middle- or upper-class parents who hoped to 'slip out of the frame some of the newspaper people put us in'. However, by September 1969, United Press International reported a 'showdown' with the same Atlanta hippies after disturbances in Piedmont Park.[65] Like members of other youth movements, hippies were socially pathologised. In news items such as 'Hippes May Get Air Travel Rules', it was suggested that American Airlines was trying to ensure anyone boarding aircraft be required to wear shoes and a representative of United Airplanes expressed the belief that anyone carrying a musical instrument that could not be lodged beneath a seat – a hippie with a guitar – should be expected to buy a half-fare ticket to transport it. Standards over hippie cleanliness were discussed in *Aviation Daily* and the American Civil Liberties Union challenged penalties exacted against hippies on the basis that 'this is the same kind of reasoning that kept Negroes in the back of the bus'.[66]

They Won't Give Peace a Chance

The anti-war movement evolved out of other social movements and was one of the most heterogeneous. The image of peace protestors as beatniks-turned-hippies protesting via love-ins was designed to damage the movement. The government's distrust of youth movements was made manifest by 1969 when Vice-President Agnew declared that young anti-war protestors were like naughty children, too easily influenced by communists. Individuals were often punished. Detroit poet John Sinclair, a member of the White Panther Party, was awarded a ten-year jail sentence for possession of two marijuana cigarettes. It was considered by many an excessive punishment meted out not for drugs but for anti-war activities. Sinclair served two-and-a-half years. The Washington demonstrations Mailer explores in *The Armies of the Night* (1968) epitomise the moment by which dissent changed to resistance, but throughout the period men and women revered as cultural experts and established intellectuals, from Dr Benjamin Spock to Rev. William Sloane Coffin, gave the lie to propaganda designed to deny the breadth and depth of the movement.

Protesting the draft meant fighting against the escalation of US troops from around 23,000 in 1964 to more than 500,000 when Johnson stepped down as President in January 1969. Journalist James Fallows in 'What Did You Do in the Class War, Daddy?' describes a draft physical in 1970, a situation satirised in the movie *Greetings* and via Arlo Guthrie's experience in *Alice's Restaurant* (1969). Fallows remembers that students like him from Harvard and MIT manipulated 'reasons' for medical exemption but that working-class young men from nearby Chelsea were accepted almost to a man. First, it was easy for influential families and middle-class young men at elite universities to extricate themselves from the war, so that when in 2004 it was posited that, 'The paucity of Americans protesting the [Iraq] war is directly related to the paucity of Americans participating in it'.[67] The logic was an ironic reminder that American family lives could be left untouched by war unless a member served. Second, as Country Joe and The Fish's anthemic song 'Feel Like I'm Fixing-to-Die Rag' dramatised, even being 'strung out' would not prevent the US military from signing up the young. Noam Chomsky's first book *American Power and the New Mandarins* (1969) was dedicated to 'the brave young men who refuse to serve in a criminal war' and Joan Baez refused to pay taxes that would contribute to the continual drafting.

It is unsurprising that Women Strike for Peace, founded in 1961 to 'End the Arms Race, Not the Human Race', should be at the forefront of protests against the draft. As Amy Swerdlow's detailed study shows, women knew how to foreground the very models of fifties-styled femininity that would give their political goals emotional weight and mothers protesting the endangerment of their children added a passion to the cause. On the other hand, the southern military college the Citadel, sixty-seven of whose alumni died in Vietnam, was vehement in its support of the war: 'the American fighting man is dying so that these bearded, draft-dodging, dope-addicted, Communist-inspired, pseudo-intellectual cowards have the liberty and sanctuary [to disparage America]'.[68] However, the Tet Offensive and the murder of dissenting students at Kent State were among the triggers for a change of culture even within the Citadel. College newspapers *The Vigil* and *The Brigadier* began to publish a spectrum of opinions including sympathy with dissent. More typically pro-and anti-war tensions were sited at the nexus of two generations, the one seeking to explain itself to the other in order to defuse the conflict that Lewis Feuer, a member of a Berkeley faculty during the FSM, summarised as a conflict between fathers and sons. The tension is dramatised in The Doors' epic song 'The End' (1967). The controversial final line Jim Morrison screams into oblivion, 'Father/ Yes son?/ I want to kill you/ Mother, I want to fuck you', is often read as the archetypal Oedipal crisis. However, it is a rejection of the Apollonian tradition of the 'father' who fails to 'picture what will be so limitless and free' for the son in his embracing of the Dionysian 'feminine' exuberance of the 'mother'. When reprised in Francis Ford Coppola's *Apocalypse Now* (1979), 'The End' is also an indictment of the desperate stakes forced on the young sacrificed by their 'fathers' in government. The question of how the US should extricate itself from the war coloured all shades of political opinion, from John Galbraith's *How To Get Out of Vietnam* (1967) and Arthur Schlesinger Jr's *The Bitter Heritage: Vietnam and American Democracy, 1941–1966* (1967) to Mary McCarthy and Diana Trilling's 'On Withdrawing from Vietnam: An Exchange' (*New York Review of Books*, 1967).

James Carroll's *An American Requiem* (1996), subtitled 'God, My Father, and the War That Came Between Us', chronicles the tension in his relationship with his father, Lieutenant General Joseph F. Carroll, director of the Defense Intelligence Agency. A priest and member of the peace movement in the late 1960s, James' anti-war sentiments force a painful breach with his father and with the idea of the nation the son has inherited. The three Carroll brothers' experiences coalesce in a succinct summary of political polarisation in the era; the eldest flees the draft, the middle son follows in his father's footsteps – Carroll Sr was an FBI man before working in government – and becomes an FBI agent charged with hunting down draft-dodgers such as his brother. Youngest son James hides his anti-war allegiance from his father and measures his timidity against Quaker Norman Morrison whose self-immolation beneath Carroll Sr and Robert McNamara's offices at the

Pentagon sickens him as it inspires his cause. Morrison's sacrificial rage was recalled by McNamara as the first protest to really compel his attention and North Vietnamese poet laureate To Huu's poem quietly commemorated the moment in which Morrison's heart grew brightest.[69]

High-profile celebrities lent their support to the anti-war effort, working within the system and pitting themselves against it. From celebrated pediatrician Dr Benjamin Spock to 'Hanoi' Jane Fonda, they publicised the steps one could take to oppose an unpopular war. Robert Bly donated the cheque he received as the winner of the 1969 National Book Award for Poetry to Resistance, organising against the draft, and John Lennon set up voter-registration booths at his American concerts in 1971 so that anti-war youth could vote against the war in voting Nixon out of power. When an established figure in American culture lent their support to the war, like John Wayne, or spoke out against it, like Jane Fonda, they symbolised the cultural divide over its continuation, no one more than CBS News anchor Walter Cronkite whose views were taken – not only by audiences but also by government – to encompass middle America's. On 27 February 1967 during an hour-long TV special on the Tet Offensive, Cronkite declared that the only 'realistic, yet unsatisfactory, conclusion' to draw was that the war was 'mired in stalemate'. This was especially devastating for the government when, as Mary McCarthy summarised, 'The meaning of a war, if it has one, ought to be discernible in the rear, where the values being defended are situated; at the front, war itself appears senseless, a confused butchery that only the gods can understand'.[70] Protests known as the Moratorium demonstrations of 15 October 1969 in which more than two million Americans were known to have participated serve as a broad-brush representation of the strength of anti-war feeling that built not only among students and radicals but also religious, civic and professional groups, politicians, from Eugene McCarthy and Edward Kennedy to George McGovern, and voters across the board.

The Vietnam Veterans Against the War (VVAW) founded in 1967 emphasised the first-hand experiences of servicemen and women in Vietnam. Despite high-profile members – John Kerry and Oliver Stone – the organisation has received much less coverage than its significance merits, especially since it continues as a non-profit organisation to support veterans. *Winter Soldier*, a little-remembered 1972 documentary, was only re-released in 2006 and is an indication that excavation of the decade's neglected cultural texts reveals a more complex mosaic of contributors to the decade's movements. Soldiers and marines testified that the war to which they were consigned, or in which they volunteered to fight, led to their having carried out 'war crimes' as the regrettable consequence of American policy. *Winter Soldier's* footage of the four day 1971 investigation is shot through with something of the emotional power of South Africa's Truth and Reconciliation Committee hearings of the 1990s, during which atrocities committed under the apartheid regime began to be addressed openly by some of those who perpetrated them. However, while the post-apartheid regime instigated the Committee's formation, Vietnam veterans themselves acted in the wake of public exposure to atrocities such as the My Lai massacre for which Lt William Calley had been made scapegoat. It is striking that in *Winter Soldier* former soldiers with long hair and beards look like student protestors whose stereotyped image had typified the way anti-war protest was represented.

Students played an important and sometimes tragic role in anti-war demonstrations, as on 4 May 1970 when four students were shot dead by National Guard at Kent State. Students were shot and wounded by the military at other universities including New York, New Mexico and Jackson State. In popular culture, tension between generations over the war and youth culture is best represented in a striking movie *Joe* (1970). Bigoted $4-an-hour factory worker Joe Curran (Peter Boyle) and $60,000-a-year advertising executive Bill Compton (Dennis Patrick) unite across class lines in their resentment of young people 'taking over the culture'. In her first role, Susan Sarandon is Melissa, Compton's daughter, hospitalised when she flips out on speed. When her father kills the young man he sees as the source of her lifestyle, Joe celebrates him as a hero: 'I'd like to kill one of them'. By the film's end, this 'ordinary Joe' has murdered three hippies. Under the influence of drugs, deciding to 'infiltrate' a commune, Joe convinces addled Bill, 'There is only one way out now. Clean. Everybody'. Bill shoots the final witness running to escape the massacre, who the camera reveals is Melissa. The four hippies murdered in *Joe* are neither guilty of drug-dealing nor of anything other than championing 'free love' and drugs, their innocence a reminder that national guardsmen also shot innocents at Kent State.

The Citadel would be among the forty-four colleges that condemned the action at Kent State and students at Mississippi's all-black Jackson State openly protested the murder of the white students. What happened next is too frequently forgotten in the commemoration of Kent State as symbolic of the anti-war student movement, perhaps because John Filo's photograph, discussed in Chapter 4, is so iconic but also because when Mississippi police fired on black protestors they did not expect to be vilified in the international press, and they were right. Nixon would describe students who protest on university campuses as 'bums'.[71] Citing sniper fire from a university building that was never proved, police fired bullets into a dormitory. Nine were wounded and two people died: Philip Gibbs studying law and a high-school student, James Earl Green, who had been taking a short cut through campus. They are commemorated by the Gibbs-Green Plaza at Jackson State, but aside from a single oral history published by Kent State in an effort to address its own symbolic centrality, the event has received little attention.

From Liberalism to Neo-Conservatism

A hardening conservatism was the liberal reaction to the most radical features of the counterculture including anti-war activism and separatist groups placing themselves in adversarial relationship to 'the nation'. Norman Poderhertz, described as 'the conductor of the neocon orchestra',[72] went so far as to initiate a campaign against 'the Movement' in *Commentary* in June 1970. Those whose youthful radicalism had been spent in the 1930s began to use what Peter Clecak calls 'the framework of nostalgia' to bolster a neo-conservative backlash. [73] *Commentary* published Midge Decter's scathing attack on the feminist movement, 'New Chastity and Other Arguments Against Women's Liberation' in 1972 but her 'Letter to the Young (and to their parents)' (*The Atlantic*, 1975) is much more commanding in its reflection on the loss of the 'most gifted' and 'the most indulged generation'. She succeeds in criticising the 'self-abasing tolerance' of liberal professors who 'abandoned' hedonistic students despite their duty of care, while quietly demonstrating how seriously a neo-conservative mother's lost hope in her nation's children should be taken.[74]

The term 'neo-conservative' did not come into vogue until the mid-1970s but the beginning of the nation's drift rightward from the 'Rooseveltian nation' has been subject to considerable scrutiny as if there were a single moment that enshrined the 'end' of liberalism and as if that moment is revealed at the ballot box. Johnson enjoyed a landslide victory in 1964 and as historian Ewan Morgan spells out: 'One out of every five people who had voted Republican in 1960 changed sides in 1964 . . . The scale of the Democratic victory persuaded some political commentators that conservatism and the Republican party

itself were moribund'.[75] However, the nomination of rightist
Republican Barry Goldwater in 1964 was a turning point for the Party.
Unlike any Republican candidate before him, he carried all the Deep
South states. Again, it could be countered that Johnson's espousal of
civil rights lost him the southern bloc. Yet his landslide in 1964 was also
revealing of a dangerous liberal complacency that allowed the
Republican right to re-group and to attract liberals whose criticisms,
like Patrick Moynihan's, Nathan Glazer's or indeed Podheretz's, best
signalled liberalism's discontents.

Conservatism gathered some force through the decade. Student
group Young Americans For Freedom (YAF) mentored by William F.
Buckley had enjoyed a much larger membership on inauguration
than SDS which would not reach its membership peak until shortly
before its demise. In *The Conscience of a Conservative* (1960) Barry
Goldwater stressed an aggressive conservatism that would unite liber-
tarians and the 'hard' right and in *Up From Liberalism* (1959) Buckley
had argued that McCathyism had already brought liberalism to boiling
point. Yet it would take until 1966 for conservatives to gain central
ground. In 1960 Nixon feared the left more than he wooed the right,
situating Republican moderates at the centre of his campaign. It was a
failing Goldwater himself would address in 1964, and that Nixon
would succeed with in 1968. Once in government Nixon licensed Vice-
President Agnew to maintain the right-wing spirit that would continually remind the electorate of the conservative strength that lay
beneath. Through Agnew's biting comments on anti-war activists as
'professional anarchists' and the liberal media as 'elitist snobs', Nixon
mobilised those radical rightists like the John Birchers and blue-collar
workers life Peter Boyle's 'Joe', as well as more sophisticated readers
of the *National Review*.

Traditional conservative attacks on federal reforms such as Johnson's
Great Society programmes, already losing ground to the war, successfully combined with neoconservative attacks on liberalism and the New
Left. In turn, the New Left had continually highlighted the weaknesses
in liberalism. In 'Culture and Politics' (1959), C. Wright Mills had
identified the young intelligentsia as the social group that would shake
the establishment, an idea taken up by Herbert Marcuse in *One-
Dimensional Man* (1964) and underlined by SNCC and SDS. However,
the 1964 and 1968 Democratic Conventions were the public theatre in
which liberalism's downturn can be best seen, as returned to at different
points across this book. When George McGovern could not turn the
political tide in 1968, it became more apparent that the Democratic

Party had lost the liberal-coalition-that-might-have-been: Robert Kennedy and Martin Luther King Jr on a platform of liberal-socialist reform at home and an end to the war abroad. Disenchanted with liberalism in the wake of violence, the surge further right took many forms: religious groups balking at the lowering of moral standards in the media and the culture; cold warriors holding out for a 'win' in Vietnam and reacting against plans to withdraw; and states' righters still smarting under the legal expectation to racially integrate.

By the 1980s Samuel Huntington was arguing that conservatism was a return to cultural norms following the 'disharmony' of the sixties while John Schwartz defended the many 'hidden successes' not always immediately apparent but now embedded in the culture that were a direct result of liberal politics in the 1960s. Such disagreements would characterise the culture wars during which liberal programmes were revisited. African American conservative Shelby Steele worked on four Great Society programmes and later espoused Black Power politics. These experiences form the basis of his 1990s critique of the 'redemptive liberalism' he believes atrophied post-1960s liberal thought, leaving only a futile sense of moral authority. He argues that African Americans lost out because the nation's need to redeem itself in the 1960s made of them a 'sociological people' who remain contingent in American life.[76]

Steele's thesis recalls a 1968 CBS programme, 'In Search of a Past', part of the Emmy-award-winning series *Of Black America* which argued that while African Americans were not yet integrated, it would prove equally impossible for them to forge a connection with Africa. In 'Toward A Future That Has No Past' (1972) Orlando Patterson argued instead that the 'historic choice' faced by African Americans was to transcend their past, 'the confines and grip of a cultural heritage', to become 'the most truly modern of all peoples – a people who feel no need for a nation, a past, or a particularistic culture.'[77] This future-oriented statement from a controversial black historian re-envisions contingency as modernity but the ironic reversal of identity politics also recalls the existentialism that Norman Mailer espoused in which the African American subject was the distillation of the modern, alienated figure at the heart of jazz and Beat culture, Hipsterdom – and Black Power politics. Criticism of affirmative-action programmes ensured that race remained a central focus of the 'hot' culture wars and 'neocons' from Irving Kristol and Glen Loury bemoaned what they saw as the state of American pluralism by targeting multiculturalism as it derived from 1960s emphases on identity politics. Conservative criticism of a supposedly 'politically correct' reification of race and ethnicity ensured members of the sixties liberal elite such as Arthur Schlesinger Jr would join the fray to argue 'multi-culti' forced a 'disuniting' of the 'vital' democratic centre that was the nation's liberal heart.

There is always a tendency for revolutions to consume and destroy their creators or for the revolutionaries to 'shift sides' or burn out. The burned-out lives of movement organisers are dramatised in Alice Walker's *Meridian* (1976) and Julius Lester's *And All Our Wounds Forgiven* (1994) and a number of those whose careers were founded on the platforms of the new social movements have been chastised in a cultural slap-in-the-face for shifting from the New Left to the neoconservative Right, as in Eric Lott's *The Disappearing Public Intellectual* (2005). However, the same grass-roots organising that opened the decade has also outlasted the sixties, often in the form of what Charles Marsh calls, respectfully, 'curmudgeonly activism',[78] like that which has kept Rev. Ed King, the white Tougaloo chaplain and one of the MFDP delegation to Atlantic City, involved in fighting for better health care in Mississippi. It is the same indefatigable community concern that made SNCC's Unita Blackwell into Mississippi's first African American woman mayor. Holding fast to 'sixties' principles or eschewing them in a disappointed conservative volte-face are equally prevalent responses to a turbulent era, reactions to which continue to dominate many contemporary debates, as summarised in the title of SNCC historian Howard Zinn's memoir *You Can't Be Neutral on a Moving Train: A Personal History of Our Times* (1994).

The Sixties and its Cultural Legacy

The ideals and the failures of the 1960s echo powerfully. Nostalgia not only harks back to a lost past but suggests the future may be lost too because American culture is still marked by some of the problems new social movements set out to solve. This may be one reason why Todd Gitlin compares his need to find a romantic foothold in the sixties with 'the myth of the magnificent French resistance [which] turns out to have been rather punier than we imagined'.[1] The deification of an 'authentic' sixties risks a loss of intellectual scepticism; the idea that any facet of the decade's culture could be 'puny' or anodyne is anathema to those who lived 'at the barricades', and for whom the decade sustains its glories and glamour regardless of failures, as Gitlin's *Letters to a Young Activist* (2003) explores. A reason to return to the decade as an ideological touchstone is to reclaim the sense of social agency in civil rights and student politics, literature and art, comedy and music. In the historical moment in which individuals came to voice and the cultural was celebrated as experiential, the importance of the individual began to be worn away in the poststructuralist move toward decentring the subject. The problem of how to recall and reproduce the urgency with which contemporary issues resonated exercises those of us who return to the era to plumb its images.

It is especially difficult when the dominant popular representation of the civil rights era has been as an integrationist success story; movies and fictions function in self-congratulatory, wish-fulfilling ways involving the amelioration of racism and white-on-black violence. Even the most incisive of 1960s directors have been co-opted to this trend. John Frankenheimer made *The Manchurian Candidate* (1962) and *Seven Days in May* (1964) as pointed critiques. When he adapted Marshall Frady's biography of George Wallace in 1997, his black aide was elevated to a central character against which the audience might measure Wallace's shifting stance on race. Wallace did have two black attendants who cared for the invalid in his last years and Eddie Holcey, at Wallace's behest in 1979, pushed him down the aisle of Dexter Avenue Baptist Church so that he could apologise for his racial misdeeds to the congregation sitting in Dr King's former church: 'I have learned what suffering means in a way that was impossible before I was shot. I think I can understand something of the pain that black people have had to endure. I know that I contributed to that pain. I can only ask you all for forgiveness'.[2] His confession was followed by the singing of 'Amazing Grace' and expressions of compassion. It is this scene that closes Frady's study of the Alabama congressman who had come as close to fascism as his populism would allow by King's death in 1968. And it is this scene that is recalled in the documentary *Four Little Girls* (1997) when Wallace embarrasses Holcey by presenting him to director Spike Lee as his 'best friend'. African American characters are often messianic and morally reliable guides but while the black character is redeemer of the white, the white is usually foregrounded.[3]

The nation's turn toward confession accelerated in the 1990s, as personified by President Clinton, and has been criticised by public intellectual Patricia Williams and lampooned by comedian Dennis Leary. The 'cult of apology' is satirised in Adam Mansbach's novel *Angry Black White Boy* (2005). Macon Detournay grows up in Boston which saw some of the most violent racial clashes over bussing, the controversial method of ensuring the racial integration of schools. In 1998 a student at Columbia University in New York, incensed by the acquittal of police indicted for beating Rodney King and inspired by hip-hop, Macon starts a riot by burning a police car, the first in a series of criminal acts he believes will avenge the African Americans he idolises and fetishises. He becomes a notorious media anti-hero in a parody of 1960s-styled performances of dissent – a persona he fails to understand or transform except into robberies and hold-ups and a futile attempt to cast off his whiteness by 'crossing over' into blackness. When he organises a 'Day of Apology' for whites to make amends for the nation's racial sins, it descends into chaos.

Writing in 1988, intellectual historian Barbara Melosh feared a 'sanitized version' of civil rights had entered 'the canon of consensus history' and bemoaned novelists' silence on this issue, silence she feared resulted from a 'modernist and postmodernist divorce between fiction and history'.[4] While political agency is made more ambivalent in postmodern terms, the shibboleth of fluidity can be undone by texts which encode racist violence and conflict in the continuous present tense, like Mansbach's novel. Julius Lester's *And All Our Wounds Forgiven* (1994) and Anthony Grooms' *Bombingham* (2001) convey post-civil rights conflict and despair. Historian Vincent Harding has noted the 'bleeding ulcers, nervous breakdowns, mysterious ailments [that] took their toll on young lives' and former activists working for voter registration in the South, such as Lester's Robert Card and Alice Walker's Meridian, suffer debilitating versions of post-traumatic stress syndrome. Grooms' Vietnam combatant Walter in *Bombingham* suffers a deep psychological and physical toll that was rarely represented at the time. Junius Edwards' *If We Must Die* (1963) and John A. Williams' *Captain Blackman* (1972) are exceptions that prove the rule. Lester plumbs the depths of post-civil rights pain via Robert Card when he is abused in jail by a white sheriff who runs his knife over Card's penis until he is aroused against his will and forces two black men to perform oral sex on him. Death would make Card a martyr and the sheriff knows how to shake his faith in self and survival without risking such distinction. Later, Card acknowledges, 'I cannot think of anyone in this century who lived in constant relationship to death like those of us who sought to make America whole and broke ourselves into pieces instead'.[5] Novelists who write beyond the historical 'ending' of the decade enter discursive terrain in which characters are emotionally disabled precisely because of the continuity they feel with the 1960s.

The Persistence of History

The history of new social movements is so recent that personal re-enactments and commemorations are legion, reinforced as mythology as well as history. In 2000, President Clinton, Coretta Scott King and civil rights leaders retraced the Selma to Montgomery March that turned into 'Bloody Sunday' on 7 March 1965, when George Wallace's state troopers and Sheriff Jim Clark's deputies beat marchers. They marked the 35th anniversary on Edmund Pettus Bridge, a solid signifier of Movement past in popular memory. However, five years later veterans who had marched every year were beginning to get worried: 'Older folks keep marching but the younger people aren't getting into it'.[6] Whether the sacrifices of older generations will continue to be commemorated is a persistent worry and a vexing question that relates to *how* the violence of the era should be remembered.

Journalist Adam Nossiter covering the 1994 trial of Byron De La Beckwith for murdering Medgar Evers in 1963 felt that 'the courtroom seesawed disorientingly, from that early 1960s world to 1994 and back again, over and over'. The age of the case was visually striking as elderly witnesses, young in 1964, repeated their testimony. A photographer described the trial as 'better than anything that anyone could conjure up on television or even on the Court Channel because it was history'.[7] The spatio-temporal distance between 1963–4 and the 1990s is collapsed again in the 1996 movie *Ghosts of Mississippi* (released in Europe as *Ghosts of the Past*): the mimetic pull of the narrative celebrates closure on thirty years' struggle for justice. Racist murders make pressing demands on collective memory and on the nation's capacity to withstand the violent history that haunts race relations. In *Ghosts of Mississippi*, a character asks, 'When are these fellows gonna get it through their heads that the 1960s are over?' but is met with silence. Whether the emphasis is deferred justice – *Never Too Late* (to do the right thing) is the title of Mississippi prosecutor Bobby DeLaughter's 2001 memoir of the trial – or on failure to find closure, the 'long' 1960s is a touchstone in memory studies.

In George Bush's inaugural address of 1989 he declared: 'The final lesson of Vietnam is that no great nation can long afford to be sundered by a memory.' Alison Lurie's *The War Between the Tates* (1974) is set in 1969–70 and its final line – 'Mommy, will the war end now?' – resonates with the knowledge that the war would not 'end' for four more years and that its effects continue, while Tim O'Brien's novel *In the Lake of the Woods* (1994) exposes the My Lai massacre as much harder to put to rest or suppress than Bush's statement might suppose. 'Bringing the war home' was the summative anti-war slogan; it signified the importance of disrupting American culture at the levels of government, politics, business and media. Michael Herr's *Dispatches* (1977), for example, closes with the mantra, 'Vietnam, Vietnam, Vietnam. We've all been there', to acknowledge the prosthetic memory of those who were never there but for whom the place, made synonymous with war in American cultural production, forms part of the consciousness of the nation.

What they did in or about Vietnam is a marker in the campaign biography of each Presidential candidate in its aftermath. This was pronounced in 2004, as satirised by Christopher Buckley: 'Neither candidate shall mention the word "Vietnam". In the event that either candidate utters said word in the course of a debate, the debate shall be concluded immediately and declared forfeit to the third-party candidate'.[8] George W. Bush was recipient of five deferments of his draft notice between 1963 and 1967 which allowed him to serve in the Texas National Guard. In Mort Sahl's blistering stand-up in 2004, the question 'What did *you* do in the war, daddy?' related to the war in Iraq and Bush's answer was deemed to be 'I started it'.[9] Former US Navy Lieutenant in Vietnam and a Vietnam Veteran Against the War, Senator John Kerry's campaign for Democratic nomination hinged on those two biographical facts and endeared him to his generation whether they fought or protested. His navy career recalled Kennedy's and his critique of Vietnam was the basis for a parallel critique of incumbent Bush's foreign policies. Joe Klein went so far as to argue in the documentary *Going Upriver: The Long War of John Kerry* (2004) that Kerry brought the Vietnam War to its real end because, thanks to his careful approach to the PoW-MIA hearings of the 1990s, he and his senate committee reported it was highly unlikely that any men missing in action remained prisoners. This pronouncement allowed Clinton to finally drop the trade embargo and resume diplomatic relations with Vietnam in 1994. However, Kerry failed to win out against Bush and a factor in that defeat was the creation of the group Swiftboat Veterans for Truth which tried to cast aspersions on Kerry's war record, securing Bush a comfortable margin over his opponent for the first time since Kerry had won the nomination. The shadow of Vietnam continues to fall over American politics.

Paul Connerton allows that how societies remember is inextricable from what they are encouraged or instructed to remember. Susan Sontag argued that collective memory could not exist but that ideologically substantiated discourse dictates precisely how a society should feel about its past. Collective memory is a mesh that connects people via institutions, traditions and conventions but there is also evidence of a powerfully personal imperative to connect individual and family history to the public sphere in the form of events and 'official' histories. Joseph Lelyveld subtitles his sixties memoir *Omaha Blues* (2005) 'A Memory Loop' and tries to distinguish 'a particular circuit of memories that I feel driven to retrace and connect, where possible, to something like an objective record or the memories of someone else, in hopes of glimpsing what was once real'.[10] Todd Gitlin opens his history of SDS with, 'I was not living in history, but in biography'.[11] Coming of age in the era involved an apocalyptic sense of doom, of waiting for 'the summer rain' made iconic in The Doors' mournful 'The End'. The omnipresent threat of nuclear disaster was drilled into schoolchildren alerted to take cover under their desks. As a child James Carroll likened himself to 'mad mascot' Alfred E. Neuman whose ironic slogan was 'What, me worry?' and Secretary of State Condoleezza Rice who was eight when Sixteenth

Figure C.1 The Doughboy Statue, Overton Park, Memphis, 10 July 1967, *Memphis Commercial Appeal*. Photographer unspecified. Mississippi Valley Collection.

Street Church was bombed allows: 'I remember more than anything, the coffins . . . The small coffins. And the sense that Birmingham wasn't a very safe place'.[12] The omnipresence of death and violence characterises sixties memoir. Jack Hoffman, brother of Abbie, drafted into the army in 1961, remembers that travelling to South East Asia as an army medic 'sounded attractive' until 'the hard heaviness of those body bags, unyielding of meaning, was my introduction to the Vietnam War'.[13]

In James Conaway's memoir *Memphis Afternoons* (1993), he recalls ordering peyote by mail, boiling the cacti into a nauseating green liquid and lying in Memphis's Overton Park waiting for something to happen but 'when the landscape turned sinister, where I most wanted to be was home'. At home is his father who, having opened his son's mail, wants to know the meaning of 'this peyote business'; while the father wants to ensure the son will not persist with drugs, the son is concerned his privacy has been violated. Their exchange is limited: 'We never discussed the peyote or the opened letter, just as we never discussed anything important that held the promise of conflict, as most things did by now, from integration to the draft'. Importantly, what remains unexpressed is the cultural shift from 'the last, lingering moment of the Adult in America, the monarch whose omnipotence comes by virtue of age and masculinity and not much else, a false entitlement shared by Dad's entire generation that would be swept away in an angry social tide I can't claim to have foreseen or taken a significant role in'.[14] What is especially revealing about Conaway's memoir is his refusal to place his youthful self at the centre of the era, as in so many memory texts by Boomers. Instead, he allows that he and his friends were insecure and apprehensive of 'the opportunities and dangers inherent in the next social order'. Dividing the generations risks losing the complexities Conaway admits into his memoir: '[T]he perspectives that made us contemptuous of the contradictions in our fathers' world would also make us suspicious of the revolutionary certitudes and pieties of the new age. We were in a sense the nowhere generation'.[15]

Conaway's southern geography contributes to his sense of not being at the centre of things yet the South of the 1960s is scrutinised time and again in ensuing decades for its symbolism as the nation's hope for racial peace. Many southern writers – farmer and environmentalist Wendell Berry (*The Hidden Wound*), novelist Ellen Douglas (*Truth: Four Stories I Am Old Enough To Tell*) and historian Tim Tyson (*Blood Done Sign My Name*) – have focused on memory as a moral resource. Tony Kushner, who grew up in Lake Charles, Louisiana returned home with the Broadway musical *Caroline, or Change* (2004), in which he conveyed how 'incredibly tiny things become metaphoric for enormous things'. When black maid Caroline (Tonya Pinkins) is instructed to keep any change her white charge Noah leaves in his pockets to teach him the value of money, a small lesson escalates into a culture clash amidst the racial wars of 1963.

Kushner has said: 'I'm interested in moments in history where a lot seems to be changing and people are either struggling to not change with the times or struggling to change'.[16]

Finding regions or cities culpable of the events that occurred in them was a media pastime in the 1960s. Chicago journalist Mike Royko, for example, made San Francisco guilty of failing to quash the hippie movement. When hippies requested a permit to demonstrate in 1968, he was ironic: permission should be granted so Chicago might teach them the lesson that San Francisco had failed to teach because Chicago is 'not as easily capitulated by fads, excited by goofs, or shocked.'[17] Chicago had its own image problems, however, not least because of high-profile violence, like that which followed Dr King's symbolic reiteration of Martin Luther when he nailed his measures for improvement in the city's race relations to the door of Chicago's City Hall, or the clashes with police that accompanied the 1968 Democratic Convention. Prior to the Convention, plywood walls were erected so that delegates staying in hotels on the Loop would not see Chicago's slums on their way to the Convention centre.[18]

The southern city provides a revealing case study of the effort it can take to change with the times. Southern cities and states were made symbolic of the national failure of liberal democracy. Inevitably, Dallas was judged and found wanting after President Kennedy's assassination: 'Dallas had claimed the ignominious reputation as a city of fanatics' and 'its name might never recover from this double infamy'.[19] A Life exposé dubbed Dallas 'smug' for dismissing the murder as a communist plot. Reporters pointed to the city's glittering skyscrapers 'shadowing ramshackle Negro homes' and 'signs of shame' such as a billboard urging 'Save our Republic' defaced by salacious graffiti and a sign urging the government to 'Impeach Earl Warren'.[20] After Dr King's murder, Memphis raised around $4 million to sell itself to a disapproving world with Mayor Loeb, whose intransigence in the face of black sanitation workers had brought King to the city, travelling to New York to lure business to Memphis. However, when a commissioned study of the city's social and economic health suggested its problems were 'old and intractable, related to a legacy of political bossism and resistance to change', the report was suppressed 'by tacit agreement among Chamber of Commerce members, politicians and the press'.[21] Much later, in 1991, the National Civil Rights Museum was conceived as a project to conserve the Lorraine Motel and to turn a site renowned only for the murder committed there into an institute for commemoration and social

change. Birmingham would follow suit enshrining and changing
Kelly Ingram Park.

But for Birmingham . . .

The Rev. Fred L. Shuttlesworth, Birmingham's longest-serving and
most assiduous fighter for civil rights, recalled that while Kennedy was
a gradualist in terms of legislation, it was Birmingham that turned the
tide for the President: 'But for Birmingham, we would not be here
today'. The phrase summarised the extent to which Alabama's most
industrial city has been the epicentre of efforts to measure the impact
of protests to secure racial justice and federal legislation. In 1961 CBS
made a television documentary *Who Speaks for Birmingham?* and
Lyndon Johnson selected the city as the target for federal enforcement
of the Voting Rights Act in 1965; in 1969 Operation New Birmingham
succeeded in bringing together civic and industry power elites in an
effort to remake the city renowned for police brutality; and in 1990,
tragically, the city 'set new records for violent deaths'.[22] Images of
Birmingham have been dominated by violence. In 2004 Warhol's
'Mustard Race Riot', inspired by *Life* magazine photographs of the
attacks on children in Kelly Ingram Park, achieved a record sum. Today,
the city is a renowned medical research centre, its Downtown dominated by University of Alabama at Birmingham; it is a banking hub and
headquarters for at least two Fortune 500 companies. In 2002 the
legend 'Heart of Dixie' that had been a fixture on the state's car licence
plates since the early 1950s was replaced by 'Stars Fell on Alabama', a
telling shift from Confederate pride to a romantic reference to an 1833
meteor shower and the popular jazz song. In 2006, Birmingham was
renamed 'The Diverse City', its traditional 'Magic City' having been
dismissed as too generic. A series of advertisements emphasise cultural
attractions including world-class entertainment, conference facilities,
fine dining – and civil rights history: 'Remember the courage of the past
to appreciate the triumphs of today in Birmingham's Civil Rights
District'.[23] In 1963, however, 'culture' had retreated, as one resident
bemoaned in *Look* magazine: 'the city has a civic symphony, civic-
theater groups, an art museum, a botanical garden and a zoo. But the
Broadway road shows are not coming to Birmingham. And our Music
Club season almost failed this year because of ticket cancellations.
Many people in Birmingham are afraid to go out after dark'.[24]

Birmingham was the largest segregated city in the US in the 1960s
and it functioned as a barometer for the racial health or sickness of the

nation. In 1963 the city was even declared 'dead'. Eulogies were typified by lawyer and resident Charles Morgan Jr's plea for a national
effort to help resuscitate the city: 'the community's life has been
snuffed out by fear and violence. What has happened here is a timely
warning of what can happen anywhere if men and women who say
they believe in American ideals – the good people – will not stand up
for their convictions ... In Birmingham, fear and cowardice have
in effect suspended the First Amendment'.[25] In the mid-1960s,
Birmingham was the nation's racial crucible from which Dr King
would write his 'Letter from Birmingham Jail'. Violence against
Freedom Riders in 1961 had already ensured that Birmingham hit the
headlines and in January 1963 SCLC launched 'Project C' for
Confrontation in the city King described as having the ugliest record
of brutality in the South, hoping for a notable civil rights victory after
the strategic indecision of the Albany campaign.

In 1963 it was the black children of Birmingham who forced
President Kennedy to act in the name of civil rights and Birmingham
city officials to finally agree to desegregation policies that had already
been before the council. Almost a thousand black children were jailed,
some as young as five or six, in the city's fairgrounds because the jails
were full. The children were moral witnesses apparently fearless in the
face of Eugene 'Bull' Connor, ironically Chief Commissioner for
Public Safety, who in that role allowed his men to unleash police dogs
and fire water cannons on the children demonstrating in Kelly Ingram
Park. The Birmingham campaign harnessed the media as no other campaign; photographs and footage of children lashed by water were dramatic and the national media mistakenly recorded a much larger group
of protesters than had actually marched.

Controversy over an iconic picture reflects contradictions in
the media's representation of Birmingham's complex racial history.
Fifteen-year-old Walter Gadsen, captured (see Figure C.2) by the
camera Bill Hudson hid in his jacket, denied in interview with *Jet* magazine that he had been involved in the demonstration. He was, he said,
an observer caught up in history when he crossed the street. He was
also a member of a black middle-class family who disagreed with the
form the protests took. Officer Dick Middleton, it has since been
argued, was actually trying to control the German Shepherd snapping
at the boy's torso. Birmingham journalist Diane McWhorter used the
image to argue in 2001 that the 'Big Truth' about segregation was never
black and white, though neither participant wished to add his thoughts
to her study.[26] However, interviewed for a British documentary in

Figure C.2 Birmingham Protest, Walter Gadsen and police dog. Photograph by Bill Hudson, 3 May 1963. AP Photos. Courtesy PA Photos.

1988 Gadsen had stated, 'I'm glad I went to the park that day because Hudson was lucky enough to catch me with his camera' and the two shook hands for the television cameras.[27] Whatever the story behind this photograph may be, despite reluctance on President Kennedy's part to intervene, and despite criticism of putting children on the movement's front lines, such images are memorable. As historians David Garrow and Peter Ling point out, the press was ready to leave Birmingham when it was decided that the 'Children's Crusade' should go ahead and, although King vacillated over the safety of allowing children to become involved, they were willing to act. Lifted into the air by the force of water cannons, bitten, bruised and jailed, the sight of American police assaulting schoolchildren was the image of brutal resistance the movement needed. The images were a turning point; they recalled Sharpeville, the 1960 anti-apartheid demonstration in South Africa when police killed sixty-nine, and they lent something of the same moral strength to the Birmingham campaign.

Remembering Birmingham in 1963 or Memphis in 1968 is to return to segregationist intransigence and in Birmingham's case to the Klan

violence that made the city a citadel of race hatred known as
'Bombingham'. Despite the success of the May demonstrations,
Sixteenth Street Baptist church was bombed on Sunday, 15 September
1963. It was the fourth bombing in a month and one of more than
twenty over the previous eight years, including one that destroyed
Rev. Fred Shuttlesworth's home. It had been preceded by the first
urban breakdown of social order in the 1960s, on 10 May 1963. When
A. G. Gaston's motel and Dr King's brother's home were bombed following a Klan rally, the city exploded too. The murder of Denise
McNair, Cynthia Wesley, Carole Robertson, and Addie Mae Collins
was the final offence in a series of Klan retaliations to the success of the
Birmingham campaign. The city's efforts to do the right thing by prosecuting the bombers were blocked when FBI's J. Edgar Hoover, no
supporter of civil rights, officially closed the investigation in 1968,
despite having the names of four men strongly believed to have been
involved. The dogged determination of Bill Baxley who pursued the
case on coming to office as Alabama Attorney General in 1971 was
crucial in ensuring it was re-opened. Slowly over subsequent decades
the city would rebuild its image by facing its past and prosecuting the
bombers. Bill Hudson's picture of Walter Gadsen epitomises the city's
overarching project to address violence as an image which has haunted
Birmingham as well as a factor of its civil rights history. It is reproduced as one of the bronze statues that forms part of James Drake's
installation of a 'Freedom Walk' through Kelly Ingram Park. The
inscription reads: ' "This sculpture is dedicated to the foot soldiers of
the Birmingham Civil Rights Movement. With gallantry, courage and
great bravery, they faced the violence of attack dogs, high powered
water hoses and bombings. They were the fodder in the advance
against injustice, warriors of a just cause. They represent humanity
unshaken in their firm belief in their nation's commitment to liberty
and justice for all. We salute these men and women who were the soldiers of the great cause" Richard Arrington Jr, Mayor of Birmingham,
May 1993'.

     In 2001 Diane McWhorter returned to memories of her childhood
in a panoramic account of Birmingham's white elite which follows
many 'returns' in various cultural forms, such as sportswriter Paul
Hemphill who in *Leaving Birmingham* (1993) recalls his blue-collar
childhood and tries to understand the climate in which racial violence
could receive public approbation. Birmingham is the setting for Vicki
Covington's novel *The Last Hotel for Women* (1996), its backdrop the
violence against Freedom Riders in 1961, and for Sena Jeter Naslund's

Figure C.3 James Drake's memorial sculpture. © Sharon Monteith.

Four Spirits (2003) in which white and black characters are focalisers through which the events of May 1963 are channelled. *Any Day Now*, a popular success on cable television's Lifetime channel, shuttled back and forth from the early 1960s to its present of 1998, an interracial friendship its focus, but of all the cultural productions that return to Birmingham, Tony Grooms' *Bombingham* is the most aesthetically interesting; it is as critically diagnostic as McWhorter's cultural history. The visceral hatred captured graphically in Charles Moore's and Bill Hudson's photographs is held back to a slow burn in this meditative novel in which a black child comes of age in Titusville where Condoleezza Rice grew up, and in Vietnam. *Bombingham* is set against a background of domestic racial terrorism and war: Birmingham in 1963 and Vietnam in the 1970s are both war zones. Walter Burke's name may be a composite of Walter Gadsen and Burke Marshall, Assistant Attorney General for civil rights and the White House's representative who was almost permanently stationed in Birmingham during 1963.

Interracial tension is palpable in Grooms' novel; rather than enu-merating what King in 'Letter from Birmingham Jail' called the 'sting-ing darts of segregation', its focus is spiralling violence. When Walter's friend Haywood dies beside him in Vietnam, the trauma triggers his memory of losing his best friend in a racist killing on 15 September 1963. In this way, Grooms commemorates the boy generally referred to as one of 'two other black children' shot on the same day as the church bombing. Grooms' Lamar Burrell is a fictional version of Virgil Lamar Ware, described in the African American-owned *Birmingham World* as a seventh-grader and 'a very quiet and Christian little boy', shot by two sixteen-year-old white boys discovered to be 'Eagle Scouts' as he rode on a bicycle.[28] Richard Rorty has argued that nov-elists are primarily 'redescriptors' of the past, but while Grooms rep-resents social breakdown by funnelling it through the story of a family breaking apart, he refuses to dilute the terror by emphasising the indi-vidual at the expense of broader historical forces: family gatherings always return to stories of lynchings and bombings. Grooms ensures that imagined characters and historical figures originate out of the same unruly and violent conditions. The subject is decentred to pre-cise effect. Walter is made permeable, seeing his sister, Lamar and Haywood as extensions of himself, and Birmingham 1963 remains a current event in this 2001 novel. Walter Benjamin argued that history can only break down images, not stories, but *Bombingham* is a repre-sentational struggle in which Grooms integrates images of Vietnam

with civil rights iconography with a striking a sense of contemporane-
ity that the US and UK's war in Iraq has only served to reinforce.
Bombingham's publication in 2001 also coincided with the conviction
of a former Klansman for the bombing of the Sixteenth Street Baptist
Church thirty-eight years previously.[29]

There is a contemporary obsession with claiming connection to
memories 'we' do not have. It is an obsession that Walter Benn
Michaels has argued is peculiarly American and animates memory
studies in their focus on 'prosthetic' memories.[30] The claim that 'I was
there' in the vanguard, participating in events that are legendary, is a
natural phenomenon. The National Voting Rights Museum in Selma,
Alabama, for example, includes a wall with the slogan 'We Were There'
followed by messages and memories written by marchers. However,
the same tendency adds a disturbing footnote to this case study of
Birmingham. A federal district judge James Ware repeatedly claimed
that Virgil Ware was his brother and that he was riding the bicycle
across Birmingham when Virgil, perched on the handlebars, was shot
dead. In fact, Virgil Ware's brother James still lived in Birmingham
when the fabrication came to light and is quoted as saying: 'I am
hopeful my brother's memory and place in history has not been
harmed by the discovery of these unfortunate events'.[31] False memories or memories of events in which a participant embellishes their role
can appear in many forms and have begun to be explored in popular
cultural productions as well as by psychologists. In an episode of television series *The Education of Max Bickford* entitled 'Revisionism'
(2001), an African American professor represents herself in speaking
engagements as a former Freedom Rider threatened in Birmingham
who protested alongside Dr King. Her 'memories' are proved false and
the kudos she has earned is dissipated by her calculated betrayal of the
past. Bickford (Richard Dreyfuss) asks whether it matters very much
if she inspires students to think about the past since the events she
described did happen. His African American university principal
(Regina Taylor) quickly educates him: 'People died. You can't take
ownership of that. It disrespects their memory'.[32]

From the Boomers to the Y Generation: 'Won't Get Fooled Again'

When Bill Clinton entered the White House, Toni Morrison praised
him as America's first 'black' President, 'blacker than any actual black
person who could ever be elected in our children's lifetime', and when

the scandal over his association with Monica Lewinsky threatened to engulf him, she named it 'Slaughtergate'.[33] Morrison's rhetoric is undergirded by sixties cultural values; Clinton had usurped power and then signally failed to assimilate. She closes her editorial with an activist flourish: she will march to Washington DC to prevent the collapse of the Constitution. With hindsight, Eric Lott has argued that with Clinton's election 'a generational legacy had at last to be confronted'.[34] The image of the 1960s has been safeguarded by around 75 million baby boomers, guardians of their youth who across the culture industries retell their coming-of-age stories and reinvest in the era. Even satirising their self-centredness and newfound well-being is frequently the province of a boomer, as in Tom Wolfe's description of 'The Me Decade' and P. J. O'Rourke's knowing irony: 'We changed the world. Life has never been the same since that "youthquake" of forty years ago ... We got married, had families, straightened out, got married again, had more families, straightened out (really). There can be no greater sacrifice than that a man lay down his lifestyle for others'.[35] While 'civil rights' often invokes a soft-focus return, the 'boomer' is a source of wry humour and knowing critique. The boomer character is complacent and/or conflicted, developing into the cut-throat corporate raider (Gordon Gecko in *Wall Street*, 1987) or flailing around as an old hippie ('The Dude' in *The Big Lebowski*, 1998). He or she is often an educator whose 'radical' sympathies the students find outmoded. In Jonathan Franzen's novel *The Corrections* (2001), for example, Chip Lambert is a conflicted university professor who gives up his radical critique of late capitalist American society: 'Criticizing a sick culture, even if the criticism accomplished nothing, had always felt like useful work. But if the supposed sickness wasn't a sickness at all . . .'[36] Like Grooms' *Bombingham*, Franzen's exploration of American culture places a family at the centre but the sickness it explores derives not a little from sixties ideas of youth as concept rather than chronology.

In 1961 at a Whitehouse conference on ageing, President Kennedy declared that adding years to the lifespan as a result of science and medicine was indeed progress, but 'our objective must be to add new life to those years'. Steve Lohr remembers Kennedy's words as he recalls progressive images of retirees in Sun City: 'The world's First Active Retirement Community' for people aged '55 and better' was built outside Phoenix, Arizona in 1960 and registers the shift whereby the freedom not to work in the retirement 'golden years' first began to be sold as a lifestyle.[37] In Christopher Buckley's *Boomsday* (2007), boomers have taken Kennedy at his word. The 'value' that boomers who put off retirement have 'added' to their twilight years is corporate corruption and the retirees toast government insolvency as they career around the golf course. *Boomsday* recalls Kurt Vonnegut's short story 'Welcome to the Monkey House' (1968) with its Federal Ethical Suicide project but is also a satirical response to topical fears about the pension payout that boomers expect and that the nation cannot easily afford. In *Boomsday*, 1960s youth has run up such social security debts that America's twenty-first-century youth led by twenty-nine-year-old blogger Cassandra Devine threatens to enforce euthanasia: a 'Natural Transitioning' whereby the 30 per cent hike in taxes for under-35s, designed to pay for retired boomers and to subsidise their longevity, will be offset by their promise to self-destruct. Cassandra breaks open a boomer monopoly on social protest: 'We aren't going to get Congress to act responsibly, to stop piling up endless debt and entitlements and passing it all on to the next generation, without a little dancin' in the street'.[38] She urges members of the beleaguered Y generation to storm the gates of retirement communities like Sun City, and to campaign against the 'Ungreatest Generation' who 'dodged the draft, snorted cocaine, made self-indulgence a virtue'.[39] She makes the cover of *Time* and – like many boomers before her – is declared the 'voice of her generation'. The youngest commissioner of Social Security in US history by the end of the novel, Cassandra prophesier of catastrophe is still trying to avert this one.

Buckley's provocative novel taps into a 1960s sub-genre that included The Doors' 'Five To One' (1968) and movies such as *Wild in the Streets* (1968) and *Gas-s-s-s* (1970), discussed in Chapter 2. It engages with an idea that conservative critic Stephen Carter advanced at the height of the culture wars, when he argued that 'most Americans despise the sixties' and that while die-hard liberals fail to apprehend this, most voters 'are tired of being blamed for everything that is wrong'.[40] However, representative sixties figures discussed in these pages have not just faded away. While the margins are seen as symbolically central across much of this study, those who occupied them in the 1960s often entered the mainstream by the end of the twentieth century – the mainstream, in turn, filling up with cultural commentators for whom dissent was a patriotic norm. Amiri Baraka, discussed in Chapter 1, is a case in point. He became the recipient of a Pen/Faulkner Award and was elected to the American Academy of Arts and Letters. Baraka's journey was a typical trajectory from radical margins to cultural centre. However, in 2002 he was castigated by the governor of New Jersey who demanded his resignation as the state's 'poet laureate' for writing the poem 'Somebody Blew up America' after the 11 September 2001 attacks. Baraka was back in the news, so much so that one commentator compared Governor McGreevey vs Baraka with Senator Joe McCarthy railing against Lenny Bruce for 'opening the door for unbridled debate on society's dark secrets'.[41]

Writers who made their names through the cult texts of the 1960s have reacted as strongly as any other boomers to the sixties re-creation in subsequent decades. In *Hocus Pocus* (1990), Kurt Vonnegut's narrator, a Vietnam veteran, named Eugene Debs Hartke after the socialist politician, is a prison guard who masterminds a prison rebellion because in late middle age in a millennial 2001 he feels 'cut loose in a thoroughly looted, bankrupt nation'. The racially segregated prison where predominantly black prisoners are served a diet of *I Love Lucy* is a quotidian reminder of social failure. The novel is an exegesis of the balancing act involved in honouring the past while using it as a psychodramatic prop through which to garner hope in the present and faith in the future.

Looking back in fiction or commentary has provoked some critical reviews of the sixties as it has impacted on subsequent decades. In 1989, Marxist Alex Callincos probed the heart of declension insofar as it relates to the perceived failure of the white middle-class members of the radical counterculture to change the world. He is relentless in his excoriation of radicals who 'settled', for whom nostalgic returns to the past stand in for lost political energy:

> What could be more reassuring for a generation drawn towards and then away from Marxism by the political ups and downs of the past . . . than to be told . . . there is nothing they can do to change the world. 'Resistance' is reduced to the knowing consumption of cultural products – perhaps the 'postmodern' works of art whose authors have sought to embody in them this kind of thinking, but if not, any old soap opera will do just as well.[42]

While in *The Making of the Counterculture* (1969) Theodore Roszak could predict that 'Technocracy's Children' were 'giving shape to something that looks like the saving vision our endangered civilization requires',[43] the radical factions that broke away were later seen as traducers of 'the sixties' as ennobled by commemorators of Kennedy and King and as recalled as enterprising rather than antinomian. In 1971 Ihab Hassan defining the 'postmodern turn' in American culture equated antinomianism, apocalypticism and annihilation with the counterculture and Eric Hobsbawm would assert in *The Age of Extremes* (1993) that the fusion of the demotic and the antinomian was the distinguishing feature of those changes, as captured in the title of Nicholas von Hoffman's *We Are the People Our Parents Warned Us Against* (1968).[44] In Philip Roth's ironically titled *American Pastoral* (1997), for example, Seymour 'Swede' Levov, a self-congratulatory product of postwar liberalism, imagines himself a version of Johnny Appleseed in his home in Arcady Hill Road. He chooses not to think about the fact that crosses were burned and swastikas daubed on the walls of his suburban haven in the recent past, or that daughter Merry Levov is beginning to symbolise the social evils he has kept at bay. But his daughter becomes 'the Rimrock bomber' and her bomb kills a man.

Over the last ten years, the number of such protagonists has risen to constitute a sub-genre. The activist who uses violence in dissent, a minor character in Joan Didion's *Play As It Lays* (1970) becomes major in E. L. Doctorow's *The Book of Daniel* (1971) and as the protagonist of Marge Piercy's *Vida* (1980) and has been re-envisioned in recent fiction as Roth's Merry, Russell Banks' Hannah in *The Darling* (2004) and Sigrid Nunez's Ann in *The Last of Her Kind* (2006), to name only a few examples of an evolving genre. The protagonists of recent representation are disaffected white, privileged sons and daughters of affluent parents who cast off their families to participate in the 'Days of Rage' of 1969; they attempt to 'bring the war home' via bombings and kidnappings; they are members of the Weathermen or the SLA; as they age, they live in prison or underground because the FBI continues to list them as its 'most wanted'. The ageing protagonists of recent fiction evince a sense of futility; broken upon the rocks of their own frustrations, to borrow Morris Dickstein's metaphor in *Leopards in the Temple*, but they hardly ever 'settle'. Sometimes the failings of the sixties that could not be resolved in life are 'resolved' in these socially symbolic fictions; sometimes the protagonists slide into regret and self-hatred; always they survive to tell a story of the 1960s that is neither self-congratulatory nor ameliorative.

Notes

Introduction

1. C. Van Woodward, *The Strange Career of Jim Crow* (New York: Oxford, 1966), pp. xii–xiii.
2. Manning Marable, *Beyond Black and White: Transforming African American Politics* (New York: Verso, 1995), p. 207; David Garrow, *Bearing the Cross: Martin Luther King Jr and the Southern Christian Leadership Conference* (New York: Harper, 1999), p. 310.
3. Jerry Wexler, quoted in Peter Guralnick, *Sweet Soul Music* (Edinburgh: Canongate, 2002), p. 18.
4. David Denby makes a similar point in 'The Moviegoer', *The New Yorker*, 12 September 2005, p. 92.
5. C. Van Woodward, *American Counterpoint: Slavery and Racism in the North-South Dialogue* (Boston, MA: Little, Brown, 1971), pp. 4–8
6. Ellen Douglas, *Black Cloud, White Cloud* (Jackson: University Press of Mississippi, 1989), p. 230.
7. Slavoj Žižek, *The Fragile Absolute* (New York: Verso, 2000), p. 3.
8. W. James Booth, *Communities of Memory: On Witness, Identity, and Justice* (Ithaca, NY: Cornell University Press, 2006), p. 23.
9. Joseph Roach, *Cities of the Dead: Circum-Atlantic Performance* (New York: Columbia University Press, 1996), p. xi.
10. Dick Hebdige, *Subculture: The Meaning of Style* (London: Routledge, 1981), p. 91.
11. Russell Baker, quoted in Richard Corliss, 'The Seventies', *Film Comment* (January–February 1980) p. 34.
12. Robert Reinhold, 'Changes Wrought by 60s Youth Linger in American Life', *New York Times*, 12 August 1979.
13. Raymond Williams, 'Culture is Ordinary', *Resources of Hope* (London: Verso, 1989), p. 4.
14. Clifford Geertz, 'Thick Description: Toward an Interpretative Theory of Culture', *The Interpretation of Cultures* (New York: Basic Books, 1973), p. 16
15. Raymond Williams, 'Base and superstructure in Marxist cultural theory', *New Left Review* 82 (1973).
16. Mike Davis, 'Urban Renaissance and the Spirit of Postmodernism', *New Left Review* 151 (1985), pp. 106–13.

17. Oscar Lewis, *Five Families: Mexican Case Studies in the Culture of Poverty* (New York: Basic Books, 1975); 'The Culture of Poverty', *Scientific American* 215 (1966), pp. 19–25.
18. Morris Dickstein, *Leopards in the Temple: The Transformation of American Fiction, 1945–1970* (Cambridge, MA: Harvard University Press, 1999), p. 101; Tom Hayden, *Reunion: A Memoir* (New York: Random House, 1988), p. 6.
19. Richard Gehman, 'That Nine Billion Dollars in Hot Little Hands', *Cosmopolitan*, November 1957, p. 72. Thanks to Alex Hinchliffe for this reference.
20. Martin Luther King Jr, 'Letter from Birmingham Jail', *Why We Can't Wait: Chaos or Community?* (Boston, MA: Beacon, 1968), p. 91.
21. Julius Lester, *Look Out Whitey! Black Power's Gon' Get Your Mama!* (New York: Dial Press, 1968), pp. 106, 104.
22. Anne Moody, *Coming of Age in Mississippi* (New York: Dell, 1968), p. 307
23. George S. Schuyler, 'King: No Help To Peace', *Racing to the Right: Selected Essays of George S. Schuyler* (Knoxville: University of Tennessee Press, 2001), pp. 104–5.
24. King, 'A Time to Break Silence', in Reese Williams (ed.), *Unwinding the Vietnam War* (Seattle, WA: Real Comet Press, 1987), p. 429.
25. King, *Why We Can't Wait*, p. 133.
26. Quoted in Stephen Oates, *Let the Trumpet Sound* (New York: New American Library, 1983), p. 110.
27. Minutes of Administrative Committee, Atlanta, Georgia, 19 October 1961, SCLC Papers 1954–70, Part 2. Records of the Executive Director and Treasurer, Project Co-ordinator Randolph Boehm (Bethesda, MD: University Publications of America, 1995), Reel 4, frames 122–4. Thanks to Peter Ling and Lee Sartain for this reference.
28. Marisa Chappell, Jenny Hutchinson and Brian Ward, ' "Dress modestly, neatly . . . as if you were going to church": Respectability, Class and Gender in the Montgomery Bus Boycott and the Early Civil Rights Movement', in Peter Ling and Sharon Monteith (eds), *Gender and the Civil Rights Movement* (New Brunswick, NJ: Rutgers University Press, 2004), pp. 69–100.
29. John W. Aldridge, 'Celebrity and Boredom', *The Devil in the Fire: Retrospective Essays on American Literature and Culture, 1951–1971* (New York: Harper's Magazine Press, 1972), p. 168.
30. Norman Mailer, *The Spooky Art: Some Thoughts on Writing* (New York: Random House, 2003).
31. Norman Mailer, 'Instinct and Influence', *The Spooky Art*, p. 99.
32. Theodore Roszak, *The Making of a Counter Culture* (London: Faber, 1970), p. 292; Norman Mailer, *The Armies of the Night: History as a Novel, The Novel as History* (London: Weidenfeld and Nicolson, 1968), p. 187.
33. Mailer, *Armies*, p. 98.
34. Ibid., p. 23.
35. Ibid., p. 3.
36. Ibid., p. 48.
37. Natalie Robins, *Alien Ink: The FBI's War on Freedom of Expression* (New Brunswick: Rutgers University Press, 1992), p. 330.
38. Mailer, *Armies*, p. 54.

39. Diana Trilling, *Encounter* (1962); Richard Poirier, *Norman Mailer* (London: Fontana, 1972), p. 98.

40. Text of 20 January 1961 inaugural speech at http://www.historyplace.com/speeches/jfk-inaug.htm

41. Don DeLillo, *Libra* (London: Viking, 1988), p. 181.

42. Theodore H. White, 'For President Kennedy: An Epilogue', *Life*, December 1963, p. 19.

43. Ibid.

44. Senator Lloyd Bentsen famously quashed the presidential ambitions of Dan Quayle with the cutting remark: 'Senator, I knew Jack Kennedy. Jack Kennedy was a friend of mine. Senator, you're no Jack Kennedy'.

45. James Carroll, *An American Requiem: God, My Father, and the War That Came Between Us* (Boston, MA: Houghton Mifflin, 1996), p. 32.

46. As demonstrated in biographies such as Robert Caro's *Means of Ascent* (1990) which argues that he undid all the good work of the Kennedy White House. The myth of Kennedy as a martyr to the cause of civil rights was even beginning to find its way into the black press, 'How JFK Surpassed Abraham Lincoln', *Ebony* 19: 4 (1964), pp. 25–34.

47. Robert Kennedy, 'A Tiny Ripple of Hope' Day of Affirmation Address at the University of Cape Town, 6 June 1966 at http://www.americanrhetoric.com/speeches/rfkcapetown.htm

48. Hunter S. Thompson, 'The Nonstudent Left', *The Nation*, 27 September 1965.

49. Abbie Hoffman, *Soon To Be A Major Motion Picture* (New York: Putnam, 1980), p. 59.

50. Robert McNamara, quoted in Todd Brewster, 'Yes, Mr. President!', *Vanity Fair*, April 2007, p. 109.

51. Mary McCarthy, *Hanoi* (London: Penguin, 1968), p. 43.

52. As quoted in Alan Shepard and Deke Slayton with Jay Barbree and Deke Slayton, *Moon Shot: The Inside Story of America's Race to the Moon* (Atlanta, GA: Turner Publishing, 1994), p. 133.

53. Lynn Spigel, 'White Flight', in Lyn Spigel and Michael Curtin (eds), *The Revolution Wasn't Televised: Sixties Television and Social Conflict* (New York: Routledge, 1997), p. 52.

54. Wallace Stegner, 'Wilderness Letter' 3 December 1960 at http://www.wilderness.org/OurIssues/Wilderness/wildernessletter.cfm

55. Warren French, ' "The Southern": Another Lost Cause', *The South in Film* (Jackson: University Press of Mississippi, 1981), pp. 3–9.

56. Charles Payne, *I've Got the Light of Freedom: The Organizing Tradition and the Mississippi Freedom Struggle* (Berkeley: University of California Press, 1995), p. 144.

57. Richard Slotkin, *Regeneration Through Violence: The Mythology of the American Frontier, 1600–1860* (Middletown, CT: Wesleyan University Press, 1973), p. 8.

58. Ellen Douglas, 'Afterword', *Black Cloud, White Cloud*, p. 230.

59. Fred Hobson, 'Booking Passage: W. J. Cash and a Southern Awakening', *The Silencing of Emily Mullen and Other Essays* (Baton Rouge: Louisiana State University Press, 2005), p. 208.

60. Howard Zinn, *The Southern Mystique* (New York: Simon and Schuster, 1972), pp. 281, 263.

61. The *Time-Life* 'Editors Preface' (1965) to Elizabeth Spencer, *The Voice at the Back Door* (1956) (New York: Time Life, 1965) n.p.; Dick Gregory, *Callus on My Soul* (New York: Kensington, 2000), p. 28.

62. Thomas Pynchon, 'Journey into the Mind of Watts', *New York Times* magazine, 12 June 1966, p. 78.

63. Otto Kermer et al., *Report of the National Advisory Commission on Civil Disorders* (New York: Dutton, 1968), p. 1.

64. Northern black conservative Shelby Steele in 'The Memory of Enemies' (1990) confides that a (white) southern accent is enough to catapult him back past what he fears may be merely 'the public relations bromide of a New South' to his stereotype of the Old: 'I could . . . condemn her and even her region, not because of her racial beliefs, which I didn't know, but because her accent had suddenly made her accountable to *my* voluminous and vivid memory of a racist South', *The Content of Our Character: A New Vision of Race in America* (New York: St. Martin's Press, 1990), p. 150.

65. Sara Evans, *Personal Politics: The Roots of Women's Liberation in the Civil Rights Movement and the New Left* (New York: Vintage, 1980), p. 60.

66. Marable, *Beyond Black and White*, p. 24.

67. Sharon Monteith, 'The Murder of Emmett Till in the Melodramatic Imagination: William Bradford Huie and Vin Packer in the 1950s', in Harriet Pollack and Christopher Metress (eds), *Emmett Till in Literary and Historical Imagination* (Baton Rouge: Louisiana State University Press, 2008), pp. 31–52.

68. George Lipsitz, 'California: The Mississippi of the 1990s', *The Possessive Investment of Whiteness* (Philadelphia: Temple University Press, 1998), pp. 211–33.

69. Carroll, *American Requiem*, p. 32.

70. Seymour M. Hersch, *The Dark Side of Camelot* (New York: Little, Brown, 1997), p. 89.

71. Carroll, *American Requiem*, p. 32; James Conaway, *Memphis Afternoons* (New York: Avon, 1994), p. 170.

72. 'When Kennedy Died', *Newsweek*, 14 September 1964, pp. 61–2.

73. Julian Bond, 'The Media and the Movement: Looking Back from the Southern Front', in *Media, Culture and the Modern African American Freedom Struggle*, ed. Brian Ward (Gainesville: University Press of Florida, 2001), p. 20.

74. Leslie Fiedler, *Waiting For the End* (London: Pelican, 1967), p. 77.

75. Wendy Kozol, *Life's America: Family and Nation in Postwar Photojournalism* (Philadelphia: Temple University Press, 1994), pp. 73–8.

76. Ibid., pp. 153–4.

77. Jill Freedman, 'Resurrection City', in Ken Light (ed.), *Witness in Our Time: Working Lives of Documentary Photographers* (Washington, DC: Smithsonian, 2000), pp. 73–4.

78. Paul Hendrickson, *Sons of Mississippi: A Story of Race and its Legacy* (New York: Alfred A. Knopf, 2003), pp. 13, 139.

79. John Gennari, 'Bridging the Two Americas: Life Looks at the 1960s', in Erika Doss (ed.), *Looking at Life: Critical Essays on America's Favorite Magazine* (Washington, DC: Smithsonian Institution Press, 2001), pp. 261–80.

80. Daniel Boorstin, *The Image: A Guide to Pseudo-Events in America* (New York: Vintage, 1961), p. 29.

81. Edgar Z. Friedenberg and Anthony Bernhard, *New York Review of Books*, 9 March 1967, in Dennis Hale and Jonathan Eisen (eds), *The California Dream* (New York: Collier Books, 1968), p. 268.

82. Irving Howe, *Decline of the New* (New York: Harcourt Brace, 1970), p. 253.

83. Vine Deloria, 'Tactics or Strategy?', *We Talk You Listen: New Tribes, New Turf* (New York: Macmillan, 1970), p. 47.

84. Fletcher Knebel, 'Scarlet O'Hara's Millions: She grossed $90 million and set off a gentlemanly battle', *Look* 27: 24 (3 December 1963), pp. 39–40, 42.

85. In 2003, three of us led a bus tour for the Organization of American Historians (OAH) of Mississippi civil rights sites: Allison Graham of the University of Memphis, Connie Curry (in the 1960s Director of the Southern Student Human Relations Project and an advisor to SNCC executive) and me. Edward Linnethal writing about our tour points out that, 'Sometimes the very lack of memorial attention to marking certain acts of racist violence on the landscape calls attention to such places for that very reason', 'Epilogue', in James Oliver and Lois Horton (eds), *Slavery and Public History: The Tough Stuff of American Memory* (New York: New Press, 2006), p. 221.

86. Randall Jarrell, 'A Sad Heart at the Supermarket', in Norman Jacobs (ed.), *Culture for the Millions: Mass Media in Modern Society* (Boston, MA: Beacon, 1964), p. 99.

87. 'Why the Craze for the Good Old Days?', *US News and World Report* 85: 20 (1973), p. 72.

88. Gary Allen, 'That Music', in Jonathan Eisen (ed.), *The Age of Rock: Sights and Sounds of the American Cultural Revolution* (New York: Vintage, 1970) p. 212.

89. Christopher Buckley, *Boomsday* (New York: Twelve, 2007), p. 63.

90. Tom Wells, 'Outrage at Sick Vietnam Napalm Game', *Sunday Mercury*, 4 April 2004; Nick Wadhams, 'Vietnam Video Game Forgets Moral Quotient', *Associated Press Online*, 6 April 2004; James Au Wagner, 'John Kerry: The Video Game', *Salon*, 13 April 2004.

91. Michael Medved, *Hollywood vs America* (New York: HarperCollins, 1993), p. 23.

92. For Agnew's speech, see Erik Barnouw, *Tube of Plenty* (New York: Oxford University Press, 1990), pp. 443–5; Department of Defense press release 3 November 1966 at http://www.dtic.mil/whs/directives/carves/html Instruction 5410.15

93. Quoted in Edward Jay Epstein, *The Big Picture: Money and Power in Hollywood* (New York: Random House, 2005), p. 328.

94. Todd Gitlin, *The Sixties: Years of Hope, Days of Rage* (New York: Bantam, 1987), p. 83.

95. Andrew Young, *An Easy Burden: The Civil Rights Movement and the Transition of America* (New York: HarperCollins, 1996), p. 413.

1. Music and Performance

1. See 'The Age of the Dream Place and the Rise of the Star System', in Paul Grainge, Mark Jancovich and Sharon Monteith, *Film Histories: An Introduction and Reader* (Edinburgh: Edinburgh University Press 2007), pp. 98–101.

2. Richard Rorty, *Contingency, Irony, Solidarity* (New York: Cambridge University Press, 1989), p. xvi.

3. Dick Gregory, quoted in Ann Powers, 'Aretha Franklin', in Barbara O' Dair (ed.), *The Rolling Stone Book of Women in Rock* (New York: Random House, 1997), p. 93.
4. Untitled informant's report, 24 March 1964, and A. L. Hopkins' investigative report, 5 April 1964, MSSC records 3–74–2 and Yasuhiro Katagiri, *The Mississippi State Sovereignty Commission* (Jackson: University Press of Mississippi, 2001) p. 154.
5. Brian Ward, *Just My Soul Responding*: *Rhythm and Blues, Black Consciousness, and Race Relations* (Berkeley: University of California Press, 1998), pp. 174, 139, 135. Although Chuck Berry sued the Beach Boys for their use of his 'Sweet Sixteen' as the underlying theme of 'Surfin' USA'.
6. Andreas Huyssen, 'Mapping the Postmodern', in Jeffrey Alexander and Steven Seidman (eds), *Culture and Society* (Cambridge: Cambridge University Press, 1984), pp. 355–67.
7. Eddie Thomas, quoted in Craig Werner, *Higher Ground* (New York: Crown, 2004), p. 80; Curtis Mayfield in 'Curtis Mayfield: Darker Than Blue', *Omnibus*, BBC Television documentary, 2004.
8. Alan Lomax, Charles Seeger and Ruth Crawford Seeger (eds), *Folk Song USA* (New York: Duell, Sloan and Pearce, 1947), p. vii.
9. Toni Cade Bambara, 'Mississippi Ham Rider,' *Gorilla, My Love* (London: The Women's Press, 1984), pp. 50–2.
10. Bob Dylan, *Chronicles: Volume One* (London: Simon and Schuster, 2005), p. 78.
11. Louis Menand, 'Bob on Bob: Dylan Talks', *The New Yorker*, 4 September 2006, p. 129.
12. John Hammond with Irving Townsend, *John Hammond on Record* (London: Penguin, 1977), p. 351.
13. Dylan, *Chronicles*, pp. 8, 83.
14. Dylan describes that epiphany more than once in *Chronicles*, pp. 244, 229; Pete Seeger, quoted in 'After A Long Hiatus, Dylan Returns', *Rolling Stone*, 24 February 1968.
15. Dylan, *Chronicles*, pp. 115–24, 147.
16. Ibid, pp. 84–6.
17. See also Mike Marqusee, *Wicked Messenger: Bob Dylan and the 1960s* (rev. from *Chimes of Freedom*, 2003; New York: Seven Stories Press, 2005), pp. 311–15, 321.
18. James Miller, *Flowers in the Dustbin: The Rise of Rock and Roll, 1947–1977* (New York: Simon and Schuster, 1999), p. 221.
19. The album would be *Planet Waves* (1974).
20. Nora Ephron and Susan Edmiston, 'Bob Dylan Interview', Summer 1965, in Jonathan Eisen (ed.), *The Age of Rock: Sights and Sounds of the American Cultural Revolution* (New York: Vintage, 1970), p. 65.
21. Gary Allen, 'That Music: There's More to It Than Meets the Ear', ibid., pp. 198–9; Griel Marcus, *Like a Rolling Stone: Bob Dylan at the Crossroads* (London: Faber, 2005), p. 149.
22. Griel Marcus, *Invisible Republic: Bob Dylan's Basement Tapes* (London: Picador, 1997), p. 70.
23. Luc Sante, 'I Is Someone Else', *New York Review of Books*, 10 March 2005, p. 35.
24. Tommie Smith, quoted Mike Marqusee, *Redemption Song: Muhammad Ali and the Spirit of the Sixties* (London: Verso, 1999), p. 244.

25. Dick Gregory with Sheila P. Moses, *Callus on my Soul* (New York: Kensington, 2000), pp. 96–7.
26. Arthur Ashe, quoted in Thomas Hauser (1991), *Muhammad Ali: His Life and Times* (London: Pan, 1997), p. 205.
27. Hauser, *Muhammad Ali*, p. 143
28. Ibid., p. 154.
29. Norman Mailer, 'Ego', *Life*, 19 March 1971. Reproduced in Gerald Early (ed.), *I'm a Little Special: A Muhammad Ali Reader* (London: Yellow Jersey Press, 1998), p. 102
30. Ibid.
31. Gordon Parks, 'The Redemption of the Champion', *Life*, 9 September 1966, reprinted in Early, p. 54.
32. Robert Lypsyte in Hauser, *Muhammad Ali*, p. 157.
33. Ibid., p. 509.
34. John Hammond with Irving Townsend, *John Hammond on Record* (London: Penguin, 1977), pp. 369–72.
35. Norman Mailer, *The Armies of the Night: History as a Novel, The Novel as History* (London: Weidenfeld and Nicolson, 1968), p. 61.
36. For a full record of *Southeastern Promotions Ltd* vs *Conrad et al.*, 420 US 546 (1975), see http://caselaw.lp.findlaw.com/scripts/getcase.pl?navby=search&court=US&case=/data/us/420/546.html
37. For example, Howard Brick, *Age of Contradiction: American Thought and Culture in the 1960s* (New York: Twayne, 1998), p. 60; Alan Kaprow, *Some Recent Happenings* (New York: Something Else Press, 1966).
38. Susan Sontag, 'Happenings: An Art of Radical Juxtaposition' (1962), in *Against Interpretation and Other Essays* (London: Eyre and Spottiswoode, 1967), pp. 263–74.
39. Ruby Cohn, *New American Dramatists 1960–1980* (London: Macmillan, 1982), p. 11.
40. Ibid., p. 77.
41. Ibid., p. 95.
42. Anatole Broyard, 'Portrait of an Inauthentic Negro: How Prejudice Distorts the Victim's Personality', *Commentary*, 10 (July 1950), pp. 56–64.
43. Paul Connerton, *How Societies Remember* (Cambridge: Cambridge University Press, 1989), p. 67.
44. Susan Sontag, 'Happenings', p. 274.
45. Michael Taussig, *The Nervous System* (New York: Routledge, 1992), p. 133.
46. For more examples, see Ronald K. L. Collins and David M. Skover, *The Trials of Lenny Bruce: The Fall and Rise of an American Icon* (Napierville, IL: Sourcebooks, 2002).
47. Lionel Trilling, 'On Lenny Bruce (1926–1966)', *The New York Review of Books*, 6 October 1966; Lionel Trilling, 'The Sad Fate of Lenny Bruce' and Jonathan Miller's 'Reply', *The New York Review of Books*, 18 November 1966.
48. Collins and Skover, *The Trials of Lenny Bruce*, p. 339.
49. Tom Lehrer, quoted in Dr Demento (aka Barry Hansen), 'Too Many Facts About Tom Lehrer', *The Remains of Tom Lehrer*, p. 15.
50. Although the US version tended to be more careful about offending its audiences with radical views than the British version.

51. Dr Demento, 'Too Many Facts', p. 18.
52. Dick Gregory with Robert Lypsyte, *Nigger: An Autobiography* (New York: Washington Square, 1964), p. 144.
53. Leslie Fiedler, *A New Fiedler Reader* (New York: Prometheus, 1999), p.
54. Devin McKinney, *Magic Circles: The Beatles in Dream and History* (Cambridge, MA: Harvard University Press, 2004)
55. Mark Kemp, *Dixie Lullaby: A Story of Music, Race and New Beginnings in a New South* (Athens: University of Georgia Press, 2006), p. 33.
56. Larry Kane's interviews were broadcast and Eppridge's candid photographs were exhibited at the celebration 'It Was Forty years Ago Today . . . The Beatles in America', Museum of Television and Radio, New York, 29 April 2004.
57. Gerri Hirshey, *Nowhere To Run: The Story of Soul Music* (London: Southbank, 2006), p. xii.
58. Ken Emerson, *Always Magic in the Air: The Bomp and Brilliance of the Brill Building Era* (London: Fourth Estate, 2006), p. 5, n. 273.
59. Ibid., p. xv.
60. Ibid., p. 266.
61. Albert Goldman, 'Detroit Retools its Rock', *Life*, 25 July 1969, p. 12.
62. Mary Wilson, *Dream Girl: My Life As A Supreme* (New York: St. Martin's Press, 1986), p. 200.
63. Berry Gordy in Adam White, 'Gordy Speaks: the Billboard Interview' (1993), Gerald Early, *One Nation Under a Groove: Motown and American Culture* (Ann Arbor: University of Michigan Press, revised 2004), pp. 150, 162.
64. Ward, *Just My Soul Responding*, p. 267.
65. Carl Davis, quoted in Robert Pruter, *Chicago Soul* (Urbana: University of Illinois Press, 1991), p. 77.
66. Marcus, pp. 113–14.
67. Brian Wilson in *Wouldn't It Be Nice* documentary; Tommy Udo, *Charles Manson: Music, Mayhem, Murder* (London: Sanctuary, 2002), pp. 188–9.
68. Marqusee, *Wicked Messenger*, p. 219.
69. Miller, *Flowers in the Dustbin*, pp. 260–1.
70. Roddy Doyle in Pat Wheeler and Jenny Newman, 'Roddy Doyle', in Sharon Monteith, Jenny Newman and Pat Wheeler, *Contemporary British and Irish Fiction: An Introduction Through Interview* (London: Arnold, 2004), p. 56.

2. Film and Television

1. Samuel Goldwyn, 'Hollywood in the Television Age', *Hollywood Quarterly*, winter 1949–1950.
2. Charles Higham, 'Hollywood Boulevard 1965', *Sight and Sound* , 34:1 (1965), p. 178.
3. Virginia Kelly, 'Hugh Downs and the Common Man', *Look*, 3 December 1963, p. 49.
4. Aniko Bodroghkozy cites student Jeff Greenwald who in an article the *New York Times Magazine* (1971) remembered TV of his childhood teaching him about adult greed (*The Price is Right*) and scheming in marriage (*I Love Lucy*) which solidified into a youthful disdain for 'an adult world that was troubled',

Groove Tube: Sixties Television and the Youth Rebellion (Durham, NC: Duke University Press, 2001), p. 33.

5. Disney was awarded a Medal of Freedom by President Johnson in 1964 but supported Republican Barry Goldwater in his Presidential campaign the same year.

6. Statement by Jack Valenti before the National Commission on the Causes and Prevention of Violence, 19 December 1968, in Stephen Prince (ed.), *Screening Violence* (New Jersey: Rutgers University Press, 2000), p. 65.

7. Pauline Kael, 'Trash, Art, and the Movies', *Going Steady: Film Writings 1968–1969* (New York: Marion Boyars, 1994), p. 96.

8. Kael, 'The Corrupt and the Primitive', *The New Yorker*, 7 December 1968; *Going Steady*, pp. 194, 199.

9. Kael, 'War as Vaudeville', *The New Yorker*, 12 October 1968.

10. Kael, '*Hud*, Deep in the Divided Heart of Hollywood', *I Lost it At the Movies* (New York: Little, Brown, 1965), pp. 78–94.

11. Kael, 'Is there a cure for film criticism?', *Sight and Sound*, 31:2 (Spring 1962), p. 57.

12. Howard Hampton, 'Such Sweet Thunder: Pauline Kael, 1919–2001', *Film Comment*, November/December 2001, p. 45.

13. Arthur Penn, 'Making Waves', in Lester D. Friedman (ed.), *Arthur Penn's Bonnie and Clyde* (Cambridge: Cambridge University Press, 2000), pp. 11–31.

14. Paul Schrader, 'Fruitful Pursuits', *Artform*, March 2001.

15. Joseph E. Mankiewicz, '*Cleopatra* Barges In – At Last', *Life*, 20 May 1963, pp. 66–74.

16. Walter Cronkite, *A Reporter's Life* (New York: Ballantine, 1996), p. 337.

17. Steven D. Classen, *Watching Jim Crow: The Struggles Over Mississippi TV, 1955–1969* (Durham, NC: Duke University Press, 2004) and my review, *Journal of American History*, 92: 1 (June 2005).

18. Though made in 1956, the film was first distributed in the US in 1958 and in the South at the beginning of the 1960s.

19. For a detailed discussion see Mary Ann Watson, 'Hungering For Heroes', *The Expanding Vista: American Television in the Kennedy Years* (Durham, NC: Duke University Press, 1994), pp. 119–20.

20. Kael, 'Apes Must Be Remembered, Charlie', *The New Yorker*, 17 February 1968.

21. Kael, 'A Fresh Star', *Going Steady*, 171–2.

22. Thomas Doherty, *Teenagers and Teenpics* (Boston, MA: Unwin Hyman, 1988), p. 194.

23. Alan Betrock, *I Was a Teenage Juvenile* (New York: St. Martin's Press, 1986), p. 103.

24. Donald Bogle, *Toms, Coons, Mulattoes, Mammies & Bucks: An Interpretive History of Blacks in American Films* (New York: Continuum, 2001), p. 200.

25. Boseley Crowther, *New York Times*, 21 September 1964, *The New York Times Film Reviews 1913–1968 Vol. 5* (New York: New York Times/Arno Press, 1970), p. 3491.

26. Roger Ebert, 1997 review in the *Chicago-Sun Times*, *Roger Ebert's Video Companion* (New York: Andrews McMeel, 1997), p. 889.

27. James Baldwin, *The Devil Finds Work* (New York: Laurel, 1976), p. 67.

28. Kael, *Going Steady*, pp. 34, 109.

29. Ron Kovic, *Born on the Fourth of July* (New York: Pocket Books, 1977), p. 112.

30. Michael Herr, *Dispatches* (London: Picador, 2002), pp. 43–4.
31. The phrase is Richard Slotkin's in *Gunfighter Nation* (New York: Atheneum, 1992). J. Hoberman in *The Dream Life: Movies Media and the Mythology of the Sixties* (New York: New Press, 2003), notes European protests against *The Green Berets* with a Stuttgart daily newspaper comparing the film to Nazi propaganda, p. 208.
32. Ralph Graves, 'Dusty and the Duke: A Choice of Heroes', *Life*, 11 July 1969.
33. 'The Bad Boy's Breakout: Steve McQueen Moves in on the Movies and Becomes its Hottest New Star', *Life*, 23 September 1963, p. 62.
34. Mayor Daley, quoted in Lewis Chester, Godfrey Hodgson and Bruce Page, *An American Melodrama: The Presidential Campaign of 1968* (London: André Deutsch, 1969), pp. 506–7.
35. For a discussion, see Adam Cohen and Elizabeth Taylor, *American Pharoah: Mayor Richard J. Daley, His Battle for Chicago and the Nation* (Boston, MA: Little, Brown, 2000).

3. Fiction and Poetry

1. Gish Jen, 'Bagels and Won Tons Served with Humor', *Seattle Post-Intelligencer*, 5 July 1996.
2. Philip Roth, 'Writing American Fiction', *Commentary*, March 1961, *Reading Myself and Others* (New York: Vintage, 2001), p. 65.
3. James Baldwin, 'Introduction', *Nobody Knows My Name: More Notes of a Native Son* (London: Penguin, 1961), p. 12.
4. Larry Neal, quoted in Eric J. Sundquist, *Cultural Contexts for Ralph Ellison's Invisible Man* (Boston, MA: Bedford/St. Martin's, 1995), p. 13.
5. Sherley Ann Williams, *Give Birth to Brightness* (New York: Dial Press, 1972), p. 24.
6. Norman Mailer, *Why Are We In Vietnam?* (Oxford: Oxford University Press, 1988), p. 13.
7. Maxwell Geismar, 'Introduction', Eldridge Cleaver, *Soul on Ice* (London: Panther, 1970), pp. 11–12.
8. Vance Bourjaily, *Confessions of A Spent Youth* (London: Corgi, 1968), p. 22.
9. Ibid., p. 262.
10. Gish Jen, *Mona in the Promised Land*, (London: Granta, 1996), p. 129.
11. Roth, *Reading Myself*, pp. 33, 18.
12. Jacob Brackman, 'The Put-On', *The New Yorker*, 24 June 1967, p. 34.
13. Leslie Fiedler, *Waiting For the End* (London: Pelican, 1967), p. 157.
14. Ross Posnock, *Color and Culture: Black Writers and the Making of the Modern Intellectual* (Cambridge, MA: Harvard University Press, 2000), p. 86.
15. Bourjaily, *Confessions*, pp. 9, 477.
16. Jacques Hermann in 'The Death of Literature', *New Literary History*, 3 (1971), pp. 31–47.
17. Fiedler, 'Come Back To the Raft Ag'in, Huck Honey!', *The New Fiedler Reader* (New York: Prometheus, 2001), p. 3.
18. Fiedler, *Love and Death in the American Novel* (London: Penguin, 1982), p. 92.
19. Fiedler, *The Return of the Vanishing American* (London: Paladin, 1972), p. 12.
20. Nina Baym, *Women's Fiction: A Guide to Novels By and About Women in America, 1820–1870* (Ithaca, NY: Cornell University Press, 1978). I use Fiedler

to situate my study of interracial friendships in southern fiction in *Advancing Sisterhood? Interracial Friendships in Contemporary Southern Fiction* (Athens: University of Georgia Press, 2000), pp. 41–3, 68, 75–6.

21. Fiedler, *Love and Death*, p. 27.
22. Fiedler, 'On Being Busted at Fifty', *The New York Review of Books*, 9: 1 (13 July 1967).
23. Fiedler, *Waiting For the End* (London: Pelican, 1967), pp. 126, 56.
24. Jay Parini, 'Being and Nothingness in New York', *The Guardian*, 26 April 2003, p. 15.
25. Ken Kesey, *One Flew Over a Cuckoo's Nest* (London: Picador, 1973), pp. 3, 8.
26. Mailer, *Cannibals and Christians* (New York: Dial, 1966), p. 85.
27. Mailer, 'The Occult', *The Spooky Art,* pp. 233–4.
28. See, for example, David P. Galloway, *The Absurd Hero in American Fiction* (1966 rev. 1970), Ihab Hassan, *Radical Innocence* (1961 rev. 1971) and Lionel Trilling, *Sincerity and Authenticity* (1972).
29. Joyce Carol Oates, 'The Teleology of the Unconscious: The Art of Norman Mailer' (pp. 179–203) in *New Heaven, New Earth: The Visionary Experience in Literature* (London: Gollancz, 1976), p. 187.
30. Norman Mailer, *The Armies of the Night: History as a Novel, The Novel as History* (London: Weidenfeld and Nicolson, 1968), p. 9.
31. John Carlos Rowe, 'Eye-Witness: Documentary Styles in the Representation of Vietnam', *Cultural Critique,* 3 (1986): pp. 126–50.
32. Hunter S. Thompson, *Fear and Loathing in Las Vegas* (London: Penguin, 1972), pp. 23, 69
33. Bob Kaufman, *Solitudes Crowded with Loneliness* (New York: New Directions, 1965), p. 53.
34. Eudora Welty, 'Preface', *The Collected Short Stories* (London: Penguin, 1983), p. xi.
35. Speech written for the inauguration of Mississippi Governor William Winter in January 1980, manuscript in The Eudora Welty Collection, Millsaps Collage, Jackson, MS.
36. William Styron, 'This Quiet Dust', *Harper's Magazine*, April 1965, p. 138.
37. Thomas R. Gray, 'The Confessions of Nat Turner', in Kenneth S. Greenberg (ed.), *The Confessions of Nat Turner and Related Documents* (Boston, MA: Bedford, 1996), pp. 40–2, 44.
38. See Tony Horwitz, 'Untrue Confessions: Is What Most of Us Know About the Rebel Slave Nat Turner Wrong?', *The New Yorker,* 13 December 1999, pp. 80–9. For more detail, see Scot French, 'Mau-Mauing the Filmmakers: Should Black Power Take the Rap for Killing Nat Turner the Movie?', in Brian Ward (ed.), *Media, Culture and the Modern African American Freedom Struggle* (Gainesville: University Press of Florida, 2001), pp. 233–54.
39. William Styron, 'Overcome', *New York Review of Books,* 1: 3 (26 September 1963).
40. Ralph Ellison, William Styron, Robert Penn Warren and moderator C. Vann Woodward, 'The Uses of History in Fiction', *Southern Literary Journal* (1968), p. 75.
41. Styron, 'This Quiet Dust', p. 139.
42. Amiri Baraka, *The Music, Reflections on Jazz and Blues* (New York: William Morrow and Company, 1987), pp. 264–5.

43. Ronald L. Fair, *Many Thousand Gone* (New York: Bantam, 1971), p. 81.

44. Nicolas Lemann, *The Promised Land: The Great Migration and How it Changed America* (London: Macmillan, 1991), p. 17. For a discussion of the new slavery in the South, Nahem Yousaf, 'A Sugar Cage: Poverty and Protest in Stephanie Black's *H-2 Worker*', in Suzanne Jones and Mark Newman (eds), *Poverty and Progress in the US South* (Amsterdam: VU Press, 2006), pp. 155–66.

45. Lyndon B. Johnson, 26 June 1964, Marvin E. Gettleman and David Mermelstein (eds), *The Great Society Reader: The Failure of American Liberalism* (New York: Vintage, 1967), p. 22.

46. Brian Ward, *Just My Soul Responding: Rhythm and Blues, Black Consciousness, and Race Relations* (Berkeley: University of California Press, 1998), pp. 205, 187.

47. Toni Cade Bambara, 'Blues Ain't No Mockin Bird', *Gorilla, My Love* (London: The Women's Press, 1984), p. 135.

48. Stephen Steinberg, *Turning Back: The Retreat from Racial Justice in American Thought and Policy* (Boston, MA: Beacon, 1995), p. 5.

49. Nicholas Lemann, 'Daniel Patrick Moynihan', *The New Yorker*, 7 April 2003, p. 98.

50. Lerone Bennett, 'The Challenge of Blackness', *Black Paper Series*, Institute of Black World Publication, April 1970.

51. Dick Gregory, *Nigger!* (New York: Washington Square, 1964); *Callus on My Soul: A Memoir* (New York: Kensington, 2000), p. 5.

52. Sharon Monteith, 'The Never-ending Cycle of Poverty: Sarah E. Wright's *This Child's Gonna Live*', *Poverty and Progress in the US South*, pp. 83–98.

53. Albert Murray, *The Omni Americans: Black Experience and American Culture* (New York: Da Capo, 1970), p. 97.

54. Sarah E. Wright, *This Child's Gonna Live* (London: Paladin, 1988), pp. 167–8.

55. Joyce Ladner, *Tomorrow's Tomorrow* (New York: Doubleday, 1971), pp. xv–xvi.

4. Art and Photography

1. Kirk Varnedoe, *Pictures of Nothing: Abstract Art Since Pollock* (Princeton, NJ: Princeton University Press, 2006), pp. 243, 8.

2. David Rosand, quoted in Amy Newman, *Challenging Art: Artforum 1962–1974* (New York: Soho Press, 2000), p. 140.

3. Guy Debord, *Society of the Spectacle*, trans. Donald Nicholson-Smith (New York: Zone Books, 1995), pp. 135–6.

4. As in the images collected for the Philip Guston exhibition, the Royal Academy, London, April 2004.

5. Joseph Kosoth explored the extent of Duchamp's influence in 'Art After Philosophy', *Studio International*, 178, pp. 915–17 (October–December 1969); *Neo-Dada: Redefining Art, 1958–62* (New York: The American Federation of the Arts/Universe Publications, 1994).

6. Marshall McLuhan, *Understanding Media: The Extensions of Man* (Cambridge, MA: MIT Press, 1997), p. 276.

7. Varnedoe, *Pictures of Nothing*, pp. 5–7, 244.

8. In 1959, Rothko refused to fulfil his commission to provide 600 feet of abstract impressionist painting for the Seagram Building, New York's finest skyscraper. His work would have covered the walls of the Four Seasons restaurant. He did

paint the murals and they hang now in the Tate Modern in London, a gift from the painter himself, but he returned the $35,000.

9. Howard Brick, *Age of Contradiction: American Thought and Culture in the 1960s* (New York: Twayne, 1998), p. 27.

10. Varnedoe, *Pictures of Nothing*, pp. 93–9.

11. Beatrice Berg, 'Susan Sontag. Intellectuals' Darling', the *Washington Post*, 8 January 1967; David Denby, 'The Moviegoer', *The New Yorker*, 12 September 2005, p. 90.

12. Susan Sontag, 'Notes on Camp', *Against Interpretation* (London: Eyre and Spottiswood, 1966), p. 273.

13. Arendt, quoted in Melvyn A.Hill (ed.), *Hannah Arendt: The Recovery of the Public World* (New York: St. Martin's Press, 1979), p. 336.

14. Craig Sleigman, *Sontag and Kael: Opposites Attract Me* (New York: Counterpoint, 2005), pp. 18, 40.

15. Journal entry 31 December 1958, excerpted in 'Susan Sontag: on Self', *New York Times*, 10 September 2006. Her journals will be published in 2008–9.

16. Guy Debord, *The Society of the Spectacle*, trans. Donald Nicolson-Smith (New York: Zone, 1995), p. 97.

17. Michael Lydon, 'Rock for Sale', in Jonathan Eisen (ed.), *The Age of Rock 2: Sights and Sounds of the American Cultural Revolution* (New York: Vintage, 1970), p. 53.

18. Thomas Crow, *The Rise of the Sixties: American and European Art in the Age of Dissent* (London: Laurence King, 2004), p. 39.

19. Roland Barthes, 'That Old Thing, Art . . .' (1980), in *The Responsibility of Forms: Critical Essays on Music, Art and Representation* (New York: Hill and Wang, 1985), p. 200.

20. Roland Barthes, 'The Photographic Message' (1961), *Image, Music, Text,* trans. Stephen Heath (London: Flamingo, 1984), p. 22.

21. Romare Bearden et al., 'The Black Artist in America', *The Metropolitan Museum of Art Bulletin*, 27: 5 (1969), pp. 245–60.

22. Matt Heron, 'The Civil Rights Movement and the Southern Documentary Project', in Ken Light (ed.), *Witness in Our Time: Working Lives of Documentary Photographers* (Washington: Smithsonian, 2000), p. 70.

23. John Rockwell, 'Preserve Performance Art? Can You Preserve the Wind?', *New York Times*, 30 April 2004, p. E5.

24. Nancy Marmer, 'LA Pop Art', in Lucy Lippard (ed.), *Pop Art* (London: Thames and Hudson, 1966), p. 139.

25. Ibid., p. 147.

26. Hal Crowther, 'The Outsider', *The Oxford American*, 51 (Fall 2005), p. 170.

27. Simon Schama, 'Twomblies of Wimmebeeldon', *The Guardian*, 17 April 2004, p. 16.

28. Jonathan Jones, 'The Last American Hurrah', *The Guardian Weekend*, 10 April 2004, pp. 40–4.

29. Jasper Johns, quoted in Calvin Tomkins, 'The Mind's Eye: the Merciless Originality of Jasper Johns', *The New Yorker*, 11 December 2006, p. 83.

30. Suzaan Boettger, *Earthworks: Art and the Landscape of the Sixties* (Berkeley: University of California Press, 2002), p. 120.

31. Max Kozloff, 'Art', *Nature*, 208: 11 (17 March 1969), p. 348.

32. Jack Flam (ed.), *The Collected Writings of Robert Smithson* (Berkeley: University of California Press, 1996), p. 237.
33. Boettger, *Earthworks*, p. 228.
34. 'The President and His Son', *Look*, 3 December 1963, pp. 26–36
35. Gordon Burn, 'King of the Day-Glo, Stiff-spined, Wise-guy Shiny Sheets', *Independent*, 8 February 1997.
36. Although Ali was at first reluctant as a Black Muslim to be photographed as a Christian icon.
37. Images on display at the exhibition 'Carl Fischer, Photographs 1963 to 1977', The Gallery at Pentagram, London, April 2004. Also available at http://web.mac.com/fischerny/Carl_Fischer_Photography_Inc./Current_Exhibition.html
38. Truman Capote, 'Richard Avedon' (1959) from *Observations*, *A Capote Reader* (London: Penguin, 1987), p. 547.
39. Susan Sontag, *On Photography*, (London: Penguin, 1979) p. 149.
40. Vernon Merritt, quoted in *The Great Life Photographers*, (ed.), The Editors of *Life* (London: Thames and Hudson, 2004), p. 358.
41. Susan Sontag, *Regarding the Pain of Others* (London: Hamish Hamilton, 2003), p. 37.
42. Robert Hughes, *Goya* (London: Harvill, 2003), p. 7.
43. My thanks to Mark Troy for introducing me to McElroy's fiction.
44. See, for example, 'TV's First War', *Newsweek*, 30 August 1965, p. 32.
45. Philip Jones Griffiths, *Vietnam Inc.* (London: Phaidon, 2005), pp. 182–3.
46. Ibid., pp. 62–3, 58–9.
47. Ibid., p. 162.
48. Ibid., p. 106
49. David Fenton (ed.), *Shots: Photographs From the Underground Press* (New York: Douglas Book Corporation, 1971), pp. 58–9.
50. *Decisive Moments: How Photography made the Sixties*, BBC, 1988, shown on BBC 2, 1997.
51. Boettger, p. 6.
52. 'TV: A Long Kept Vigil', *New York Times*, 9 June 1968, p. 60.
53. Bill Eppridge, quoted in *The Great Life Photographers*, p. 148.
54. I was drawn to the photographs when I saw them first in 'The Long Goodbye', *The Guardian*, 9 October 1999, accompanied by Mailer's essay, pp. 9–24 in advance of the publication of *Funeral Train*.
55. Michael Harrington, 'Introduction: Poverty in the Seventies', *The Other America: Poverty in the United States* (London: Penguin, rev. ed. 1981), p. xx.
56. Paul Fusco, 'Afterword', *RFK: Funeral Train* (New York: Magnum Photos Inc./Umbrage Editions, 2000), n.p.
57. The simple grave site was changed at the family's request in 1971.
58. Miwon Kwon, *One Place After Another: Site-Specific Art and Locational Identity* (Cambridge, MA: MIT Press, 2004), p. 43.

5. New Social Movements and Creative Dissent

1. Alice Walker, 'The Civil Rights Movement: What Good Was It?' (1967), *In Search of Our Mothers' Gardens* (London: The Women's Press, 1984), p. 122; Gary Wills, *The Kennedy Imprisonment* (Boston, MA: Little, Brown, 1984), p. 301.

2. James Peck, *Freedom Ride* (New York: Grove, 1962), pp. 10, 102–3.

3. *The Movement: Documentary of a Struggle for Equality* (New York: Simon and Schuster, 1964), p. 52.

4. Clarke was testifying as to how 'riots' like the one in Watts in 1965 might be addressed differently from riots in Chicago in 1919, *Report of the National Commission on Civil Disorders* (New York: Bantam, 1968), pp. 482–3.

5. Tom Hayden in Cheiyl Lynn Greenberg (ed.), *A Circle of Trust: Remembering SNNC* (New Brunswick: Rutgers University Press, 1998), pp. 212–13.

6. James Baldwin, 'Down At The Cross: Letter from a Region in My Mind', *The Fire Next Time* (London: Penguin, 1964), p. 83.

7. Martin Luther King Jr, 'Where Are We?', in *Where Do We Go From Here: Chaos or Community?* (Boston, MA: Beacon, 1968), p. 22; Robert K, Roney, 'A Different Kind of Woodstock', *Integrated Education*, 11: 2 (March–April 1973), p. 3.

8. Julius Lester, *All Is Well: An Autobiography* (New York: William Morrow, 1976), p. 68.

9. Martin Luther King Jr, 'Letter from Birmingham Jail', *Why We Can't Wait* (New York: Signet, 2000), p. 68; David Dellinger in Lewis Chester, Godfrey Hodgson and Bruce Page, *An American Melodrama: The Presidential Campaign of 1968* (London: Deutsch, 1969), p. 516.

10. Ed King in Charles Marsh, *God's Long Summer* (Princeton: Princeton University Press, 1997), p. 29.

11. Memorandum on SNCC Summer Mississippi Summer Project, University of Southern Mississippi, McCain Library and at http://anna.lib.usm.edu/%7Espcol/crda/ellin/ellin062.html

12. Julian Bond, quoted in Francesca Polletta, *Freedom is an Endless Meeting* (Chicago: University of Chicago Press, 2004), p. 105.

13. Fannie Lou Hamer, 'Foreword', Tracey Sugarman, *Strangers at the Gates: A Summer in Mississippi* (New York: Hill and Wang, 1966), pp. viii–ix.

14. *Voices of Freedom* (New York: Vintage, 1995), p. 183.

15. Cited in Milton Voist, *Fire in the Streets: America in the 1960s* (New York: Simon and Schuster, 1979), p. 229; Edward P. Morgan, *The 60s Experience: Hard Lessons About Modern America* (Philadelphia: Temple University Press, 1991), p. 61.

16. 'SNCC Position Paper (Women in the Movement), Name Withheld by Request', November 1964, in Sara Evans, *Personal Politics: The Roots of Women's Liberation in the Civil Rights Movement and the New Left* (New York: Vintage, 1979), p. 234.

17. Mario Savio, 'Thirty Years Later: Reflections on the FSM', in Roger Cohen and Reginald E. Zelnik (eds), *The Free Speech Movement: Reflections of Berkeley in the 1960s* (Berkeley: University of California Press, 2002), p. 64.

18. Clayborne Carson, *In Struggle: SNCC and the Black Awakening of the 1960s* (Cambridge, MA: Harvard University Press, 1981), p. 2.

19. Mrs Hamer, interview with Neil McMillen, 14 April 1972, Mississippi Oral History Program, McCain Library, University of Southern Mississippi, Hattiesburg.

20. Lester Sobol, *Civil Rights 1960–1966* (New York: Facts on File, 1967), pp. 190–1.

21. Mrs Hamer, 'To Praise Our Bridges', in Dorothy Abbott (ed.), *Mississippi Writers: Reflections of Childhood and Youth* (Jackson: University Press of Mississippi, 1986), p. 324.

22. Gordon Parks, 'Black Muslims Cry Grows Louder . . . What Their Cry Means to Me: A Negro's Own Evaluation', *Life International*, 9 September 1963, p. 32.

23. James Baldwin, 'The Dungeon Shook', *The Fire Next Time* (London: Penguin, 1964), p. 17.

24. Michael Harrington, *The Other America: Poverty in the Unites States* (London: Penguin, 1981), p. x.

25. David Murray, 'Sovereignty and the Struggle for Representation in American Indian Nonfiction', in Eric Cheyfitz (ed.), *The Columbia Guide to American Indian Literatures of the United States Since 1945* (New York: Columbia University Press, 2006), pp. 324–5.

26. Vine Deloria, 'Others', *We Talk You Listen: New Tribes, New Turf* (New York: Macmillan, 1970), p. 85.

27. Deloria, 'The Liberal Problem', *We Talk*, p. 79.

28. Deloria, 'The Red and the Black', *Custer Died For Your Sins* (New York: Avon, 1969), p. 169.

29. Deloria, 'Preface' and 'The Burden of Indian Education', *Spirit and Reason* (Golden, CO: Fulcrum, 1999), pp. xii, 176.

30. Deloria, 'The Red and the Black', p. 172.

31. Deloria, 'Stereotyping', *We Talk*, p. 91.

32. Deloria, 'Tactics or Strategy?', Ibid., p. 51.

33. Sylvia Plath, 'Context' (1962), in Ted Hughes (ed.), *Johnny Panic and the Bible of Dreams and Other Prose Writings* (London: Faber, 1977), p. 93; Betty Friedan, *The Feminine Mystique* (New York: Dell, 1964), p. 318.

34. Plath, 'America! America!' (1963), *Johnny Panic*, pp. 37–8.

35. Marianne DeKoven, *Utopia Limited: The Sixties and the Emergence of the Postmodern* (Durham: Duke University Press, 2004), p. 268.

36. Kenneth C. Davis, *Two-Bit Culture: The Paperbacking of America* (Boston, MA: Houghton Mifflin, 1984), p. 304.

37. Sylvia Fleis Fava, 'Book Review', *American Sociological Review*, 28: 6 (December 1963), pp. 1053–4.

38. Lynn Spigel, 'From the Dark Ages to the Golden Age: Women's Studies and Television Re-Runs', *Screen*, 36: 1 (1995), pp. 16–33.

39. 'No More Miss America!', *Sisterhood is Powerful*, ed. Robin Morgan (New York: Vintage, 1970), pp 584–9.

40. John D'Emilio, 'Placing Gay in the Sixties', in Alexander Bloom (ed.), *Long Time Gone: Sixties America Then and Now* (Oxford: Oxford University Press, 2001), p. 210.

41. Lucian Truscott IV, 'Gay Power Comes to Sheridan Square', *The Village Voice*, 3 July, 1969.

42. Gay dissent was embedded in Burroughs' fiction as in Allen Ginsberg's poetry. Ginsberg's 'Please Master' (1968) broke new ground in its graphic description of a homosexual encounter.

43. Martin Duberman, *Cures: A Gay Man's Odyssey* (New York: Penguin, 1991), p. 161.

44. Paul Welch, 'The Gay World Takes to the City Streets'; 'Homosexuality: A Secret World Grows Open and Bolder', *Life*, 27 July 1964, pp. 44–58.

45. Henry D. Thoreau, Henry David Thoreau, Owen Thomas (ed.), *Walden and Civil Disobidience*, (New York: Norton 1966), p. 62, 186.

46. Rachel Carson, *Silent Spring* (London: Penguin, 2000).
47. Ibid., p. 29.
48. Priscilla Coit Murphy, *What A Book Can Do: The Publication and Reception of Silent Spring* (Amherst: University of Massachusetts Press, 2005), p. 4.
49. Ibid., p. 14.
50. Cited in Martha Freeman (ed.), *Always Rachel. The Letters of Rachel Carson and Dorothy Freeman*, 1953–1964 (Boston, MA: Beacon, 1994), p. 394.
51. Murphy, *What A Book Can Do*, p. 190.
52. Juliet Eilperin, 'Bush Uses Market Incentives; Kerry Focuses on Rules', *Washington Post*, 26 October 2004, p. A05.
53. Martin Luther King Jr, *Where Do We Go From Here?*, p. 116.
54. 'Battling in a Verdant Hell', *Life*, 27 January 1964.
55. Wallace Stegner, *All the Little Live Things* (New York: Penguin, 1991), p. 35.
56. Ibid., p. 278.
57. Wallace Stegner, 'Wilderness Letter', 3 December 1960 at http://www.wilderness.org/OurIssues/Wilderness/wildernessletter.cfm
58. Alice Echols, 'Hope and Hype in Sixties Haight-Ashbury', in *Shaky Ground: The 60s and its Aftershocks* (New York: Columbia University Press, 2002), p. 18.
59. 'Are Hippies Fading Away or Becoming Part of the Community?', *Memphis Press-Scimitar*, 27 December 1967, p. 15.
60. Zay N. Smith, 'The Flower Children Still Bloom', *Memphis Commercial Appeal*, 26 July 1981.
61. http://www.thefarm.org
62. Warren Hickle, 'A Social History of the Hippies' (1967), in Gerald Howard (ed.), *The Sixties* (New York: Washington Square Press, 1982), p. 208.
63. Paul Warshow, 'Easy Rider', *Sight and Sound* (Winter 1969/1970), pp. 36–8.
64. 'Hippies Leaving – Dope Peddlers, Hoodlums Taking Their Place', *Memphis Commercial Appeal*, 27 July 1968.
65. 'Atlanta Becomes New Mecca for Flower Children', *Memphis Commercial Appeal*, 21 October 1967; '1,000 Hippies in Showdown with Atlanta's Policemen', *Memphis Press-Scimitar*, 22 September 1969.
66. Orville Hancock, 'Hippies May Get Air Travel Rules' *Memphis Press-Scimitar*, 15 November 1967.
67. James Fallows, *Washington Monthly*, October 1975; Peter Beinhart, 'Two Countries', *New Republic*, 10 May 2004.
68. 'The Citadel War Record: Vietnam's Casualties', Citadel Archives, Charleston, South Carolina, quoted in Alex Macauley, 'An Oasis of Order: the Citadel, the 1960s and the Vietnam Anti-War Movement', *Southern Cultures* (Fall 2005), p. 46.
69. Cited in Taylor Branch, *At Canaan's Edge* (New York: Simon and Schuster, 2006), pp. 359–61.
70. Mary McCarthy, *Hanoi* (London: Penguin, 1968), p. 75.
71. Richard Nixon, *The Memoirs* (New York: Grosset and Dunlap, 1978), p. 453.
72. Joshua Muravchik, 'The Neoconservative Cabal', *Commentary*, 23 September 2003, p. 26.
73. Peter Clecak, *America's Quest for the Ideal Self: Dissent and Fulfillment in the 60s and 70s* (New York: Oxford University Press, 1983), pp. 76–91.

74. Midge Decter, 'Letter to the Young (and to their parents)', in Mark Gershon and James O. Wilson (eds), *The Essential Neo-Conservative Reader* (Reading, MA: Addison Wesley, 1996), pp. 64–75.
75. Iwan W. Morgan, *Beyond the Liberal Consensus: A Political History of the United States Since 1965* (London: Hurst, 1994), p. 41.
76. Shelby Steele, 'The Loneliness of the Black Conservative', *The Dream Deferred: The Second Betrayal of Black Freedom in America* (New York: HarperCollins, 1998), esp. pp. 43–70.
77. Orlando Patterson, 'Toward . . . Past: Reflections on the Fate of Blacks in the Americas', *The Public Interest*, 27 (Spring 1972), pp. 60–1.
78. Marsh, *God's Long Summer*, p. 197.

Conclusion

1. Todd Gitlin, *Letters to a Young Activist* (New York: Basic Books, 2003), p. 19.
2. Marshall Frady, *Wallace* (New York: Random House, 1996), pp. 288–90.
3. Sharon Monteith, *Advancing Sisterhood: Interracial Friendship in Contemporary Southern Fiction* (Athens: University of Georgia Press, 2000).
4. Barbara Melosh, 'Historical memory in Fiction: The Civil Rights Movement in Three Novels', *Radical History Review* (Winter 1988), pp. 64, 75.
5. Sharon Monteith, 'Revisiting the 1960s in Contemporary Fiction: "Where Do We Go From Here?" ', in Peter Ling and Sharon Monteith (eds), *Gender and the Civil Rights Movement* (New Brunswick, NJ: Rutgers University Press, 2004), pp. 228–9; Julius Lester, *And All Our Wounds Forgiven* (New York: Harcourt and Brace, 1994), p. 190.
6. Floyd Tolbert, quoted in Samira Jafari, 'Marchers Want Youth to Follow in Footsteps', *The Herald-Sun*, Durham, NC, 6 March 2005, p. A10.
7. Adam Nossiter, *Of Long Memory: Mississippi and the Murder of Medgar Evers* (Reading, MA: Addison-Wesley, 1994), pp. 249–52; photographer David Rae Morris, quoted in Willie Morris, *The Ghosts of Medgar Evers: A Tale of Race, Murder, Mississippi, and Hollywood* (New York: Random House, 1998), p. 57.
8. Christopher Buckley, 'Rules of Engagement', *The New Yorker*, 4 October 2004, p. 51.
9. Mort Sahl, The Village Theater, New York City, 29 April 2004.
10. Joseph Lelyveld, *Omaha Blues: A Memory Loop* (New York: Picador, 2006), p. 18.
11. Todd Gitlin, *The Sixties: Years of Hope, Days of Rage* (New York: Bantam, 1987), p. 1.
12. Condoleezza Rice, quoted in Antonia Felix, 'The black "slip of a girl" who grew up in the segregated Deep South', *Sunday Times*, 21 November 2004, Section 5, p. 2.
13. Jack Hoffman and Daniel Simon, *Run, Run, Run: The Lives of Abbie Hoffman* (New York: Putnam, 1996), pp. 63–4.
14. James Conaway, *Memphis Afternoons* (New York: Avon, 1994), p. 175.
15. Ibid., p. 174.
16. Kushner, quoted in Harry Haun, 'A Range of Change', author's playbill for the performance of *Caroline, or Change* at Eugene O'Neill Theater, New York City, 4 May 2004, p. 10.

17. Mike Royko, 'Flower Children Planting Seeds for Chicago But-In', *Memphis Commercial Appeal*, 31 March 1968.
18. Fred Halstead, *Out Now! A Participant's Account of the American Movement Against the Vietnam War* (New York: Monad, 1971), p. 411.
19. Thomas Thompson, 'Aftermath of Shame – And Detection', *Life*, 30 December 1963, p. 21.
20. 'Dallas: Smug But Beginning to Think', *Life*, 30 December 1963, pp. 14–15; Robert Wallace, 'A Beer Can and a Bouquet: What Dallas Is Like and How It Got to Be That Way', *Life*, 30 December 1963, pp. 16–17.
21. Conaway, *Memphis Afternoons*, p. 196.
22. Glenn T. Eskew, *But for Birmingham: The Local and National Movements in the Civil Rights Struggle* (Chapel Hill, NC: University of North Carolina Press, 1997), p. 333.
23. See, for example, the Birmingham Convention and Visitors Bureau at http://www.bcvb.org/about-ads
24. Charles Morgan Jr, as told to Thomas B. Morgan, 'I Saw A City Die: Birmingham', *Look*, 27: 24, 3 December 1963, pp. 23–4.
25. Ibid., p. 24.
26. Diane McWhorter, 'The Moment That Made a Movement', *The Washington Post*, 2 May 1993 and *Carry Me Home: Birmingham Alabama, The Climactic Battle of the Civil Rights Revolution* (New York: Simon and Schuster, 2001), pp. 372–5.
27. *Decisive Moments: The Photographs That Made History* (Yorkshire Television, 1988).
28. 'Funeral for Virgil Ware, Allegedly Killed by White Youth, Set for Sunday, Sept. 22', *Birmingham World*, 21 September 1963, p. 1.
29. Thomas Blanton was only the second person to be brought to justice since Robert Chambliss' conviction in 1977. Blanton was given four life terms for each of the schoolgirls the bomb killed. Of the other bombers, members of Eastview's Klavern 13, Bobby Frank Cherry would finally be tried in 2002 and would die in prison in 2004. A fourth man died before he was charged
30. Walter Benn Michaels, 'You Who Never Was There: Slavery and the New Historicism, Deconstruction and the Holocaust', *Narrative*, 4 (1996), pp. 1–16.
31. NPR, 8 November 1997; 'Fellow Judge Discovered Ware's Lie About Identity; Article About Racist Attack Boosted Suspicion', *Washington Post*, 9 November 1997.
32. 'Revisionism', *The Education of Max Bickford*, CBS, 21 November 2001.
33. Toni Morrison, 'The Talk of the Town', *The New Yorker*, 5 October 1995, pp. 31–2.
34. Eric Lott, *The Disappearance of the Liberal Intellectual* (New York: Basic Books, 2006), p. 133.
35. P. J. O'Rourke, 'The Veterans of Domestic Disorder Memorial', *Atlantic Monthly*, April 2003, p. 40–1.
36. Jonathan Franzen, *The Corrections* (London: Fourth Estate, 2002), p. 93.
37. Steve Lohr, 'The Late, Great "Golden Years"', *New York Times*, 6 March 2005, pp. 1, 6.
38. Christopher Buckley, *Boomsday: A Novel* (New York: Twelve, 2007) pp. 70–1.
39. Ibid., p. 94.

40. Stephen Carter, 'The Dialectics of Race and Citizenship', *Transition*, 56 (1992), pp. 80–99.
41. Rotan E. Lee, 'The Baraka Flap: Lenny Bruce Revisited', *Philadelphia Tribune*, 11 October 2002.
42. Alex Callincos, *Against Postmodernism* (Berkeley: University of California Press, 1989), p. 170.
43. Theodore Roszak, *The Making of a Counter Culture* (Berkeley: University of California Press, 1995), p. 1
44. Ihab Hassan, *The Postmodern Turn: Essays in Postmodern Theory and Culture* (Columbus, OH: Ohio State University Press), p. 19; Eric Hobsbawm, *The Age of Extremes* (London: Michael Joseph, 1994), p. 78.

Bibliography

General

Raymond Arsenault, *Freedom Riders: 1961 and the Struggle for Racial Justice* (New York: Oxford University Press, 2006).

Alexander Bloom and Wini Breines (eds), *'Takin' it to the Streets': A Sixties Reader* (New York: Oxford University Press, 2003).

Daniel Boorstin, *The Image: A Guide to Pseudo-Events in America* (New York: Vintage, 1961).

Howard Brick, *Age of Contradiction: American Thought and Culture in the 1960s* (New York: Twayne, 1998).

Ann Charters (ed.), *The Portable Sixties Reader* (London: Penguin, 2003).

David Farber (ed.), *The Sixties: From Memory to History* (Chapel Hill, NC: University of North Carolina Press, 1994).

James J. Farrell, *The Spirit of the Sixties: Making Postwar Radicalism* (New York: Routledge, 1997).

David Garrow, *Bearing the Cross: Martin Luther King, Jnr., and the Southern Christian Leadership Conference* (London: Vintage, 1993).

Clifford Geertz, *The Interpretation of Cultures* (New York: Basic Books, 1973).

Todd Gitlin, *The Sixties: Years of Hope, Days of Rage* (New York: Bantam, 1987).

Dennis Hale and Jonathan Eisen (eds), *The California Dream* (New York: Collier Books, 1968).

Michael J. Heale, *Sixties in America* (Edinburgh: Edinburgh University Press, 2001).

Seymour M. Hersch, *The Dark Side of Camelot* (New York: Little, Brown, 1997).

Gerald Howard (ed.), *The Sixties: The Art, Attitudes, Politics, and Media of Our Most Explosive Decade* (New York: Washington Square Press, 1982).

Irving Howe, *Decline of the New* (New York: Harcourt Brace, 1970).

Norman Jacobs (ed.), *Culture for the Millions: Mass Media in Modern Society* (Boston, MA: Beacon, 1964).

Fredric Jameson, *The Ideologies of Theory: Essays, 1971–1986* (Minneapolis: Minnesota, 1988).

Otto Kermer et al., *Report of the National Advisory Commission on Civil Disorders* (New York: Dutton, 1968).

Wendy Kozol, *Life's America: Family and Nation in Postwar Photojournalism* (Philadelphia: Temple University Press, 1994).

Christopher Lasch, *The Culture of Narcissism: American Life in an Age of Diminishing Expectations* (New York: Norton, 1979).

Claude Levi-Strauss, *Structural Anthropology* (New York: Basic Books, 1963).

Peter Ling, *Martin Luther King, Jr* (London: Routledge, 2002).

Edward P. Morgan, *The 60s Experience: Hard Lessons About Modern America* (Philadelphia: Temple University Press, 1991).

Joan Morrison and Robert K. Morrison, *From Camelot to Kent State* (New York: Times Books, 1987).

Joseph Roach, *Cities of the Dead: Circum-Atlantic Performance* (New York: Columbia University Press, 1996).

Natalie Robins, *Alien Ink: The FBI's War on Freedom of Expression* (New Brunswick, NJ: Rutgers University Press, 1992).

Theodore Roszak, *The Making of a Counter Culture* (London: Faber, 1970).

Nora Sayre, *Sixties Going on Seventies* (London: Constable, 1974).

Sohnya Sayres et al., *The 60s Without Apology* (Minneapolis: University of Minnesota Press, 1984).

Arthur Schlesinger Jr, *History of US Political Parties: Factions to Parties* (New York: Chelsea House Publishers, 1973).

Richard Slotkin, *Regeneration Through Violence: The Mythology of the American Frontier, 1600–1860* (Middletown, CT: Wesleyan University Press, 1973).

Shelby Steele, *The Content of Our Character: A New Vision of Race in America* (New York: St. Martin's Press, 1990).

Irwin Unger and Debi Unger (eds), *The Times Were a Changin': The Sixties Reader* (New York: Three Rivers Press, 1998).

Brian Ward (ed.), *Media, Culture and the Modern African American Freedom Struggle* (Gainesville: University Press of Florida, 2001).

C. Van Woodward, *The Strange Career of Jim Crow* (New York: Oxford, 966).

Andrew Young, *An Easy Burden: The Civil Rights Movement and the Transition of America* (New York: HarperCollins, 1996).

Howard Zinn, *The Southern Mystique* (New York: Simon and Schuster, 1972).

Music and Performance

Amiri Baraka, *The Music, Reflections on Jazz and Blues* (New York: William Morrow and Company, 1987).

Stephen J. Bottoms, *Playing Underground: A Critical History of the 1960s Off-Off-Broadway Movement* (Ann Arbor: University of Michigan Press, 2005).

Lewis Chester, Godfrey Hodgson and Bruce Page, *An American Melodrama: The Presidential Campaign of 1968* (London: André Deutsch, 1969).

Adam Cohen and Elizabeth Taylor, *American Pharaoh: Mayor Richard J. Daley, His Battle for Chicago and the Nation* (Boston, MA: Little, Brown, 2000).

Ruby Cohn, *New American Dramatists 1960–1980* (London: Macmillan, 1982).

Ronald K. L. Collins and David M. Skover, *The Trials of Lenny Bruce: The Fall and Rise of an American Icon* (Napierville, IL: Sourcebooks, 2002).

Neil Corcoran (ed.), *'Do You Mr Jones?': Bob Dylan with the Poets and Professors* (London: Pimlico, 2003).

Peter Coyote, *Sleeping Where I Fall* (Washington, DC: Counterpoint, 1998).

R. G. Davis, *The San Francisco Mime Troupe: The First Ten Years* (Palo Alto, CA: Ramparts, 1975).

Serge R. Denisoff, *Great Days Coming: Folk Music and the American Left* (Urbana: University of Illinois Press, 1971).

Robert Draper, *Rolling Stone Magazine: The Uncensored History* (New York: Bantam, 1990).

Gerald Early (ed.), *I'm a Little Special: A Muhammad Ali Reader* (London: Yellow Jersey Press, 1998).

Gerald Early, *One Nation Under a Groove: Motown and American Culture* (Ann Arbor: University of Michigan Press, 2004).

Jonathan Eisen (ed.), *The Age of Rock: Sights and Sounds of the American Cultural Revolution* (New York: Vintage, 1970).

Ken Emerson, *Always Magic in the Air: The Bomp and Brilliance of the Brill Building Era* (London: Fourth Estate, 2006).

Benjamin Filene, *Romancing the Folk: Public Memory and American Roots Music* (Chapel Hill, NC: University of North Carolina Press, 2000).

Paul Friedlander, *Rock and Roll: A Social History* (Boulder, CO: Westview Press, 1996).

Martin Goldsmith, *The Beatles Come to America* (London: Wiley, 2004).

Michael Gray, *Song and Dance Man III: The Art of Bob Dylan* (London: Continuum, 2000).

Marcus Griel, *Invisible Republic: Bob Dylan's Basement Tapes* (London: Picador, 1997).

Marcus Griel, *Like a Rolling Stone: Bob Dylan at the Crossroads* (London: Faber, 2005).

Peter Guralnik, *Sweet Soul Music* (Edinburgh: Canongate, 2002).

David Hajdu, *Positively 4th Street: The Lives and Times of Bob Dylan, Joan Baez, Mimi Baez Farina and Richard Farina* (London: Bloomsbury, 2001).

Thomas Hauser, *Muhammad Ali: His Life and Times* (London: Pan, 1997).

Gerri Hirshey, *Nowhere To Run: The Story of Soul Music* (London: Southbank, 2006).

Jack Hoffman and Daniel Simon, *Run, Run, Run: The Lives of Abbie Hoffman* (New York: Putnam, 1996).

Alan Kaprow, *Some Recent Happenings* (New York: Something Else Press, 1966).

Mark Kemp, *Dixie Lullaby: A Story of Music, Race and New Beginnings in a New South* (Athens: University of Georgia Press, 2006).

Alan Lomax, Charles Seeger and Ruth Crawford Seeger (eds), *Folk Song USA* (New York: Duell, Sloan and Pearce, 1947).

Devin McKinney, *Magic Circles: The Beatles in Dream and History* (Cambridge, MA: Harvard University Press, 2004).

Mike Marqusee, *Redemption Song: Muhammad Ali and the Spirit of the Sixties* (London: Verso, 1999).

Mike Marqusee, *Wicked Messenger: Bob Dylan and the 1960s* (New York: Seven Stories Press, 2005).

James Miller, *Flowers in the Dustbin: The Rise of Rock and Roll, 1947–1977* (New York: Simon and Schuster, 1999).

Barbara O'Dair (ed.), *The Rolling Stone Book of Women in Rock* (New York: Random House, 1997).

Robert Pruter, *Chicago Soul* (Urbana: University of Illinois Press, 1991).

Tommie Smith with David Steel, *Silent Gesture* (Philadelphia: Temple University Press, 2007).

Howard Sounes, *Down the Highway: The Life of Bob Dylan* (London: Black Swan, 2002).
Tommy Udo, *Charles Manson: Music, Mayhem, Murder* (London: Sanctuary, 2002).
Richie Unterberger, *Turn! Turn! Turn!; The 60's Folk-Rock Revolution* (San Francisco: Backbeat Books, 2002).
Brian Ward, *Just My Soul Responding* (Berkeley: University of California Press, 1998)
Brian Ward, *Radio and the Struggle for Civil Rights in the South* (Gainesville: University of Florida Press, 2004).

Film and Television

James Baldwin, *The Devil Finds Work* (New York: Laurel, 1976).
Erik Barnouw, *Tube of Plenty* (New York: Oxford University Press, 1990).
John Baxter, *Hollywood in the Sixties* (London: Tantivy Press, 1972).
Aniko Bodroghkozy, *Groove Tube: Sixties Television and the Youth Rebellion* (Durham, NC: Duke University Press, 2001).
Will Brantley (ed.), *Conversations with Pauline Kael* (Jackson: University Press of Mississippi, 1999).
Douglas Brode, *The Films of the Sixties* (Secaucus, NJ: Citadel Press, 1980).
Douglas Brode, *From Walt to Woodstock: How Disney Created the Counterculture* (Austin: University of Texas Press, 2003).
Robert Burgoyne, *Film Nation: Hollywood Looks at US* (Minneapolis: University of Minnesota Press, 1997).
Seth Cagin and Philip Dray, *Hollywood Films of the Seventies: Sex, Drugs, Violence, Rock 'n' Roll & Politics* (New York: Harper and Row, 1984).
Steven D. Classen, *Watching Jim Crow: The Struggles Over Mississippi TV, 1955–1969* (Durham, NC: Duke University Press, 2004).
Jim Collins, *Architectures of Excess: Cultural Life in the Information Age* (New York: Routledge, 1995).
John E. Connor (ed.), *American History, American Television: Interpreting the Video Past* (New York: Frederick Unger, 1983).
Corrigan, Timothy, *A Cinema Without Walls: Movies and Culture After Vietnam* (New Brunswick, NJ: Rutgers University Press, 1991).
Edward Jay Epstein, *The Big Picture: Money and Power in Hollywood* (New York: Random House, 2005).
Lester D. Friedman (ed.), *Arthur Penn's Bonnie and Clyde* (Cambridge: Cambridge University Press, 2000).
Paul Grainge, Mark Jancovich and Sharon Monteith, *Film Histories: An Introduction and Reader* (Edinburgh: Edinburgh University Press, 2007).
Jim Hoberman, *The Dream Life: Movies Media and the Mythology of the Sixties* (New York: The New Press, 2003).
David E. James, *Allegories of Cinema: American Film in the Sixties* (Princeton, NJ: Princeton University Press, 1989).
Pauline Kael, *I Lost It At The Movies* (New York: Little, Brown, 1965).
Pauline Kael, *Going Steady: Film Writings 1968–1969* (New York: Marion Boyars, 1994).
Stephen Prince (ed.), *Screening Violence* (New Jersey: Rutgers University Press, 2000).

Richard Schickel, *The Disney Version: The Life, Times, Art and Commerce of Walt Disney* (New York: Simon and Schuster, 1972).

Lynn Spigel and Michael Curtin (eds), *The Revolution Wasn't Televised: Sixties Television and Social Conflict* (New York and London: Routledge, 1997)

Ella Taylor, *Prime Time: Television Culture in Postwar America* (1989)

The New York Times Film Reviews 1913–1968 Vol. 5 (New York: New York Times/Arno Press, 1970).

Parker Tyler, *Underground Cinema* (London: Pelican, 1969).

Mary Ann Watson, *The Expanding Vista: American Television in the Kennedy Years* (Durham, NC: Duke University Press, 1990).

Fiction and Poetry

John W. Aldridge, *The Devil in the Fire: Retrospective Essays on American Literature and Culture, 1951–1971* (New York: Harper's Magazine Press, 1972).

Marc Chenetier, *Beyond Suspicion: New American Fiction since 1960* (Liverpool: Liverpool University Press, 1996).

John Henrik Clarke (ed.), *Ten Black Writers on Nat Turner* (Boston, MA: Beacon, 1968).

Marianne DeKoven, *Utopia Limited: The Sixties and the Emergence of the Postmodern* (Durham, NC: Duke University Press, 2004).

Morris Dickstein, *Gates of Eden: American Culture in the Sixties* (New York: Basic Books, 1977).

Morris Dickstein, *Leopards in the Temple: The Transformation of American Fiction, 1945–1970* (Cambridge, MA: Harvard University Press, 1999).

Leslie Fiedler, *Waiting For the End* (London: Pelican, 1967).

Leslie Fiedler, *The Return of the Vanishing American* (London: Paladin, 1972).

Leslie Fiedler, *Love and Death in the American Novel* (London: Penguin, 1982).

Leslie Fiedler, *A New Fiedler Reader* (New York: Prometheus, 2001).

David P. Galloway, *The Absurd Hero in American Fiction: Updike, Styron, Bellow, Salinger* (Austin, TX: University of Texas Press, 1982).

Kenneth S. Greenberg (ed.), *The Confessions of Nat Turner and Related Documents* (Boston, MA: Bedford, 1996).

Ihab Hassan, *Radical Innocence, Studies in the Contemporary American Novel* (Princeton, NJ: Princeton University Press, 1961).

Jacques Hermann, 'The Death of Literature', *New Literary History*, 3 (1971), pp. 31–47.

Tony Horwitz, 'Untrue Confessions: Is What Most of Us Know about the Rebel Slave Nat Turner Wrong?', *The New Yorker*, 13 December 1999, pp. 80–9.

Kathryn Hume, *American Dream, American Nightmare: Fiction Since 1960* (Champaign, IL: University of Illinois Press, 2000).

Nicolas Lemann, *The Promised Land: The Great Migration and How it Changed America* (London: Macmillan, 1991).

Albert Murray, *The Omni Americans: Black Experience and American Culture* (New York: Da Capo, 1970).

Joyce Carol Oates, *New Heaven, New Earth: The Visionary Experience in Literature* (London: Gollancz, 1976).

Raymond Michael Olderman, *Beyond 'The Waste Land': A Study of the American Novel in the Nineteen-Sixties* (New Haven, CT: Yale University Press, 1972).

Ross Posnock, *Color and Culture: Black Writers and the Making of the Modern Intellectual* (Cambridge, MA: Harvard University Press, 2000).

Manfred Putz, *The Story of Identity: American Fiction of the Sixties* (Stuttgart: Metzler, 1979).

Albert E. Stone, *The Return of Nat Turner: History, Literature and Cultural Politics* (Athens: University of Georgia Press, 1992).

Lionel Trilling, *Sincerity and Authenticity* (Cambridge, MA: Harvard University Press, 1974).

Sherley Ann Williams, *Give Birth to Brightness* (New York: Dial Press, 1972).

Art and Photography

Julia Ault, *Come Alive: The Spirited Art of Sister Corita* (London: Four Corners, 2007).

Richard Avedon, *The Kennedys: Portrait of a Family* (New York: Thames and Hudson, 2007).

Suzaan Boettger, *Earthworks: Art and the Landscape of the Sixties* (Berkeley: University of California Press, 2002).

Pierre Bourdieu, *Photography: A Middle-Brow Art* (London: Polity Press, 1996).

Truman Capote, *Observations, A Capote Reader* (London: Penguin, 1987).

Denise Chang, *The Girl in the Picture: The Remarkable Story of Vietnam's Most Famous Casualty* (London: Simon and Schuster, 1999).

Thomas E. Crow, *The Rise of the Sixties: American and European Art in the Era of Dissent* (New York: Harry N. Abrams, 1996).

Jennifer Doyle, Jonathan Flatley and José Esteban Muñoz, *Pop Art: Queer Warhol* (Durham, NC: Duke University Press, 1996).

Martin Duberman, *Black Mountain College, An Exploration in Community* (New York: Dutton, 1972).

Horst Faas and Tim Page, *Requiem: By the Photographers who Died in Vietnam and Indochina* (London: Jonathan Cape, 1997).

John Alan Farmer, *The New Frontier: Art and Television 1960–65* (Austin, TX: Austin Museum of Art, 2000)

Jack Flam (ed.), *The Collected Writings of Robert Smithson* (Berkeley: University of California Press, 1996).

Thomas Frank, *The Conquest of Cool: Business Culture, Counterculture, and the Rise of Hip Consumerism* (Chicago: University of Chicago Press, 1997).

Paul Fusco, *RFK: Funeral Train* (New York: Magnum Photos Inc./Umbrage Editions, 2000).

Stuart Hall and Tony Jefferson (eds), *Resistance Through Rituals: Youth Subcultures in Post-War Britain* (London: Routledge, 1993).

Mary Emma Harris, *The Arts at Black Mountain College* (Cambridge, MA: MIT Press, 1987).

Barbara Haskell, *Claes Oldenburg: Object into Moment* (Pasadena, CA: Pasadena Art Museum Catalogue, 1971).

Seymour Hersch, *May Lai 4: A Report on the Massacre and Its Aftermath* (New York: Random House, 1970).

Robert Hughes, *American Visions: Epic Hisory of Art in America* (London: Harvill Press, 1997).

Vincent Katz, (ed.), *Black Mountain College: Experiment in Art* (Cambridge, MA: MIT Press, 2002).

Anthony W. Lee, *Diane Arbus: Family Albums* (New Haven, CT: Yale University Press, 2003).

Lucy Lippard, *Six Years: The Dematerialisation of the Art Object from 1966–1972* (Berkeley: University of California Press, 2001).

Charles Moore, *Powerful Days, The Civil Rights Photography of Charles Moore* (New York: Stewart, Tabori and Chang, 1991).

Robert C. Morgan, *Conceptual Art: An American Perspective* (Jefferson, NC: McFarland, 1994).

Amy Newman, *Challenging Art: Artforum 1962–1974* (New York: Soho Press, 2000).

John O'Brien (ed.), *Clement Greenberg, The Collected Essays and Criticism. Volume 4: Modernism with a Vengeance* (Chicago: University of Chicago Press, 1993).

Anne Rorimer, *New Art in the 60s and 70s: Redefining Reality* (London: Thames and Hudson, 2001).

Clifford Ross (ed.), *Abstract Expressionism* (New York: Harry N. Abrams, 1991).

Craig Seligman, *Sontag and Kael: Opposites Attract Me* (New York: Counterpoint, 2005).

Susan Sontag, *On Photography* (London: Penguin, 1979).

Susan Sontag, *Regarding the Pain of Others* (London: Hamish Hamilton, 2003).

Ronald Steel, *In Love with Night: The American Romance with Robert Kennedy* (New York: Simon and Schuster, 2000).

Kirk Varnedoe, *Pictures of Nothing: Abstract Art Since Pollock* (Princeton: Princeton University Press, 2006).

New Social Movements

Judith Clavir Albert and Stewart Edward Albert (eds), *The Sixties Papers: Documents of a Rebellious Decade* (Westport, CT: Praeger, 1984).

David Allyn, *Make Love, Not War: The Sexual Revolution: An Unfettered History* (New York: Routledge, 2001).

Terry H. Anderson, *The Movement and the Sixties* (New York: Oxford University Press, 1995).

John A. Andrew, *The Other Side of the Sixties: Young Americans for Freedom and the Rise of Conservative Politics* (New Brunswick, NJ: Rutgers University Press, 1997).

Geoff Andrews et al., *New Left, New Right and Beyond: Taking the Sixties Seriously* (Houndmills: Palgrave, 1999).

Edward Baccioco, *The New Left in America: Reform to Revolution, 1956–1970* (Palo Alto, CA: Hoover Institution Press, 1974).

Tom Bates, *Rads: The 1970 Bombing of the Army Math Research Center at the University of Wisconsin and Its Aftermath* (New York: HarperCollins, 1992).

Warren J. Belasco, *Appetite for Change: How the Counterculture Took on the Food Industry* (Ithaca, NY: Cornell University Press, 2006).

Robert Bellah et al., *Habits of the Heart: Individualism and Commitment in American Life* (London: Harper Perennial, 1985).

Joseph Boskin and Robert A. Rosenstone, *Seasons of Rebellion: Protest and Radicalism in Recast America* (New York: Holt, Rinehart and Winston, 1972).

Taylor Branch, *Parting the Waters: America in the King Years, 1954–63* (New York: Touchstone, 1988).

Winifred Breines, *Community and Organization in the New Left: 1962–1968* (New Brunswick, NJ: Rutgers University Press, 1989).

Lindsey Brink, *The Age of Abundance: How Prosperity Transformed America's Politics and Culture* (London: HarperCollins, 2007).

Paul Buhle (ed.), *History and the New Left: Madison, Wisconsin, 1950–1970* (Philadelphia: Temple University Press, 1990).

Stewart Burn, *Social Movements of the 1960s: Searching for Democracy* (Boston, MA: Twayne, 1990).

Ellen Cantarow, *Moving the Mountain: Women Working for Social Change* (New York: Feminist Press, 1980).

Milton Canton, *The Divided Left: American Radicalism, 1900–1975* (New York: Hill and Wang, 1978).

Stokely Carmichael, *Black Power: The Politics of Liberation in America* (London: Cape, 1967).

David Carter, *Stonewall: The Riots That Sparked The Gay Revolution* (New York: St. Martin's Press, 2004).

William H. Chafe, *Civilities and Civil Rights* (New York: Oxford University Press, 1980).

Peter Clecak, *Radical Paradoxes: Dilemmas of the American Left, 1945–1970* (New York: Harper and Row, 1973).

James H. Cone, *Martin and Malcolm and America: A Dream or a Nightmare* (New York: Orbis Books, 1991).

CORE, *Cracking the Color Line: Non-Violent Direct Action Methods of Eliminating Racial Discrimination* (New York: CORE, 1960).

Maurice Cranston (ed.), *The New Left: Six Critical Essays* (London: Bodley Head, 1970).

Nick Crossley, *Making Sense of Social Movements* (Milton Keynes: Open University Press, 2002).

Marcy Darnovsky, Barbara Epstein and Richard Flacks (eds), *Cultural Politics and New Social Movements* (Philadelphia: Temple University Press, 1995).

Charles DeBenedetti and Charles Catfield, *An American Ordeal: The Anti-War Movement of the Vietnam War* (New York: Syracuse University Press, 1990).

Gerard J. DeGroot (ed.), *Student Protest: The Sixties and After* (London: Addison Wesley Longman, 1998).

Gary A. Donaldson, *Liberalism's Last Hurrah* (New York: M. E. Sharpe, 2003).

Martin Duberman, *Stonewall* (New York: Dutton, 1993).

Sara Evans, *Personal Politics: The Roots of Women's Liberation in the Civil Rights Movement and The New Left* (New York: Vintage, 1980).

Adam Fairclough, *To Redeem the Soul of America* (Athens, GA: University of Georgia Press, 1987).

Adam Fairclough, *Race and Democracy: The Civil Rights Struggle in Louisiana, 1915–1972* (Athens, GA: University of Georgia Press, 1995).

Daniel Foss, *Freak Culture: Life-style and Politics* (New York: Dutton, 1972).

Ronald Fraser et al., *1968: A Student Generation in Revolt* (New York: Macmillan, 1972).

George M. Fredrickson, *The Comparative Imagination: On the History of Racism, Nationalism and Social Movements* (Berkeley: University of California Press, 2000).

Jo Freeman (ed.), *Social Movements of the Sixties and Seventies* (London: Longman, 1983).

L. H. Gann and Peter Duignan, *The New Left and the Cultural Revolution of the 1960s: A Re-evaluation* (Stanford, CA: Hoover Institute, 1995).

Mark Gerson (ed.), *The Essential Neoconservative Reader* (Reading: Addison-Wesley, 1996).

Joanna Grant, *Ella Barker: Freedom Bound* (New York: John Wiley, 1980).

David Halberstam, *The Children* (New York: Fawcett Books, 1998).

Fred Halstead, *Out Now! A Participant's Account of the American Movement Against the Vietnam War* (New York: Monad, 1978).

Samuel Huntingdon, *American Politics: the Promise of Disharmony* (Cambridge, MA: Belknap, 1981).

Maurice Isserman, *If I Had a Hammer: The Death of the Old Left and the Birth of the New Left* (New York: Basic Books, 1987).

Rhodri Jeffreys-Jones, *Peace Now!: American Society and the Ending of the V War* (New Haven, CT: Yale University Press, 1999).

Richard King, *Civil Rights and the Idea of Freedom* (Oxford: Oxford University Press, 1990).

Enrique Larana et al., *New Social Movements: From Ideology to Identity* (Philadelphia, PA: Temple University Press, 1994).

Linda Lear, *Rachel Carson: Witness for Nature* (London: Penguin Books, 1997).

John Lewis, *Walking in the Wind: A Memoir of the Movement* (New York: Simon and Schuster, 1998).

Peter Ling and Sharon Monteith (eds), *Gender and the Civil Rights Movement* (New Jersey: Rutgers University Press, 2004).

Danny Lyon, *Memories of the Southern Civil Rights Movement* (Chapel Hill: University of North Carolina Pres, 1992).

William J. McGill, *The Year of the Monkey: Revolt on the Campus, 1968–1969* (New York: Basic Books, 1982).

Kay Mills, *This Little Light of Mine: The Life of Fannie Lou Hamer* (New York: Dutton, 1993).

Aldon Morris, *The Origins of the Civil Rights Movement: Black Communities Organising for Change* (London: Collier Macmillan, 1984).

Anthony Oberschall, *Social Conflict and Social Movements* (Englewood Cliffs, NJ: Prentice-Hall, 1973).

Frances Fox Piven and Richard Cloward, *Poor People's Movements* (New York: Pantheon Books, 1977).

Charles Payne, *I've Got the Light of Freedom: The Organizing Tradition and the Mississippi Freedom Struggle* (Berkeley: University of California Press, 1995).

Howell Raines, *My Soul is Rested* (New York: Penguin, 1977).

W. J. Roraborough, *Berkeley at War: The 1960s* (New York: Oxford University Press, 1989).

John Schwartz, *America's Hidden Successes: A Reassessment of Public Policy from Kennedy to Reagan* (New York: Norton, 1988).

Alan Scott, *Ideology and New Social Movements* (London: HarperCollins, 1990).

Tim Tyson, *Radio Free Dixie: Robert F. Williams and the Roots of Black Power* (Chapel Hill: University of North Carolina Press, 1999).

Jeremy Varon, *Bringing the War Home: the Weather Underground, the Red Army Faction, and Revolutionary Violence in the Sixties and Seventies* (Berkeley: University of California Press, 2004).

Milton Viorst, *Fire in the Streets: America in the 1960s* (New York: Simon and Schuster, 1979).

Jack L. Walker, *Sit-Ins in Atlanta* (New York: McGraw-Hill, 1964).

Robert Penn Warren, *Who Speaks for the Negro?* (New York: Vintage, 1965).

Nancy Zaroulis and Gerald Sullivan, *Who Spoke Up? American Protest Against the War in Vietnam* (Garden City, NY: Doubleday, 1984).

Howard Zinn, *SNCC: The New Abolitionists* (Boston, MA: Beacon, 1964).

Cultural Legacy

Paul Berman (ed.), *Debating P.C.: The Controversy Over Political Correctness on College Campuses* (New York: Laurel, 1992).

Michael Bérubé and Cary Nelson (eds), *Higher Education Under Fire: Politics, Economics, and the Crisis of the Humanities* (New York: Routledge, 1995).

Allan Bloom, *The Closing of the American Mind* (New York: Simon and Schuster, 1987).

W. James Booth, *Communities of Memory: On Witness, Identity, and Justice* (Ithaca, NY: Cornell University Press, 2006).

Robert Bork, *Slouching Towards Gomorrah: Modern Liberalism and American Decline* (London: HarperCollins, 1997).

David Burner, *Making Peace with the 60s* (Princeton, NJ: Princeton University Press, 1996).

Walter H. Capps, *The Unfinished War: Vietnam and the American Conscience* (Boston, MA: Beacon, 1982).

Ron Chepesiuk, *Sixties Radicals Then and Now: Candid Conversations with Those Who Shaped the Era* (Jefferson, NC: McFarland and Company, 1995).

Peter Collier and David Horowitz, *Destructive Generation: Second Thoughts About the Sixties* (New York: Free Press, 1989).

Craig Cox, *Storefront Revolution: Food Co-ops and the Counterculture* (New Brunswick, NJ: Rutgers University Press, 1994).

Alice Echols, *Shaky Ground: The '60s and its Aftershocks* (New York: Columbia University Press, 2002).

Richard J. Ellis, *The Dark Side of the Left: Illiberal Egalitarianism in America* (Lawrence, KS: University of Kansas Press, 1998).

Robert S. Ellwood, *The Sixties Spiritual Awakening: American Religion Moving from Modern to Postmodern* (New Brunswick, NJ: Rutgers University Press, 1994).

Glenn T. Eskew, *But for Birmingham: The Local and National Movements in the Civil Rights Struggle* (Chapel Hill: University of North Carolina Press, 1997).

James J. Farrell, *The Spirit of the Sixties: The Making of Postwar Radicalism* (New York: Routledge, 1997).

Steve Fraser, *The Rise and Fall of the New Deal Order, 1930–1980* (Princeton, NJ: Princeton University Press, 1999).

Lawrence H. Fuchs, *The American Kaleidoscope: Race, Ethnicity, and the Civic Culture* (Middletown, CT: Wesleyan University Press, 1990).

Henry Louis Gates, *Loose Canons: Notes on the Culture Wars* (New York: Oxford University Press, 1993).

Gary Gerstle *American Crucible: Race and Nation in the Twentieth Century* (Princeton, NJ: Princeton University Press, 2001).

Todd Gitlin, *The Twilight of Common Dreams: Why America Is Wracked by Culture Wars* (New York: Henry Holt and Company, 1995).

Paul Gottfried, *The Conservative Movement* (Boston, MA: Twayne, 1993).

Jonathon Green, *All Dressed Up: The Sixties and the Counterculture* (London: Pimlico, 1999).

Kenneth Heineman, *Campus Wars: The Peace Movement on American Campuses in the Vietnam Era* (New York: New York University Press, 1992).

Robert Hughes, *The Culture of Complaint: The Fraying of America* (London: Harvill, 1994).

James Davison Hunter, *Culture Wars: The Struggle to Define America* (New York: Basic Books, 1991).

Maurice Isserman and Michael Kazin, America Divided: The Civil War of the 1960s (Oxford: Oxford University Press, 2003).

Ron Jacobs, *The Way the Wind Blew: A History of the Weather Underground* (London: Verso, 1997).

Robin D. G. Kelley, *Yo' Mama's Disfunktional: Fighting the Culture Wars in Urban America* (Boston, MA: Beacon Press, 1997).

Lauren Kessler, *After All These Years: Sixties Ideals in a Different World* (New York: Thunder's Mouth Press, 1990).

Roger Kimball, *Tenured Radicals: How Politics Has Corrupted Our Higher Education* (New York: Harper and Row, 1990).

Christopher Lasch, *The True and Only Heaven: Progress and its Critics* (New York: Norton, 1991).

Christopher Lasch, *The Revolt of the Elites and the Betrayal of Democracy* (New York: Norton, 1995).

Lawrence W. Levine, *The Opening of the American Mind* (Boston, MA: Beacon, 1996).

Steven Macedo (ed.), *Reassessing the Sixties: Debating the Political and Cultural Legacy* (New York and London: Norton, 1997).

Andrew M. Manis, *A Fire You Can't Put Out: The Civil Rights Life of Birmingham's Reverend Fred Shuttlesworth* (Tuscaloosa, AL: University of Alabama Press, 1984).

Willie Morris, *The Ghosts of Medgar Evers: A Tale of Race, Murder, Mississippi, and Hollywood* (New York: Random House, 1998).

Gary B. Nash, *History on Trial: Culture Wars and the Teaching of the Past* (New York: Alfred A. Knopf, 1997).

Melvin Small, *Covering Dissent: The Media and the Anti-Vietnam War Movement* (New Brunswick: Rutgers University Press, 1994).

Stephen Steinberg, *Turning Back: The Retreat from Racial Justice in American Thought and Policy* (Boston, MA: Beacon, 1995).

Jack Whalen and Robert Flacks, *Beyond the Barricades: The Sixties Generation Grows Up* (Philadelphia, PA: Temple University Press, 1989).

Lawrence Wright, *In the New World: Growing Up with America from the Sixties to the Eighties* (New York: Vintage, 1987).

Index